MOUNTAIN BIKE!
The Great Lakes States

MOUNTAIN BIKE!

The Great Lakes States

A GUIDE TO THE CLASSIC TRAILS

MINNESOTA
WISCONSIN
MICHIGAN

PHIL VAN VALKENBERG
WITH JACK MCHUGH

Menasha
Ridge
Press

Printed in the United States of America
Published by Menasha Ridge Press
Second Edition, first printing

Library of Congress Cataloging-in-Publication Data
is available from the Library of Congress.

Photos by authors unless otherwise credited
Maps by Tim Krasnansky
Cover photo by Phil Van Valkenberg

Menasha Ridge Press
P.O. Box 43059
Birmingham, Alabama 35243

All the trails described in this book are legal for mountain bikes. But rules can change—especially for off-road bicycles, the new kid on the outdoor recreation block. Land access issues and conflicts between bicyclists, hikers, equestrians, and other users can cause the rewriting of recreation regulations on public lands, sometimes resulting in a ban of mountain bike use on specific trails. That's why it's the responsibility of each rider to check and make sure that he or she rides only on trails where mountain biking is permitted.

CAUTION
Outdoor recreation activities are by their very nature potentially hazardous. All participants in such activities must assume the responsibility for their own actions and safety. The information contained in this guidebook cannot replace sound judgment and good decision-making skills, which help reduce risk exposure, nor does the scope of this book allow for disclosure of all the potential hazards and risks involved in such activities.

Learn as much as possible about the outdoor recreation activities you participate in, prepare for the unexpected, and be safe and cautious. The reward will be a safer and more enjoyable experience.

Table of Contents

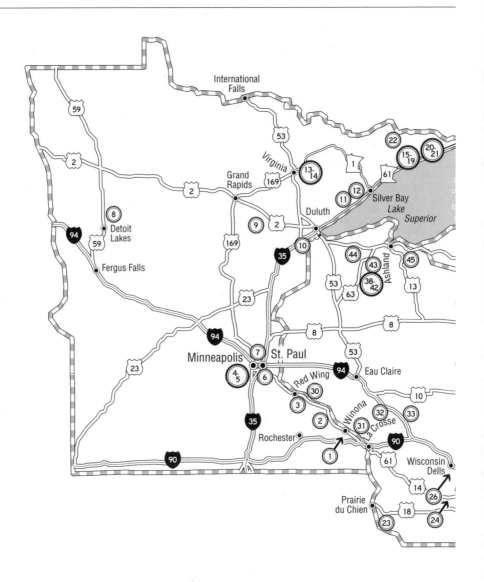

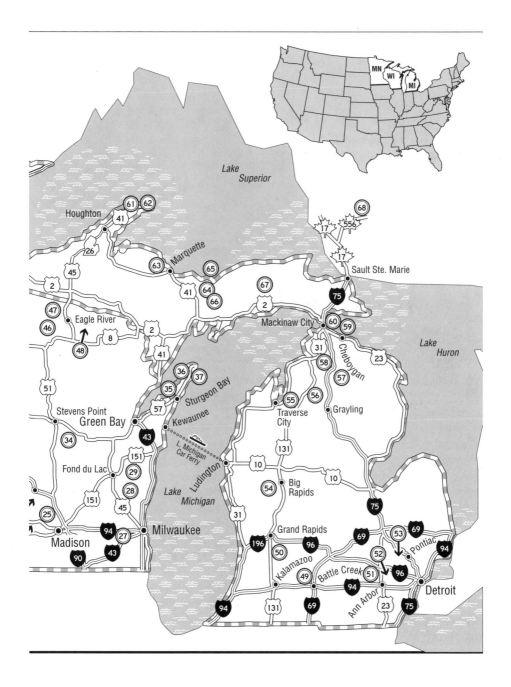

List of Maps

AMERICA BY MOUNTAIN BIKE *MAP LEGEND*

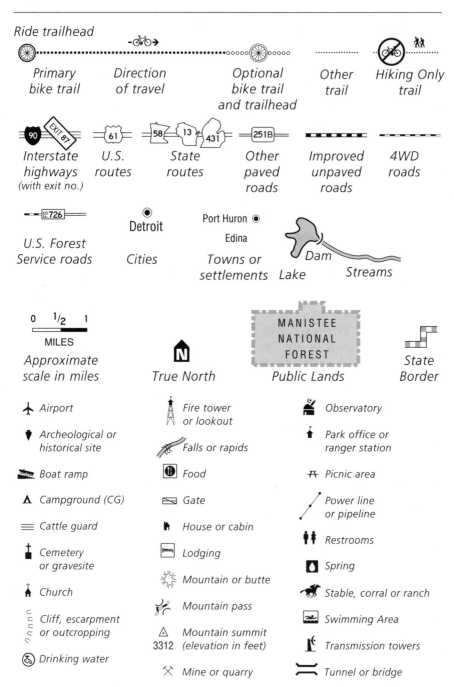

Ride trailhead

Primary
bike trail

Direction
of travel

Optional
bike trail
and trailhead

Other
trail

Hiking Only
trail

Interstate
highways
(with exit no.)

U.S.
routes

State
routes

Other
paved
roads

Improved
unpaved
roads

4WD
roads

U.S. Forest
Service roads

Cities

Towns or
settlements

Lake

Dam

Streams

Approximate
scale in miles

True North

Public Lands

State
Border

✈ Airport

♥ Archeological or
historical site

Boat ramp

▲ Campground (CG)

≡ Cattle guard

Cemetery
or gravesite

Church

Cliff, escarpment
or outcropping

Drinking water

Fire tower
or lookout

Falls or rapids

Food

Gate

House or cabin

Lodging

Mountain or butte

Mountain pass

Mountain summit
(elevation in feet)

Mine or quarry

Observatory

Park office or
ranger station

Picnic area

Power line
or pipeline

Restrooms

Spring

Stable, corral or ranch

Swimming Area

Transmission towers

Tunnel or bridge

Foreword

Welcome to *America by Mountain Bike,* a series designed to provide all-terrain bikers with the information they need to find and ride the very best trails everywhere in the mainland United States. Whether you're new to the sport and don't know where to pedal, or an experienced mountain biker who wants to learn the classic trails in another region, this series is for you. Drop a few bucks for the book, spend an hour with the detailed maps and route descriptions, and you're prepared for the finest in off-road cycling.

My role as editor of this series was simple: First, find a mountain biker who knows the area and loves to ride. Second, ask that person to spend a year researching the most popular and very best rides around. And third, have that rider describe each trail in terms of difficulty, scenery, condition, elevation change, and all other categories of information that are important to trail riders. "Pretend you've just completed a ride and met up with fellow mountain bikers at the trailhead," I told each author. "Imagine their questions, be clear in your answers."

As I said, the *editorial* process—that of sending out riders and reading the submitted chapters—is a snap. But the work involved in finding, riding, and writing about each trail is enormous. In some instances our authors' tasks are made easier by the information contributed by local bike shops or cycling clubs, or even by the writers of local "where-to" guides. Credit for these contributions is provided, when appropriate, in each chapter, and our sincere thanks goes to all who have helped.

But the overwhelming majority of trails are discovered and pedaled by our authors themselves, then compared with dozens of other routes to determine if they qualify as "classic"—that area's best in scenery and cycling fun. If you've ever had the experience of pioneering a route from outdated topographic maps, or entering a bike shop to request information from local riders who would much prefer to keep their favorite trails secret, or know how it is to double- and triple-check data to be positive your trail info is correct, then you have an idea of how each of our authors has labored to bring about these books. You and I, and all the mountain bikers of America, are the richer for their efforts.

You'll get more out of this book if you take a moment to read the Introduction explaining how to read the trail listings. The "Topographic Maps" section will help you understand how useful topos will be on a ride, and will also tell you where to get them. And though this is a "where-to," not a "how-to" guide, those of you who have not traveled the backcountry might find "Hitting the Trail" of particular value.

In addition to the material above, newcomers to mountain biking might want to spend a minute with the glossary, page 269, so that terms like *hard-pack, single-track,* and *water bars* won't throw you when you come across them in the text.

Finally, the tips in the Afterword on mountain biking etiquette and the land-use controversy might help us all enjoy the trails a little more.

All the best.

Dennis Coello
St. Louis

Preface

You probably wouldn't be looking at this book if you didn't already love the outdoors. Since the creation of the mountain bike, millions of people have discovered that it is perfect for exploring nature's silent world. *Mountain Bike! The Great Lakes States* is your ticket to outdoor adventure and excitement on over 700 miles of mountain bike routes in the wonderland cradled by Lake Superior, Lake Michigan, and Lake Huron.

Lake Superior is the "big sea water," Gitchee Gumi in the native Ojibwe and in Longfellow's poem "Hiawatha." On rides included here, you can gaze at its deep blue expanse from the Sawtooth Mountains of Minnesota and from Michigan's Lookout Mountain and Grand Island. Lake Huron is the backdrop for rides on Michigan's Mackinac and Bois Blanc islands. Three rides trace the quiet shores of Lake Michigan in Wisconsin's Door County.

There is more to the region than the Great Lakes. On one ride you can cruise to a sleepy river town and trace the edge of the mighty Mississippi on an obscure Wisconsin gravel road that actually passes under the rock wall of a towering river bluff. We'll take you to Hell—the village of Hell, Michigan that is—where you'll follow the twists and turns of the famous Potawatomi Trail as it winds past blue lakes and through deep forests. You can explore the trails of Wisconsin's Chequamegon Forest, a land of clear lakes and vast stands of timber that annually attract thousands of off-roaders to the nation's largest mountain bike race. How about getting eyeball-to-eyeball with giant moose in the borderland wilderness of Minnesota's Gunflint Trail? Then there's the challenge of the rough-and-tumble topography of Wisconsin's beautiful Kettle Moraine State Forest on your choice of three trail systems.

In all, you can choose from a premier collection of 68 routes ideal for novice to veteran riders. Some routes follow quiet gravel roads while others are on cross-country ski trail systems, which are plentiful in this region.

Mountains? We used to have them. Big as the Rockies they were. That was billions of years ago in what they call the Precambrian era. We still call some of these protuberances mountains, although out East they'd be foothills and out West who knows what. Our justification is that the early French explorers called them mountains, too. But, what did they know? They thought China was on the other side.

Actually, the upper Great Lakes region has something better than mountains. Massive continental glaciers, a mile thick, once pushed down from Canada, four of them in fact in the last million years. They bulldozed our mountains, leaving only their tough, rocky cores. The last one was awesome.

The handiwork of the industrious beaver can alter any rider's plans.

Called the Wisconsin Glacier, it created the galaxy of small lakes that the region is famous for, carved the basins of the inland seas (Superior, Michigan, and Huron), and scoured out the valley of the Mississippi.

Best of all, the glacier created some of the finest off-road riding you'll find anywhere. Not to take anything away from the mountain states—I've loved the grand scenery and challenge of off-roading in the East and the West—but I have to say it's more humane here. Off-roading is a more attainable adventure for a much broader cross section of the riding public and, I dare say, it's more fun. A homesick Midwest expatriate friend of mine who lives in the Rockies told me recently, "I know that on any ride I take I'm going to be grinding uphill for an hour to two hours." The mountains are a great challenge, but riding on them every day may not be as appealing as a ramble through the woods of the Great Lakes region.

As with many other parts of the country, hikers' and bikers' groups have conflicted in our region. As International Mountain Bicycling Association (IMBA) Executive Director Tim Bluementhal pointed out, nature seekers want the wilderness to themselves these days. Time was when few cared, but today enough people have learned to appreciate a soothing self-propelled experience in nature that we find ourselves in conflict with kindred spirits. Hikers and bikers seem to love the same music, but different rhythms.

The conflicts have cooled somewhat in recent years, thanks to the efforts of IMBA and local organizations like RIDE (Recreation for Individuals

Dedicated to the Environment), WORBA (Wisconsin Off-Road Bicycle Association), MMBA (Michigan Mountain Biking Association), MMBRG (Metro Mountain Biking Resource Group–Twin Cities of Minnesota), and CAMBA (Chequamegon Area Mountain Bike Association–Northern Wisconsin). They have articulated the needs and opinions of off-road riders, which has resulted in access to trails that would have otherwise been closed. Before their efforts, closing trails to off-road riders seemed to be the most expedient solution when conflicts arose.

One of the access success stories in the region came through the efforts of RIDE and WORBA in Wisconsin's Kettle Moraine State Forest. Trails in the southern area of the forest that had been used by off-roaders for years were suddenly closed. The work of these organizations and concerned citizens, bicycle dealers, and manufacturers ensured that trails would be open for off-road riding in the Kettle Moraine Southern Unit as well as dozens of other state parks and forests.

Despite the efforts of so many dedicated people, I have chosen not to include the trails of the Kettle Moraine Southern Unit in this guide. My feeling, and that of others whose opinions I trust, is that the area is overused, or is at least near its capacity. Its proximity to Chicago and Milwaukee make it the convenient choice for many mountain bikers. It is good that the state and the mountain biking community are committed to maintaining and expanding riding trails there, but it doesn't seem to be an area I should encourage more people to use.

The delicate matter of land access, overuse, and riding etiquette is covered very well by Series Editor Dennis Coello in the Afterword section. I recommend paying serious attention to these tips, both for your sake and for the future of off-road riding. Several additional thoughts apply to the Great Lakes area.

First, there is no such thing as free and open land, except perhaps in your dreams. All land is managed by some agency or other. This guide only lists routes where mountain biking is 100% legal; we have also sought out areas where off-roaders will feel welcome. It is up to you not to wear out this welcome. Obey all signage and rules whether you understand the reasons behind them or not.

Land managers function in a difficult world. Charged with the stewardship of the land, they face increased demand for use from many sectors and, at the same time, they face limited or declining budgets. In this region, concern over trail damage from mountain biking in wet conditions is a large issue in many of the more populated areas. I know of perfectly wonderful riding experiences that are now completely closed to mountain bikers because some riders would not obey the "trails closed" signs erected during wet periods. One park manager told me of confronting a rider all covered in mud who told him, "I'm not hurting the trails." The manager asked the rider where he thought the mud had come from.

Riders who abuse the land have the same mentality as the gun users we decry when we see a shot-up information sign. Always phone ahead to check on trail status before heading out and if you find any riders violating the rules, give them a piece of your mind. They will probably be unarmed.

Last, always pay any associated fees or give generous donations if they are suggested. Riders can often easily avoid doing so, but we must put some bucks behind the facilities we need to enjoy off-roading. All of the trail and park fees you could possibly pay in a season would amount to a tiny fraction of the investment you've made in equipment. If the choice comes down to buying a titanium bolt or coughing up the park fee, you'd better have your head on straight.

I also have just a few suggestions to add to Dennis Coello's extensive tips in the Introduction. Riding in the deep woods, which is a wonderful part of the experience on many of these tours, requires a few special considerations. The dense cover can prevent normal direction reckoning from the position of the sun. On a cloudy day the light can be quite dim. While we have tried to choose trails that are well-signed or present a minimal chance of disorientation, it is still remarkably easy to become lost or at least confused.

I recommend carrying a compass, an inexpensive, easy-to-use tool that makes you feel like a real explorer. They all have a magnetized needle that points north (unless held near a ferric metal object). Your trail map will have a symbol indicating the direction of north. With these two aids you should be able to extricate yourself from any confusing situation. Read up on compass use and practice when you are not lost. Finally, don't ride alone and don't begin your ride late in the day. The deep woods get dark a lot earlier than open areas, and it will be hard to read a compass or map in the dark.

No project as ambitious as this guide can be the product of only two people. Fortunately, many people have assisted Jack McHugh and me. In particular we'd like to thank Doug Shidell, John Drewes, Jim and Mary Richards, Mark Spinler, John Filander, Ivy Hocking, Bruce Kerfoot, Tom Klein, Harry Spehar, Dick Moran, Dave Olson, Will Goddard, Gary Crandall, Bruce Germond, Ken Lawrence, J. Watt, Brian Delany, Dave Maurer, Dwain Abramowski, and Steve and Stephanie Rowe.

Phil Van Valkenberg

P.S. In our trail descriptions, you will come across the term DNR (the Department of Natural Resources). It has state agencies in Minnesota, Wisconsin, and Michigan, and is charged with management of state forests, parks, and trails.

MOUNTAIN BIKE!

The Great Lakes States

Introduction

TRAIL DESCRIPTION OUTLINE

TRAIL DESCRIPTION OUTLINE

Information on each trail in this book begins with a general description that includes length, configuration, scenery, highlights, trail conditions, and difficulty. Additional description is contained in eleven individual categories. The following will help you understand all of the information provided.

Trail name: Trail names are as designated on United States Geological Survey (USGS) or Forest Service or other maps, and/or by local custom.

Length: The overall length of a trail is described in miles, unless stated otherwise.

Configuration: This is a description of the shape of each trail—whether the trail is a loop, out-and-back (that is, along the same route), figure eight, trapezoid, isosceles triangle, or if it connects with another trail described in the book.

Difficulty: This provides at a glance a description of the degree of physical exertion required to complete the ride, and the technical skill required to pedal it. Authors were asked to keep in mind the fact that all riders are not equal, and thus to gauge the trail in terms of how the middle-of-the-road rider—someone between the newcomer and Ned Overend—could handle the route. Comments about the trail's length, condition, and elevation change will also assist you in determining the difficulty of any trail relative to your own abilities.

Condition: Trails are described in terms of being paved, unpaved, sandy, hardpacked, washboarded, two- or four-wheel-drive, single-track or double-track. All terms that might be unfamiliar to the first-time mountain biker are defined in the Glossary.

Scenery: Here you will find a general description of the natural surroundings during the seasons most riders pedal the trail, and a suggestion of what is to be found at special times (like great fall foliage or cactus in bloom).

Highlights: Towns, major water crossings, historical sites, etc., are listed.

General location: This category describes where the trail is located in reference to a nearby town or other landmark.

Elevation change: Unless stated otherwise, the figure provided is the total gain and loss of elevation along the trail. In regions where the elevation variation is not extreme, the route is simply described as flat, rolling, or possessing short steep climbs or descents.

Season: This is the best time of year to pedal the route, taking into account trail condition (for example, when it will not be muddy), riding comfort (when the weather is too hot, cold, or wet), and local hunting seasons.

Note: Because the exact opening and closing dates of deer, elk, moose, and antelope seasons often change from year to year, riders should check with the local Fish and Game department, or call a sporting goods store (or any place that sells hunting licenses) in a nearby town before heading out. Wear bright clothes in fall, and don't wear suede jackets while in the saddle. Hunter's-orange tape on the helmet is also a good idea.

Services: This category is of primary importance in guides for paved-road tourers, but is far less crucial to most mountain bike trail descriptions because there are usually no services whatsoever to be found. Authors have noted when water is available on desert or long mountain routes, and have listed the availability of food, lodging, campgrounds, and bike shops. If all these services are present, you will find only the words "All services available in . . ."

Hazards: Special hazards like steep cliffs, great amounts of deadfall, or barbed-wire fences very close to the trail are noted here.

Rescue index: Determining how far one is from help on any particular trail can be difficult due to the backcountry nature of most mountain bike rides. Authors therefore state the proximity of homes or Forest Service outposts, nearby roads where one might hitch a ride, or the likelihood of other bikers being encountered on the trail. Phone numbers of local sheriff departments or hospitals have not been provided because phones are almost never available. If you are able to reach a phone, the local operator will connect you with emergency services.

Land status: This category provides information regarding whether the trail crosses land operated by the Forest Service, Bureau of Land Management, a city, state, or national park, whether it crosses private land whose owner (at the time the author did the research) has allowed mountain bikers right of passage, and so on.

Note: Authors have been extremely careful to offer only those routes that are open to bikers and are legal to ride. However, because land ownership changes over time, and because the land-use controversy created by mountain bikes still has not completely subsided, it is the duty of each cyclist to look for and to heed signs warning against trail use. Don't expect this book to get you off the hook when you're facing some small-town judge for pedaling past a "Biking Prohibited" sign erected the day before. Look for these signs, read them, and heed the advice. And remember there's always another trail.

Maps: The maps in this book have been produced with great care, and, in conjunction with the trail-following suggestions, will help you stay on course. But as every experienced mountain biker knows, things can get tricky in the backcountry. It is therefore strongly suggested that you avail yourself of the detailed information found in the 7.5 minute series USGS (United States Geological Survey) topographic maps. In some cases, authors have found that specific Forest Service or other maps may be more useful than the USGS quads, and tell how to obtain them.

Finding the trail: Detailed information on how to reach the trailhead and where to park your car is provided here.

Sources of additional information: Here you will find the address and/or phone number of a bike shop, governmental agency, or other source from which trail information can be obtained.

Notes on the trail: This is where you are guided carefully through any portions of the trail that are particularly difficult to follow. The author also may add information about the route that does not fit easily in the other categories. This category will not be present for those rides where the route is easy to follow.

ABBREVIATIONS

The following road-designation abbreviations are used in the *America by Mountain Bike* series:

CR	County Road
FR	Farm Route
FS	Forest Service road
I-	Interstate
IR	Indian Route
US	United States highway

State highways are designated with the appropriate two-letter state abbreviation, followed by the road number. *Example:* MN 6 = Minnesota State Highway 6.

Postal Service two-letter state codes:

AL	Alabama	CT	Connecticut
AK	Alaska	DE	Delaware
AZ	Arizona	DC	District of Columbia
AR	Arkansas	FL	Florida
CA	California	GA	Georgia
CO	Colorado	HI	Hawaii

ID	Idaho	NY	New York
IL	Illinois	NC	North Carolina
IN	Indiana	ND	North Dakota
IA	Iowa	OH	Ohio
KS	Kansas	OK	Oklahoma
KY	Kentucky	OR	Oregon
LA	Louisiana	PA	Pennsylvania
ME	Maine	RI	Rhode Island
MD	Maryland	SC	South Carolina
MA	Massachusetts	SD	South Dakota
MI	Michigan	TN	Tennessee
MN	Minnesota	TX	Texas
MS	Mississippi	UT	Utah
MO	Missouri	VT	Vermont
MT	Montana	VA	Virginia
NE	Nebraska	WA	Washington
NV	Nevada	WV	West Virginia
NH	New Hampshire	WI	Wisconsin
NJ	New Jersey	WY	Wyoming
NM	New Mexico		

TOPOGRAPHIC MAPS

The maps in this book, when used in conjunction with the route directions present in each chapter, will in most instances be sufficient to get you to the trail and keep you on it. However, you will find superior detail and valuable information in the 7.5 minute series United States Geological Survey (USGS) topographic maps. Recognizing how indispensable these are to bikers and hikers alike, many bike shops and sporting goods stores now carry topos of the local area.

But if you're brand new to mountain biking you might be wondering "What's a topographic map?" In short, these differ from standard "flat" maps in that they indicate not only linear distance, but elevation as well. One glance at a "topo" will show you the difference, for "contour lines" are spread across the map like dozens of intricate spider webs. Each contour line represents a particular elevation, and at the base of each topo a particular "contour interval" designation is given. Yes, it sounds confusing if you're new to the lingo, but it truly is a simple and wonderfully helpful system. Keep reading.

Let's assume that the 7.5 minute series topo before us says "Contour Interval 40 feet," that the short trail we'll be pedaling is two inches in length on the map, and that it crosses five contour lines from its beginning to end.

What do we know? Well, because the linear scale of this series is 2,000 feet to the inch (roughly 2 3/4 inches representing 1 mile), we know our trail is approximately 4/5 of a mile long (2 inches × 2,000 feet). But we also know we'll be climbing or descending 200 vertical feet (5 contour lines × 40 feet each) over that distance. And the elevation designations written on occasional contour lines will tell us if we're heading up or down.

The authors of this series warn their readers of upcoming terrain, but only a detailed topo gives you the information you need to pinpoint your position exactly on a map, steer yourself toward optional trails and roads nearby, plus let you know at a glance if you'll be pedaling hard to take them. It's a lot of information for a very low cost. In fact, the only drawback with topos is their size—several feet square. I've tried rolling them into tubes, folding them carefully, even cutting them into blocks and photocopying the pieces. Any of these systems is a pain, but no matter how you pack the maps you'll be happy they're along. And you'll be even happier if you pack a compass as well.

In addition to local bike shops and sporting goods stores, you'll find topos at major universities and some public libraries, where you might try photocopying the ones you need to avoid the cost of buying them. But if you want your own and can't find them locally, write to:

USGS Map Sales
Box 25286
Denver, CO 80225

Ask for an index while you're at it, plus a price list and a copy of the booklet *Topographic Maps*. In minutes you'll be reading them like a pro.

A second excellent series of maps available to mountain bikers is that put out by the United States Forest Service. If your trail runs through an area designated as a national forest, look in the phone book (white pages) under the United States Government listings, find the Department of Agriculture heading, and then run you finger down that section until you find the Forest Service. Give them a call and they'll provide the address of the regional Forest Service office, from which you can obtain the appropriate map.

TRAIL ETIQUETTE

Pick up almost any mountain bike magazine these days and you'll find articles and letters to the editor about trail conflict. For example, you'll find hikers' tales of being blindsided by speeding mountain bikers, complaints from mountain bikers about being blamed for trail damage that was really caused by horse or cattle traffic, and cries from bikers about those "kamikaze" riders who through their antics threaten to close even more trails to all of us.

The authors of this series have been very careful to guide you to only those trails that are open to mountain biking (or at least were open at the time of their research), and without exception have warned of the damage done to our sport through injudicious riding. My personal views on this matter appear in the Afterword, but all of us can benefit from glancing over the following International Mountain Bicycling Association (IMBA) Rules of the Trail before saddling up.

1. *Ride on open trails only.* Respect trail and road closures (ask if not sure), avoid possible trespass on private land, obtain permits and authorization as may be required. Federal and State wilderness areas are closed to cycling.

2. *Leave no trace.* Be sensitive to the dirt beneath you. Even on open trails, you should not ride under conditions where you will leave evidence of your passing, such as on certain soils shortly after rain. Observe the different types of soils and trail construction; practice low-impact cycling. This also means staying on the trail and not creating any new ones. Be sure to pack out at least as much as you pack in.

3. *Control your bicycle!* Inattention for even a second can cause disaster. Excessive speed can maim and threaten people; there is no excuse for it!

4. *Always yield the trail.* Make known your approach well in advance. A friendly greeting (or a bell) is considerate and works well; startling someone may cause loss of trail access. Show your respect when passing others by slowing to a walk or even stopping. Anticipate that other trail users may be around corners or in blind spots.

5. *Never spook animals.* All animals are startled by an unannounced approach, a sudden movement, or a loud noise. This can be dangerous for you, for others, and for the animals. Give animals extra room and time to adjust to you. In passing, use special care and follow the directions of horseback riders (ask if uncertain). Running cattle and disturbing wild animals is a serious offense. Leave gates as you found them, or as marked.

6. *Plan ahead.* Know your equipment, your ability, and the area in which you are riding—and prepare accordingly. Be self-sufficient at all times. Wear a helmet, keep your machine in good condition, and carry necessary supplies for changes in weather or other conditions. A well-executed trip is a satisfaction to you and not a burden or offense to others.

For more information, contact IMBA, P.O. Box 7578, Boulder, CO 80306, (303) 545-9011.

HITTING THE TRAIL

Once again, because this is a "where-to," not a "how-to" guide, the following will be brief. If you're a veteran trail rider these suggestions might serve to remind you of something you've forgotten to pack. If you're a newcomer, they might convince you to think twice before hitting the backcountry unprepared.

Water: I've heard the questions dozens of times. "How much is enough? One bottle? Two? Three?! But think of all that extra weight!" Well, one simple physiological fact should convince you to err on the side of excess when it comes to deciding how much water to pack: a human working hard in 90-degree temperature needs approximately ten quarts of fluids every day. Ten quarts. That's two and a half gallons—12 large water bottles, or 16 small ones. And, with water weighing in at approximately 8 pounds per gallon, a one-day supply comes to a whopping 20 pounds.

In other words, pack along two or three bottles even for short rides. And make sure you can purify the water found along the trail on longer routes. When writing of those routes where this could be of critical importance, each author has provided information on where water can be found near the trail—if it can be found at all. But drink it untreated and you run the risk of disease. (See *Giardia* in the Glossary.)

One sure way to kill both the bacteria and viruses in water is to boil it for ten minutes, plus one minute more for each 1,000 feet of elevation above sea level. Right. That's just how you want to spend your time on a bike ride. Besides, who wants to carry a stove, or denude the countryside stoking bonfires to boil water?

Luckily, there is a better way. Many riders pack along the effective, inexpensive, and only slightly distasteful tetraglycine hydroperiodide tablets (sold under the names Potable Aqua, Globaline, and Coughlan's, among others). Some invest in portable, lightweight purifiers that filter out the crud. Yes, purifying water with tablets or filters is a bother. But catch a case of Giardia sometime and you'll understand why it's worth the trouble.

Tools: Ever since my first cross-country tour in 1965 I've been kidded about the number of tools I pack on the trail. And so I will exit entirely from this discussion by providing a list compiled by two mechanic (and mountain biker) friends of mine. After all, since they make their livings fixing bikes, and get their kicks by riding them, who could be a better source?

These two suggest the following as an absolute minimum:

    tire levers
    spare tube and patch kit
    air pump
    allen wrenches (3, 4, 5, and 6 mm)
    six-inch crescent (adjustable-end) wrench
    small flat-blade screwdriver
    chain rivet tool
    spoke wrench

But, while they're on the trail, their personal tool pouches contain these additional items:

    channel locks (small)
    air gauge
    tire valve cap (the metal kind, with a valve-stem remover)
    baling wire (ten or so inches, for temporary repairs)
    duct tape (small roll for temporary repairs or tire boot)
    boot material (small piece of old tire or a large tube patch)
    spare chain link
    rear derailleur pulley
    spare nuts and bolts
    paper towel and tube of waterless hand cleaner

First-Aid Kit: My personal kit contains the following, sealed inside double Ziploc bags:

    sunscreen
    aspirin
    butterfly-closure bandages
    Band-Aids
    gauze compress pads (a half-dozen 4″ × 4″)
    gauze (one roll)
    ace bandages or Spenco joint wraps
    Benadryl (an antihistamine, in case of allergic reactions)
    water purification tablets
    Moleskin / Spenco "Second Skin"
    hydrogen peroxide, iodine, or Mercurochrome (some kind of antiseptic)
    snakebite kit

Final Considerations: The authors of this series have done a good job in suggesting that specific items be packed for certain trails—raingear in particular seasons, a hat and gloves for mountain passes, or shades for desert jaunts. Heed their warnings, and think ahead. Good luck.

Dennis Coello
St. Louis

MINNESOTA

Southern Minnesota

The Mississippi River influences the character of many rides in southern Minnesota. North America's greatest river begins as a small stream in the north woods, but by the time it reaches the metro area of Minneapolis and St. Paul it begins to show its mighty character. The system of river locks and dams that makes the river a highway for barges and tugs ends in the Twin Cities. As impressive as it is, the Mississippi is a trickle compared to what it once was. When the continental glacier melted, the river filled the valley from rim to rim, carving the gorges, bluffs, and palisades that make it the scenic wonder it is today.

Tucked into the niches of the Mississippi bluffs are three rides that take advantage of the river's handiwork. Riders will find extremely challenging mountain biking on the Holzinger Lodge Trail on the edge of the river city of Winona. At the more isolated Snake Creek Trail, set in a side valley of the great river, riders can enjoy a moderate route in an almost alpine setting. On the All-Terra Tour, a system of gravel roads creates a moderate ride through the hills and orchards just south of the historic river city of Red Wing.

The river greatly influences the Twin Cities area (where over half of the state's population lives), but the riding terrain in the metro area is a product of the glacier's ice sheets rather than its runoff. Evidence of the glacier doesn't get any more impressive than on the Murphy-Hanrehan Trails. The extremely challenging riding there covers steep, rocky moraine laid down by the melting ice. It is part of the Hennepin Parks system, which preserves nature's legacy and provides many kinds of recreation around the metro area. Buck Hill is a private alpine ski area that offers the enthusiastic mountain biking public a challenging experience in a controlled area that takes in almost all of the vertical feet that skiers enjoy. Lebanon Hills also offers challenging riding on a short, but exciting loop on steep glacial moraine. At Elm Creek, another Hennepin Park ride, the riding is easy and shows that the glacier also created marshes and scenic lakes surrounded by low hills.

RIDE 1   *HOLZINGER LODGE TRAIL*

A ride at Holzinger Lodge offers two possible loops along the wooded bluffs at the edge of the city of Winona. You will be amazed how isolated the routes seem, especially if you take the upper loop. Your only clue that you're in an urban area may be a glimpse of a rooftop through the trees or the sound of a lawn mower. The proximity of Winona is a big plus for riders interested in

RIDE 1 *HOLZINGER LODGE TRAIL*

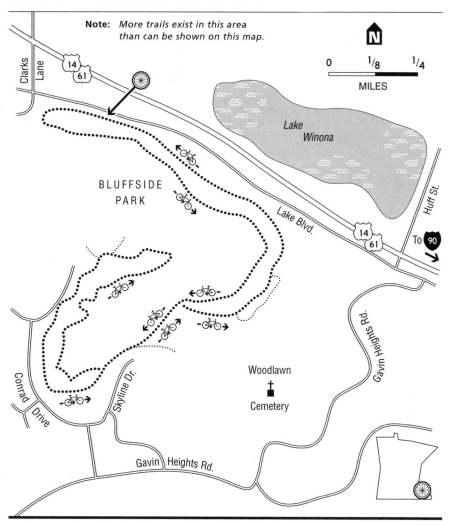

Note: *More trails exist in this area than can be shown on this map.*

N

0   1/8   1/4

MILES

Clarks Lane

14 61

Lake Winona

BLUFFSIDE PARK

Lake Blvd.

14 61

To 90

Huff St.

Gavin Heights Rd.

Woodlawn

Cemetery

Conrad Drive

Skyline Dr.

Gavin Heights Rd.

food, lodging, and historic sites. Parts of the city still retain much of the character of the days when the paddle wheel steamboat was the only link with the outside world.

Holzinger Lodge is a rustic warming building used during the cross-country ski season. No, the skiers do not use the trails that climb to the blufftop. The lower loop, which must be ridden if you want to take the climb, is 2.4 miles long and moderately difficult for the average rider. The loop is on an eight-foot-wide cross-country ski trail. It's a rolling ride with a long, fast downhill run to the finish. The surface is a mix of hardpack and grass with rocks and roots on the steeper sections. About 170 feet of elevation is gained in one circuit. Except for a mowed lawn at the start at Holzinger Lodge and a mowed park at the west end, you will ride through dense oak and maple woods for the whole route.

The upper loop adds another 2.4 miles of extremely challenging single-track trail. Over 380 feet of elevation are gained in addition to that on the lower loop. The initial climb is real hero stuff, and much of the elevation is gained in one quarter-mile-long grind. The surface is a mix of hardpack, grass, rocks, and roots. Shortly after the steepest part of the climb, the trail splits and you follow a snaking course along the bluff edge that will test anyone's skill. You'll find a mix of rocks, roots, hummocks, close trees and branches, and tricky ravine crossings with small, rough, log-covered bridges always found at the bottom of a steep pitch.

At the run's eastern end you can take a few steps off the trail to an open area on the edge of the bluff overlooking Woodlawn Cemetery and parts of the city. Soaring hawks, vultures and, at times, eagles are seen here. The return route is much easier as it rolls gently through the blufftop woods on a hard-packed surface.

General location: On the south side of the city of Winona.

Elevation change: The ride begins at 740′ and rises to 1,090′. If you only ride the lower loop you will climb to 910′.

Season: Any time there is no snow and it's not extremely wet. The area is well drained. Hot and humid in the summer; insect populations flourish under these conditions.

Services: All services are available in Winona, including bicycle sales and repair.

Hazards: The trails are open to hikers. Deer are often scared up and may bolt across the trail. Good riders like to hammer here and the need to concentrate on the terrain may cause surprises. Rocks, roots, and fallen logs and branches will be encountered on the lower loop, and it is possible to catch air on the long downhill to the finish. All of the above plus hummocks, tricky ravine crossings, and close trees and branches will be found on the upper loop. If you are in doubt or get off line, walk. A spill will likely result in a tumble down the brushy bluff side. Speed must be moderated almost constantly on the steep descent.

Rescue index: Help is available in Winona. Many service businesses are located along US 14 / 61 just west of the route. On the upper loop you are never far from blufftop residences.

Land status: City of Winona park land.

Maps: No maps that show the trails are available. The Chamber of Commerce city map will help you locate Lake Boulevard and other points of interest.

Where's the city? Surprise, you're still in it.

Finding the trail: Holzinger Lodge is located along Lake Boulevard which parallels US 14 / 61 on the south side of Winona. It is most easily found by turning south on Huff Street, which is a major intersection on US 14 / 61. Turn right on Lake Boulevard and follow it .7 mile to the west. Holzinger Lodge, a log building, and a parking area are on the left.

Sources of additional information:

Winona Convention and Visitors Bureau
P.O. Box 870
67 Main Street
Winona, MN 55987
(507) 452-2272

Notes on the trail: There is almost no signage on the trail. From Holzinger Lodge, ride west along the mowed area a short distance to the trailhead. Both loops are noteworthy for a total lack of signage. This is not a problem on the lower loop, which is an easily identifiable cross-country ski trail. The only confusion may come at the start, where you should take the right trail, and about a quarter-mile later when you emerge into an open, mowed park area. At this point make a 180-degree left turn around a masonry fire pit to find the trail again. Be sure to ride all loops in a counter-clockwise direction to keep with the flow of rider traffic.

There are many more short trails in this area than can be shown on this map. To locate the upper loop, a bicycle computer on the trip distance setting will be of great help. At 1.5 miles on the lower loop the trail makes a 180-degree turn back toward the lodge. Two trails fork off to the west at this point. The left trail leads to a long, steep climb up the bluff after a short dip. The right trail is a short dead end. Continue climbing on a steady course until 1.9 miles, where you turn right and ride a short distance down to a ravine crossing. You will be on the most difficult single-track section of the route with the downhill side on your right until 2.6 miles, when the direction reverses sharply from east to west. Many trails intersect on the blufftop, but if you remember that the downhill should be on the left and any homes or buildings on the right, you will stay on course. At 3.5 miles you will have the option of heading sharply downhill. This is the trail you came up on. If you become lost you can always push your bike through to a neighborhood and ride back down on Gavin Heights Road.

RIDE 2   *SNAKE CREEK TRAIL*

The two-mile cross-country ski loop at Snake Creek is a quiet little trail that ranks at the low end of moderate difficulty for the average rider. It is a good step-up trail for those who are just beyond the novice stage and are ready to take on something a bit tougher. The difficulty comes from 150 feet of climbing with some very steep pitches early on, plus a few fast downhills. Trail surfaces are mostly grassy which, although a bit rough in the beginning, require little technical skill. Toward the end of the loop there is a downhill where you could get airborne if you fail to moderate your speed.

Much of the loop is in a dense woods where oak predominate. Around the half-way point you break out into the open for a gorgeous view of the valley to the south. The short length of the loop and fine scenery invite riders to try multiple laps. A seven-mile snowmobile trail loop to the southeast can also be mountain biked. It is considerably more challenging, because it scales the full 340-foot height of the bluffs twice. You can access it on the south side of the gravel road you came in on about .4 mile west of the cross-country ski trailhead. Use caution: the snowmobile trail is also open to motorized all-terrain vehicles during warm weather months.

General location: Ten miles southeast of Wabasha.
Elevation change: One gradual to steep 150′ climb, one 100′ downhill.
Season: Trails should be clear of snow and ice April through November. Expect cool temperatures at the extremes of this period.
Services: There are no services at the trail site. All services are available in Wabasha except bicycle retail and repair, which can be found 15 miles farther north on US 61 at Red Wing.

RIDE 2   *SNAKE CREEK TRAIL*

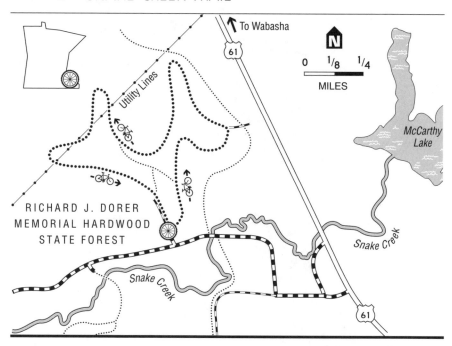

Hazards: Trails are well maintained, but windfall trees and branches are always a possible hazard. Washout ruts may be found on steep slopes. On a downhill run near the end of the loop you may get airborne if you don't moderate your speed.

Rescue index: Help is available in the village of Kellogg, just off of US 61, 4.5 miles north of the trail.

Land status: Richard J. Dorer Memorial Hardwood State Forest

Maps: An excellent map, "Richard J. Dorer Memorial Hardwood State Forest Trail Map, Snake Creek Management Unit," is available from the Department of Natural Resources.

Finding the trail: From US 61 drive onto a gravel road at the official brown State Forest sign "Access Snake Creek Trail," 9.5 miles south of Wabasha. Drive 1 mile east to the Snake Creek Forest Management Unit cross-country ski area.

Sources of additional information:

Minnesota Department of Natural Resources
Division of Parks and Recreation Information Center
500 Lafayette Road
St. Paul, MN 55155-4040
(612) 296-6157

Spring storms carved this gulley.

Mississippi Valley Partners
c/o John Hall
Anderson House
333 West Main Street
Wabasha, MN 55981
(507) 565-4524

Notes on the trail: The trail is very well marked for one-way travel in a counter-clockwise direction with cross-country ski trail signs and blue diamonds with direction arrows. From the trailhead you will ride past a gate and make an immediate right to follow the trail.

RIDE 3   *ALL-TERRA TOUR*

This ride is a 19.9-mile paved and gravel spur-and-loop road tour centered on the steep bluffs and valleys east of the small historic city of Red Wing. The route is used as part of a tour organized by local bicycling enthusiast John Drewes for law enforcement and correctional officers. It is held annually on the first weekend of October. The first 6.2 miles and the last 2.3 miles are on paved streets and highways, just enough distance to warm up and cool down. A thorough warm-up is a good idea since riders will take on steep grades on 270-, 340-, and 400-foot climbs. The gravel roads are well maintained for two-wheel-drive vehicles that serve the many farms in the area. The grades merit a moderate difficulty rating, but no technical ability beyond handling the bike at high speed is needed.

You will find a scenic mix of dense hardwood forest on the steep slopes and farmland in the valleys and on the blufftops. Red Wing offers historic sites and interesting opportunities for dining, lodging, shopping, and antiquing. There are also six miles of moderate to difficult single-track cross-country ski trails in Memorial Park where mountain biking is allowed. The trails can be accessed from Golf Links Road at the northeast corner of the clubhouse parking lot. A large map sign illustrates the trail layout.

General location: Red Wing, 55 miles southeast of the Twin Cities.

Elevation change: Over 1,200′ of elevation will be gained and lost.

Season: Anytime snow and ice are not a problem (roughly March through November).

Services: All services including bicycle retail and repair are available in Red Wing at The Outdoor Store. There is a country store in the village of Frontenac at the intersection of County Road 2, 3.6 miles east of the route.

Hazards: There is considerable traffic on US 63/61, but if you ride clockwise, all turns are to the right and there is a wide paved shoulder. Loose gravel may be present on any of the unpaved roads. All roads are open to motor vehicle traffic. Speed should be moderated on steep downhill grades.

Rescue index: Help is available in Red Wing. There are many farms along the route, and farmers are usually friendly and helpful.

Land status: Public roadways through private land.

Maps: USGS 7.5 minute quads for Red Wing, Bay City, and Lake City NW show all of the roads except Golf Links Road, which is a recent addition. None of the roads except the U.S. highways are named and, unless you are a map freak who likes to see every contour, the USGS maps are unnecessary. Nearly all of the roads are well signed.

Finding the trail: From US 61 (Main Street) in the city of Red Wing, turn north on Broad Street and travel one block to the intersection of Levee Street;

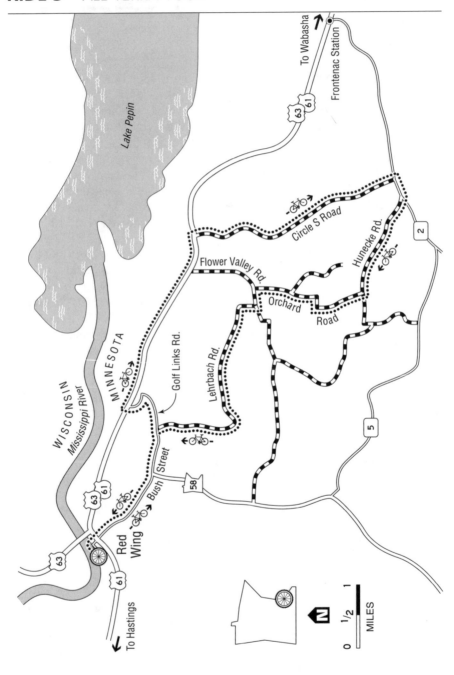

Thick woods line hillside roads south of the city of
Red Wing.

park in the lots for the Red Wing Area Chamber of Commerce, which is in
the old railroad depot building.

Sources of additional information:

Red Wing Area Chamber of Commerce
420 Levee Street
Red Wing, MN 55066
(612) 388-4719

(For the organized All-Terra tour)
John Drewes
1079 Highway 292, MCF-RW
Red Wing, MN 55066
(612) 388-7154 ext. 296

Notes on the trail: From the Red Wing Depot and Chamber of Commerce, ride one block east on Levee Street and turn right on Bush Street. Bush Street leads you out of town and becomes Golf Links Rd. All roads are two-way, but it is best to ride in a clockwise direction as this eliminates cross-traffic turns on US 61/63 and allows more paved road riding for warming up. Signage consists of official U.S. Highway and county road signs.

Town roads are well marked with green street-type signs except for the intersection of Hunecke and Orchard roads, where there is no sign. This intersection is 1.9 miles from the start of Hunecke Road at County Road 2. Orchard Road is narrow and descends sharply. At the bottom, Orchard Road ends in a **T** intersection with County Road 21 (Flower Valley Road). Turn left on CR 21 and, after a short distance, turn right on Lehrbach Road.

Returning into Red Wing on Bush Street, you will be forced to veer off to the right on Plum Street around the 10th Street intersection. Continue on Plum Street to 7th Street and turn left. Turn right on Bush Street one block later and retrace your out-bound route back to the trailhead.

RIDE 4   *MURPHY-HANREHAN TRAILS*

"Extreme" best describes the riding at Murphy-Hanrehan Park Reserve. This 6.1-mile ride includes a 1.5-mile (each way) out-and-back trail and a three-mile inner loop. There are some steep sections on the out-and-back trail, but they are just a warm-up. The inner loop makes this a very challenging ride for the average rider. Grades are long and steep. You need technique to keep the front wheel on the ground going up and to keep your body off the ground going down. Though the route is on wide cross-country ski trails, the inner loop hills are often rough, rocky, and subject to washouts that create sandy, cobble-filled gullies. The loop begins with a max-out 130-foot climb and it's a roller coaster ride from there on. Shooting up one hill, you risk becoming airborne at the crest just before a sharp left turn. Sometimes there will only be one good line on the downhills. There is no level ground on the inner loop.

If you can handle Murphy, there are many rewards to riding it. You have a chance to warm up and cool down on a relatively easy, grassy trail with a smooth hardpack track worn in. The scenery in the deep oak, maple, aspen, and birch forest is punctuated by placid lakes, ponds, and bogs. The trail itself gets a bit boggy during rainy periods.

General location: In the Twin Cities suburb of Prior Lake.
Elevation change: The terrain is constantly rolling. Extremely steep grades of 50′ to 80′ are common and one climb and descent is 130′.

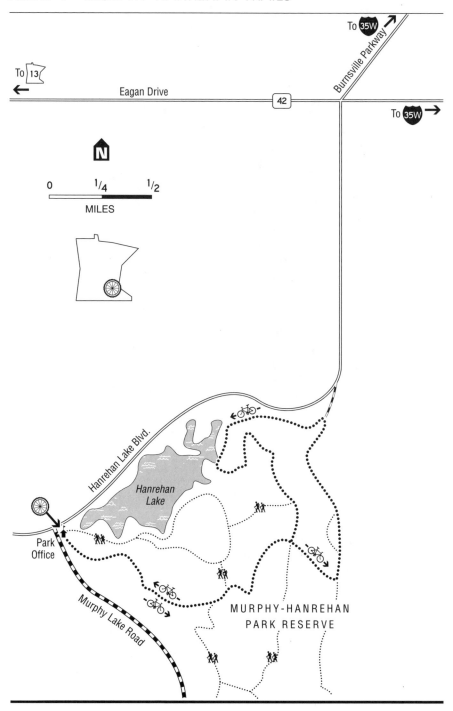

It's either up or down on the trails at Murphy-Hanrehan.

Season: Trails are open for biking August through October.

Services: All services are available in Burnsville, to the east, including bicycle retail and repair.

Hazards: Trails are well maintained, but downed trees and branches may be encountered. Grades are extremely steep and rough. Deep, rocky washouts are common on steep slopes and soft mud and sand are common at the bottom. Halfway around the inner loop is an uphill where you can easily get airborne at the crest. It is followed by a hidden left turn. Hikers may be encountered on all trails.

Rescue index: Help can be summoned by phone at the trailhead. There is frequent rider traffic on the trails. Halfway around the inner loop a gated trail leads north to busy Hanrehan Lake Boulevard.

Land status: Hennepin Park, Scott-Hennepin Park Authority. A $4 daily or $20 annual parking sticker is required to drive into the park.

Maps: A detailed trail map is available at the trailhead.

Finding the trail: Heading south on Interstate 35W, exit at County Road 42 and turn west. Heading north on I-35, exit at Crystal Lake Road and turn west; at a **T** intersection turn north on County Road 5 and at CR 42 turn west. At Burnsville Parkway turn south (this becomes Hanrehan Lake Boulevard). At Murphy Lake Road turn south and after a short distance turn left into Murphy-Hanrehan Park Reserve.

Sources of additional information:

Hennepin Parks
12615 County Road 9
Plymouth, MN 55441-1248
(612) 559-9000

Greater Minneapolis Convention and Visitors Association
4000 Multi Foods Tower
33 South 6th Street
Minneapolis, MN 55402
(612) 661-4700

Notes on the trail: A parking fee is required (see Land status). The trails are well marked with blue signs featuring climbing mountain bike silhouettes and periodic "you are here" map signs. Trails where riding is not allowed are gated and marked. After riding three miles on the inner loop you will come to a cross intersection where the trail straight ahead is gated. Turn left to ride another lap of the inner loop or right to return to the trailhead.

RIDE 5   *BUCK HILL TRAILS*

The tough slopes of Buck Hill Ski Area have been known to Twin Cities off-roaders for years as the site of the popular Tour de Bump mountain bike race held in early August. More recently Buck's trails have been open to the riding public for recreation and training Wednesdays through Sundays. A highly successful team racing series is held on Thursday evenings. Riding this 3.4-mile loop at Buck Hill with over 500 feet of climbing will definitely challenge the average rider. In another event held here, the "24 Hours at Buck," featuring teams of four riding for worthy causes, the winners covered 76 laps. Think about it.

Riding at Buck Hill entails a lot more than going up and down open ski slopes. In fact, you almost never do. Most of the trails are single or slightly wider tracks on the mixed wooded and open land that comprises the northern third of the area. Only the southern loop is entirely in the open; there the

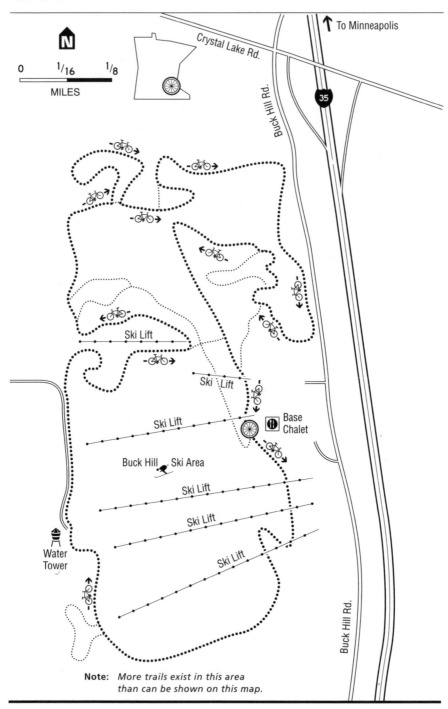

Note: *More trails exist in this area than can be shown on this map.*

route follows an unimproved access road up and around to the back of the ski hill. Up on the back side you will find a block-long stretch of paved surface that will rocket you toward the woods. Trail surfaces vary from grassy, to sandy, to earthen surface. All downhills are rough with undulating surfaces or roots and rocks—or both.

You can look like a pro by catching air as you burst out of the woods on Don's Descent. If catching your breath is more your speed, you can pause for a fine view of Crystal Lake at the top of the Enchanted Forest loop. While it's not the wilderness (you can see the interstate and suburban development from up there too), there is something reassuring about riding in an area where someone knows you're out there.

General location: One mile south of downtown in the Twin Cities suburb of Burnsville.
Elevation change: You are either going up or down at Buck Hill. One lap will take you up a steep 250′ climb, a 70′ climb, and a 100′ climb in addition to a number of shorter grades.
Season: Buck Hill Ski Area is open for mountain biking mid-May through October.
Services: Water, soft drinks, bicycle repair and rental, and helmet rental (helmets are required) are available at the trailhead. All services are available in Burnsville, including bicycle retail and repair.
Hazards: Expect very steep downhills with rough surfaces and, in places, soft sand.
Rescue index: Help is available at the trailhead. Trails are swept periodically.
Land status: Buck Hill Ski Area is private land. A trail fee of $5 per day is charged. A season pass is available for $75.
Maps: A detailed map that includes topographical information is available at the trailhead.
Finding the trail: Heading south on Interstate 35W, exit at County Road 42 and proceed straight onto Buck Hill Road, a frontage road. Heading north on I-35, exit at Crystal Lake Road and turn west, cross over the interstate, and turn south on Buck Hill Road.

Sources of additional information:

Buck Hill Ski Area
15400 Buck Hill Road
Burnsville, MN 55306
(612) 435-7174

Greater Minneapolis Convention and Visitors Association
4000 Multi Foods Tower
33 South 6th Street
Minneapolis, MN 55402
(612) 661-4700

Woods and steep terrain attract riders to Buck Hill.

Notes on the trail: A trail pass is required to ride at Buck Hill (see Land status). The trails are almost all one-way. They are well marked with name signs and blue-and-red posts and ribbon. There are more trails in the area than can be shown on this map. Because of the complexity of the system, a few "you are here" signs at intersections would be helpful, but with the small confines of the area the system soon becomes familiar.

From the trailhead follow the Burma Road, High Traverse, Skunk Hollow, Give it a Whirl, Enchanted Forest, The Swirly, Beaver Downhill, Pipeline, Steamer Lane, and Don's Descent to complete the 3.4-mile route shown on this map.

RIDE 6   *LEBANON HILLS TRAIL*

It's short, but that doesn't mean it's sweet. At 2.3 miles the Lebanon Hills loop trail dishes out a lot of adversity per linear foot. Steep, rocky, sandy uphills and downhills make it a challenging ride for those of average off-roading ability. If you take it on, you will only have to share the trail with other mountain bikers. Hiking trails banned to riding is a common situation. This is the case at Lebanon Hills, too, but here the mountain bike trails are also restricted and hiking is not allowed.

Surfaces on the park's wide cross-country ski trails vary from hardpack to loose rock and sand. The loop begins on a sunny, open unimproved road. This might tempt you to wear your cool mirrored sunglasses, but the shades will make you almost blind in the woods. Most of the trail winds through an oak forest so thick that little light filters through, even on a bright day. And you will need to see the trail. The southern part of the loop features a succession of three rocky uphills where the ability to choose a line through the rocks is as important as strength. All downhills are rocky and there is a series of **S** curves. The last one is the meanest. It tempts you to ride high on its banking as you swing to the right. If you do, you could be pitched into several trees on the outside of the following left turn. A shortcut trail runs north to south in the middle of the loop, but it does not eliminate this difficult section.

General location: In the southwest corner of the Twin Cities suburb of Eagan.
Elevation change: The terrain is almost constantly rolling. There are a half-dozen steep or very steep climbs in the 50′ range and one 90′ downhill.
Season: Lebanon Hills trails are open for mountain biking May through October.
Services: All services are available along Cliff Road to the west of Interstate 35E, including bicycle retail and repair.
Hazards: The trail is well maintained, but downed trees or branches may be found at any time. Most downhills are very rocky. One tricky **S** curve has trees at the outside of the second corner.
Rescue index: Help can be summoned at numerous businesses on Cliff Road to the west of I-35E.
Land status: Dakota County Regional Park.
Maps: Trail maps are available at the trailhead or from the Dakota County Parks Department.
Finding the trail: In the Twin Cities suburb of Eagan, exit Interstate 35E at Cliff Road and travel .75 mile to the east. Turn south on Johnny Cake Ridge Road and travel one-half mile to the parking lot for Dakota County Lebanon Hills Regional Park on the right.

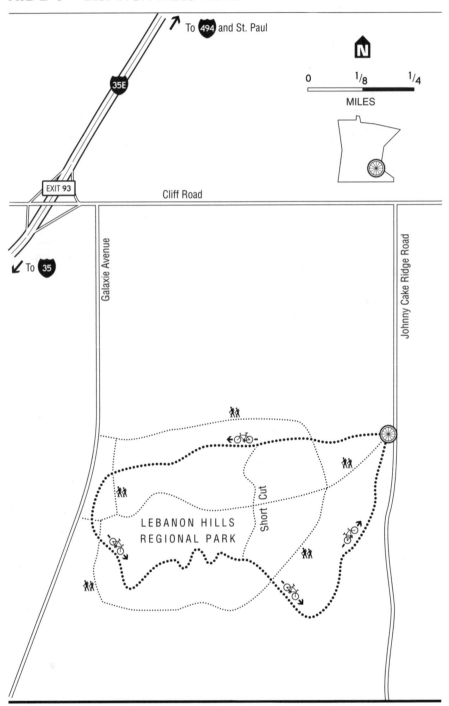

To **494** and St. Paul

35E

EXIT 93

To **35**

Cliff Road

N

0   1/8   1/4
MILES

Galaxie Avenue

Johnny Cake Ridge Road

Short Cut

LEBANON HILLS
REGIONAL PARK

Hiking is not allowed on the mountain bike trails at
Lebanon Hills.

Sources of additional information:

Dakota County Parks Department
8500 127th Street East
Hastings, MN 55033
(612) 437-6608

Greater Minneapolis Convention and Visitors Association
4000 Multi Foods Tower
33 South 6th Street
Minneapolis, MN 55402
(612) 661-4700

Notes on the trail: This one-way trail is well marked with brown and white
mountain bike silhouette signs and frequent "you are here" map signs. Riding
is not allowed on the numerous hiking trails, which are marked with two

signs: the green and white hiker silhouette sign and the brown and white bike sign—this time with a red circle and slash on it. This circle and slash is not always visible in the dark forest, but to stray onto any hiking trail, you would have to make a radical turn.

At about 1.5 miles there is a series of **S** curves. Use extra caution on the last one, which swings to the right with a high banking. Riding way up on the banking at high speed can throw you into several trees at the outside of the next curve. There is a shortcut mountain bike trail at .2 mile from the trailhead parking lot, but it rejoins the outside loop before the series of **S** curves. At 2.3 miles you will see an "exit" sign, which will lead you to the parking lot a few feet away, or you can turn left on a bypass trail and begin another lap.

RIDE 7   *ELM CREEK TRAILS*

Elm Creek Park Reserve's trails are the easy riders of off-roading in the Twin Cities Metro area. The 4.6-mile loop shown here is a good introduction to off-road riding for the novice or a nice cruise for the more advanced rider. The park's swimming beach can make a visit to Elm Creek even more fun. Terrain is flat to gently rolling with a few short, steep grades to test your climbing ability. The route follows wide grassy cross-country ski trails with a hardpack track worn in for most of the distance. There is also a block-long stretch of boardwalk crossing a marsh that offers a great view of the tall cattails and of Mud Lake. The scenery is a mix of marshland, open area with sumac bushes, and hardwood forest with many maple trees. Near the northern part of the loop you enter a dark tunnel through the maples and ride on the bare earthen floor. There are a few short stretches of black muck in low spots.

General location: In the northern Twin Cities suburb of Maple Grove, northwest of Osseo.

Elevation change: The terrain is flat to rolling. Some short, steep climbs of 30′ to 50′ will be encountered.

Season: Elm Creek mountain bike trails are open April through October. They may be closed due to wet conditions, so be sure to call ahead.

Services: All services, except a bicycle shop, are available in Osseo. Bicycle retail and repair are available to the east in Brooklyn Park.

Hazards: Trails are well maintained, but fallen trees and branches are always a possibility. There is a significant lip on the boardwalk through the marsh about a quarter-mile from the trailhead. Hikers may be encountered on all trails.

Rescue index: Help is available at the Visitor Center at the trailhead and at the Eastman Nature Center. Trails are well traveled.

RIDE 7 *ELM CREEK TRAILS*

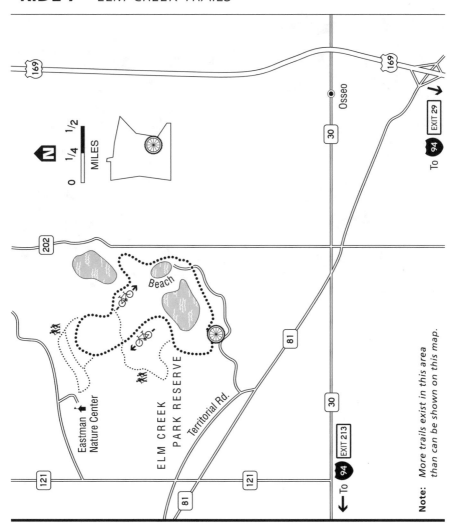

Land status: Hennepin County Park Reserve. A \$4 daily or \$20 annual parking sticker is required to drive into the park.

Maps: A detailed trail map is available at the trailhead.

Finding the trail: From US 169 turn west on County Road 81. Travel through Osseo and turn right on Territorial Road. After a tenth of a mile turn right into Elm Creek Park Reserve and follow the road three-quarters of a mile to the Visitor Center on the left.

The boardwalk is the best way to see the marsh at Elm Creek. *Photo courtesy of Hennepin Parks.*

Sources of additional information:

Hennepin Parks
12615 County Road 9
Plymouth, MN 55441-1248
(612) 559-9000

Greater Minneapolis Convention and Visitors Association
4000 Multi Foods Tower
33 South 6th Street
Minneapolis, MN 55402
(612) 661-4700

Notes on the trail: A parking fee is required (see Land status). The trails are generally well marked with brown and white mountain bike signs and periodic "you are here" map signs. The paved bike trails (nine miles total) are marked with the same signs; trails where riding is not allowed use these signs with the additional red circle and slash. The red slash is not always easy to see in the forest. There are more trails in the park than can possibly be depicted on this map.

The trails are signed for two-way travel, but these directions are for riding counter-clockwise. From the Visitor Center trailhead, follow the gravel road to the right of the building and make an immediate right onto a grassy off-road trail. Make a sharp right at the bottom of the hill, following signs directing you to the Creek Trail. At 2.3 miles you are dumped out onto a paved bike trail for about ten yards before the off-road trail splits off to the right. At this point you will be on the Lake Trail. At 2.7 miles you will briefly ride on paved trail again before veering right onto the off-road trail.

At an intersection at 2.9 miles both trails are marked for mountain biking. Take the left trail. At 3.1 miles you are again out on a paved bike trail. Stay on it, crossing several roads, until 3.8 miles, where a grassy trail signed for mountain bikes makes a sharp right. If you come to the Hennepin Corridor Trail, a paved bike trail that junctions from the left, you have gone about fifteen yards too far. At 4.4 miles you ride the paved trail again for a tenth of a mile before turning right on an off-road trail; this takes you back to the trailhead parking lot after another tenth of a mile.

Northern Minnesota

When you get "out state" as they say, which means beyond the Twin Cities, the land starts to resemble the wilderness that existed in pre-Columbian times, especially if you go north. The state license plates claim that Minnesota is the land of 10,000 lakes; most of them are in northern Minnesota. Minnesota-speak for summer vacation is "going up to the lake."

The big lake in Minnesota is Lake Superior. Geologically speaking, it is a graben. Over a billion years ago, fissures opened in the western lake area, and molten lava welled up from the earth's core, eventually forming a mass five miles thick. The tremendous weight of the flows caused the earth's crust to subside and form the Lake Superior basin, a perfect trough to channel glacial ice into Minnesota.

Northern Minnesota is also the location of the Mesabi Range (pronounced Mess-ah-bah), a vast swath of iron ore–bearing earth that has been scoured for its resources for a hundred years. The ore pits were so huge that they were among the few man-made features astronauts could see from outer space.

On the Maplelag trails you can enjoy the northern forest land of lakes on an easy ride. This unique private area features rustic accommodations, unmatched hospitality, and a great network of cross-country ski trails in a maple forest.

Minnesota's State Park system has responded to the interest in mountain biking with designated riding trails. Four are included in northern Minnesota. Lakes and forests mark the moderately difficult route at Savanna Portage State Park. At Jay Cooke State Park, three loops from easy to moderately difficult shadow the St. Louis River as it flows toward Lake Superior. An easy loop at Gooseberry Falls State Park will leave plenty of time to relax beside the park's five scenic waterfalls. Split Rock State Park packages Lake Superior's most picturesque lighthouse with moderately difficult riding trails that will show you a fantastic view of the lake.

Giants Ridge Recreation Area is an outdoor sports development in the heart of the Iron Range that has become a center for off-roading activity. The area promotes the state's most popular fat tire festival on Labor Day weekend. Two Giants Ridge trails, the Silver and the Laurentian, offer contrasting, challenging, and moderate riding experiences in the same area.

RIDE 8   *MAPLELAG TRAILS*

Note: *More trails exist in this area than can be shown on this map.*

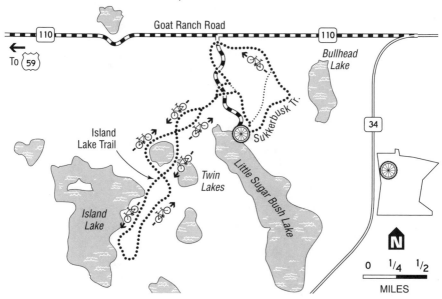

RIDE 8   *MAPLELAG TRAILS*

This easy 6.4-mile cruise on Maplelag's cross-country ski trails is a loop ride through a forest that has been powering the self-propelled for hundreds of years. As the name of Jim and Mary Richards's rustic resort implies, Maplelag stands amidst maple trees. In fact, they are sugar maples that were tapped for sap to produce high-energy maple syrup and sugar by the native Ojibwe and early Finnish settlers.

The Richards family has created the perfect atmosphere for enjoying a north woods mountain bike vacation. Their ever-expanding collection of accommodations is augmented by an eclectic assortment of memorabilia, the Cadillac of hot tubs, and lots of home cooking. You don't have to stay there to ride the wide, smooth, mowed grass cross-country ski trails, but it's a shame to pass them by. There is much more mountain biking than just the loop shown here. There are over 30 miles of trails. The Richards's son Jay is an outstanding mountain bike racer, and he has designed three miles of challenging single-track for biking only. Riders may find some swampy sections,

The maple forest at Maplelag.

but the payoff will be lake views and chances to spot beaver, swans, and other wildlife. Maplelag also holds an annual mountain bike race, Laddie's Loppet, in late September, which is usually the height of the fall color season.

General location: Nine miles east of the village of Callaway, which is on US 59.
Elevation change: Moderate grades in the 50′ elevation range will be found.
Season: Maplelag's trails are open for mountain biking in May, September, and October, and in November until the snow flies.
Services: Water, food, beverage, and lodging are available at Maplelag.
Hazards: Trails are smooth and well maintained, but new windfall trees and branches are always a possible hazard.
Rescue index: Help is available at the trailhead and County Road 110 is well traveled.
Land status: Private land with some easements on public land.
Maps: An excellent map showing topographical information and all cross-country ski trails is available from Maplelag.

Finding the trail: Follow large Maplelag signs. From the village of Callaway travel a half-mile north on US 59 and turn east on County Road 14. After 3 miles, turn north on County Road 23 at a **T** intersection. After 1.7 miles turn east on County Road 110 (gravel, Goat Ranch Road) and travel 3.5 miles to the Maplelag entrance on the south side of the road.

Sources of additional information:

Maplelag
Route 1, Box 52
Callaway, MN 56521-9741
(218) 375-4466, (800) 654-7711 (lodging reservations only)

Notes on the trail: Be sure to check in at the resort before riding. There are many more trails at Maplelag than can be shown on this map, but the cross-country ski map shows them all. Trails are well marked with ski signs. Most of the trails are one-way, but the route begins on the two-way Sukkerbusk loop. Pick up the trail behind the Norwegian log cabin and ride it in either direction until you junction with the Island Lake Trail. Follow the one-way Island Lake loop as it crisscrosses the lakes and forest before returning to the Sukkerbusk loop.

RIDE 9   *SAVANNA PORTAGE STATE PARK TRAILS*

This 7.3-mile loop follows gravel roads and cross-country and snowmobile trails. It passes through dense oak woods, past lakes, and across the watershed between the Mississippi River and Lake Superior in historic Savanna Portage State Park. The area was once the site of a French fur trade route, and a hiking trail (which is off-limits to bikes) traces its course. The gravel roads are wide and well surfaced. The trails are always wide enough for a four-wheeled ATV and the surface varies from grassy to soft and mucky where boardwalks are sometimes used to assure passage.

This is a moderate ride and a good challenge for the novice. No technical skill is needed except for the ability to control a bike on downhills and the will to negotiate soft surfaces. Wildlife abound in the park and deer, wolves, moose, bear, and coyotes may be seen. Two scenic views on the trail overlook Wolf Lake and Loon Lake.

General location: Seventeen miles northeast of McGregor, 50 miles west of Duluth.
Elevation change: The terrain is flat to gently rolling except for the mostly moderate 100′ climb on the gravel park road and the watershed trail.
Season: May through October. Always call ahead to make sure the trails are open.

RIDE 9   *SAVANNA PORTAGE STATE PARK TRAILS*

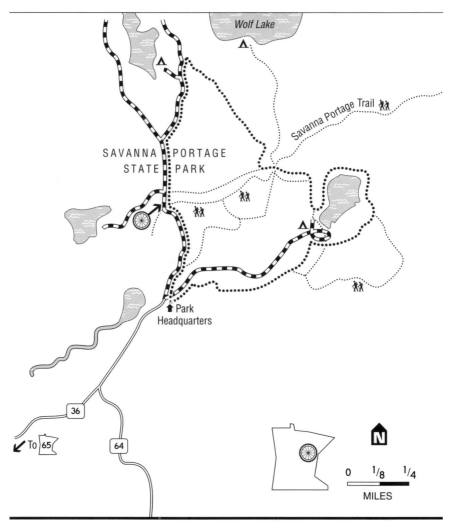

Services: All services except bicycle retail and repair are available in McGregor.

Hazards: Trails and roads are well maintained, but windfall branches and logs are a possibility. Gravel roads are open to motor vehicle traffic, which should be light. Trails are open to hikers. Expect a rough ride if you don't control your speed coming down the Continental Divide Trail.

Rescue index: Help is available at the park headquarters.

Scenic woods line the trails at Savanna Portage State Park.

Land status: Minnesota State Park. A daily or annual admission sticker is required for motor vehicles in the park ($4 daily, $20 annually). Bicycles ridden into the park are not charged.

Maps: An excellent map is available at the park headquarters or from the Minnesota DNR.

Finding the trail: Follow County Road 14/36 northeast from McGregor to Savanna Portage State Park. Follow the gravel park road north from the park headquarters building to the Savanna Portage Historical Marker parking area.

Sources of additional information:

Minnesota Department of Natural Resources
Division of Parks and Recreation Information Center
500 Lafayette Road
St. Paul, MN 55155-4040
(612) 296-6157

Savanna Portage State Park Manager
Route 3
McGregor, MN 55760
(218) 426-3271

Notes on the trail: The route can be ridden in either direction, but I recommend going clockwise. This will allow a warm-up on gravel roads. From the Savanna Portage Historic Site parking lot, ride north on the gravel park road one-half mile, where you will turn right on the gravel road to the Savanna Lake group campground. Continue straight past the left turn into the campground approximately two-tenths of a mile and turn right on the Continental Divide Trail. There is little in the way of specific marking for mountain biking, but frequent "you are here" signs help keep you oriented and off of hiking trails where riding is prohibited.

RIDE 10 *JAY COOKE STATE PARK TRAILS*

This 13.6-mile route includes 7.3 miles on the paved railroad grade, Willard Munger State Trail. The remaining 6.3 miles consists of cross-country and snowmobile trails in Jay Cooke State Park. The park preserves a scenic section of the St. Louis River that is one of the finest whitewater kayaking rivers in the state. The off-road sections consist of three separate loops of different characters.

The first is an easy 1.9-mile, near dead-flat, grassy snowmobile loop trail that runs along the tilted slate shore of Forbay Lake before returning to the Munger Trail. The second loop, the 3.3-mile Triangle Trail, is the toughest, but still garners a moderate rating. The cross-country ski trail winds through the dense maple and birch forest. The surface is a mix of grass, hardpack, and soft low spots. A one-mile round trip spur trail, where riding is not allowed, leads to a scenic overlook of the St. Louis River. The third loop, the Oak Trail, is also a cross-country ski trail and has a surface similar to the Triangle Trail, but it only covers 120 feet of elevation.

It is possible to access these trails from the park headquarters by riding the .9 mile-long Forbay Trail, but I recommend starting at the village of Carlton. This way you can use the paved road to warm up and you can also enjoy the view from the stressed iron bridge over the St. Louis River three-quarters of a mile from the start. This is a good introductory off-road experience because the Munger Trail and Forbay Lake loop are very easy, the Oak Trail is easy to moderate, and the Triangle Trail is moderate. The Munger Trail goes all the way to the south end of Duluth, a distance of 14 miles.

General location: Fifteen miles west of the city of Duluth and 5 miles east of the city of Cloquet.

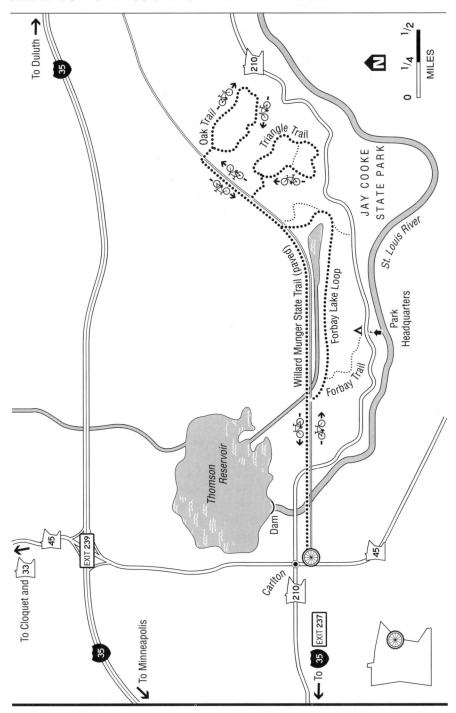

Steep layers of tilted rock plunge to the St. Louis River at
Jay Cooke State Park.

Elevation change: If you ride all three loops you will gain and lose 460′ of
elevation.

Season: May through October. Always call ahead to make certain the trails
are open. Bug season reaches its height in June and July.

Services: There is a restaurant, motel, and tavern in Carlton. All services,
including bicycle retail and repair, are available 15 miles away in Duluth. All
services except bicycle retail and repair are available 5 miles away in Cloquet.

Hazards: The trails are all well maintained and, while open to hikers, shouldn't
attract many. Fallen branches and logs are always possible hazards.

Rescue index: Help is available in Carlton and at park headquarters.

Land status: Minnesota State Park. A daily or annual admission sticker is
required for motor vehicles in the park ($4 daily, $20 annually). Bicycles ridden
into the park are not charged and there is no fee for riding on the Willard
Munger Trail, but trail donations are appreciated.

The Munger trail cuts through jagged basalt on its way
to the city of Duluth.

Maps: An excellent map is available from the Minnesota DNR or at park
headquarters.
Finding the trail: If you are traveling north on I-35, exit at MN 210 and follow it two miles east to Carlton. If you are coming from Duluth, exit at MN
45 and drive one mile south.

Sources of additional information:

Minnesota Department of Natural Resources
Division of Parks and Recreation Information Center
500 Lafayette Road
St. Paul, MN 55155-4040
(612) 296-6157

Jay Cooke State Park Manager
Carlton, MN 55718
(218) 384-4610

Duluth Convention and Visitors Bureau
Endion Station
100 Lake Place Drive
Duluth, MN 55802
(800) 438-5884.

Notes on the trail: Start at the Willard Munger State Trail parking area in Carlton. The off-road trails are marked with small brown and white mountain bike signs that are hard to spot from the Munger Trail. The Forbay Lake loop starts 1.8 miles from the parking lot. The Triangle Trail is .6 mile from where the Forbay Lake Loop returns to the Munger Trail and the Oak Trail is another .6 mile beyond.

RIDE 11 GOOSEBERRY FALLS STATE PARK TRAILS

An easy 2.8-mile loop on cross-country ski and snowmobile trails takes you into the dense birch and conifer forest of Gooseberry Falls State Park. As you can tell from the name, the park is known for its waterfalls. There are five of them, and all are easily accessible by foot. The first four are large 30- to 60-foot falls a short distance above and below the US 61 bridge where the Gooseberry River flows into Lake Superior. Visitors always love these falls. The Fifth Falls is much smaller and some distance up stream. It can easily be accessed on foot from the mountain bike trail and viewed from a footbridge without the crowds. Deer and gulls are common, and the black bear is also counted among the park residents.

The trails are grassy with a walking/riding path worn down the middle. The grass may be tall since the trails are only mowed in the fall. Some loose rock may be found on steeper sections. All are wide enough for a four-wheel-drive ATV. This is an easy, introductory off-road experience. The ride begins with a gradual uphill. There are a few steeper pitches beyond Fifth Falls. The snowmobile trail is a moderate mile-long descent back to the Interpretive Center.

General location: Forty miles northeast of Duluth.
Elevation change: The terrain rolls quite a bit in the middle section. The high point reached is 200′ above the starting point.
Season: Late April through October. Insect populations are high from late May to August. Temperatures can be very cool at any time of the year in this region. The daily low temperature is below freezing for half of the year.

RIDE 11   *GOOSEBERRY FALLS STATE PARK TRAILS*

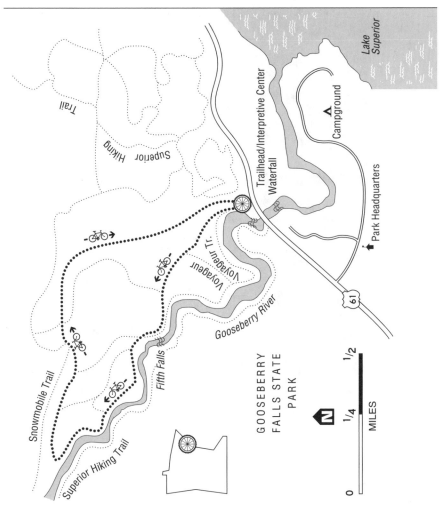

Services: None at all along the route. All services except bicycle retail and repair are available in Two Harbors. All services including bicycle retail and repair are available in Duluth.

Hazards: Downed trees and branches may be found at any time. Hiking is allowed on all trails, but foot traffic is light.

Rescue index: Help is available at park headquarters or the Interpretive Center.

Land status: Minnesota State Park. A daily or annual admission sticker is required for motor vehicles in the park ($4 daily, $20 annually). Bicycles ridden into the park are not charged and it is not necessary to pay the motor

Upper Falls is one of the five cascades at Gooseberry
Falls State Park.

vehicle fee if you park at the Interpretive Center or in the lots along
US 61.

Maps: An excellent map showing topographic and trail information is
available from the Minnesota DNR or at park headquarters.

Finding the trail: The Gooseberry Falls State Park Interpretive Center is
on the north side of the US 61 Gooseberry River bridge, 40 miles north of
Duluth.

Sources of additional information:

Minnesota Department of Natural Resources
Division of Parks and Recreation Information Center
500 Lafayette Road
St. Paul, MN 55155-4040
(612) 296-6157

Two Harbors Chamber of Commerce
P.O. Box 39
Two Harbors, MN 55616
(218) 834-2600

Notes on the trail: From the right side of the Interpretive Center parking lot, follow the Voyageur Trail to the northeast. Do not follow the Voyageur Trail from the left side of the lot where it descends to follow the river. This trail section and the Fifth Falls Trails are the only ones on the north side of the river where riding is restricted. Special signage for biking does not exist, but blue cross-country ski signs, orange snowmobile signs, and frequent "you are here" map signs make getting lost less likely. Other than the point at .3 mile from the start, where the Voyageur Trail turns left, if you always choose the left trail at any intersection until you reach the snowmobile trail, you will follow the route perfectly.

RIDE 12   *SPLIT ROCK STATE PARK TRAILS*

A 5.8-mile spur-and-loop ride on the Lake Superior shoreline in Split Rock Lighthouse State Park offers views of one of Minnesota's most scenic attractions. The Split Rock Lighthouse and Museum, perhaps the most photographed beacon in the country, was built in 1909, a few years after a storm wrecked six ships in the area. The park features unique cart-in campsites where carts are used to haul equipment to tent-only campsites. White tail deer are common and an occasional moose or black bear may be seen.

On the south side of US 61 the trails are covered with fairly firm, crushed red gravel for the most part. This makes a fast, rolling surface, but also a popular one for hikers. Away from the highway the trail is grassy, and rocks, roots, and soft surfaces may be found. The loose rock on the climb to the lookout point on the Merrill Logging Trail will challenge the skill of any rider. The ride is moderate to difficult; the main difficulty comes on the lookout climb. Several other scenic overlooks can be reached by foot. The Top of the Day Trail scales a 100-foot hill for a fantastic view of the lighthouse and the lake. Bring your camera.

General location: Forty-seven miles northeast of Duluth.
Elevation change: The terrain is almost constantly rolling. From the low point to the high point, the elevation change is 270′. The climb to the high point, the lookout on the Merrill Logging Trail, is 140′, a one-in-seven average grade for a quarter mile. This climb can be avoided by taking the short bypass trail, which also saves .2 mile.

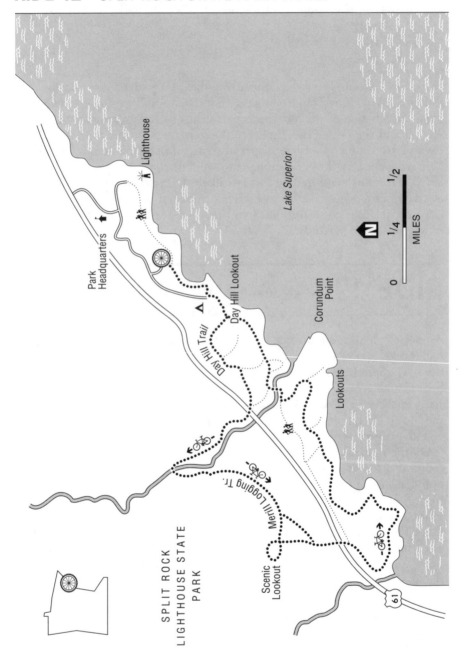

Split Rock Lighthouse stands on a jagged rock above the shore of Lake Superior.

Season: Late April through October. Insect populations are high from late May to August. Temperatures can be very cool at any time of the year in this region. The daily low temperature is below freezing for half of the year.

Services: None at all along the route. All services except bicycle retail and repair are available in Two Harbors. All services including bicycle retail and repair are available in Duluth.

Hazards: Downed trees and branches may be found at any time. Hiking is popular and allowed on all of the trails. Rocks, roots, and logs laid across soft spots require caution. Traffic on US 61 travels at highway speeds, so make a full stop before crossing.

Rescue index: Help is available at park headquarters.

Land status: Minnesota State Park. A daily or annual admission sticker is required for motor vehicles in the park ($4 daily, $20 annually). Bicycles ridden into the park are not charged admission.

Maps: An excellent map showing topographic and trail information is available from the Minnesota DNR and at park headquarters.

Finding the trail: The entrance road to Split Rock Lighthouse State Park is on the south side of US 61, 47 miles north of Duluth. Take the park road that splits to the right just beyond the park headquarters to the picnic shelter parking lot. Take the trail at the west end of the lot.

Sources of additional information:

> Minnesota Department of Natural Resources
> Division of Parks and Recreation Information Center
> 500 Lafayette Road
> St. Paul, MN 55155-4040
> (612) 296-6157

> Split Rock Lighthouse Park Manager
> 2010A Highway 61 East
> Two Harbors, MN 55616
> (218) 226-3065

> Two Harbors Chamber of Commerce
> P.O. Box 39
> Two Harbors, MN 55616
> (218) 834-2600

Notes on the trail: An admission sticker is required for motor vehicles in the park (see Land status). The ride starts at the west end of the picnic shelter parking lot. This trail does not go to the shelter. A short downhill will take you to a **T** intersection where you will turn right on the Little Two Harbors Trail. There is no special signage for mountain biking, but "you are here" map signs appear frequently. At the Day Hill Trail, keep to the right. Hike to the top on the Top of the Day Trail for a great view. Cross US 61 with caution. On the Merrill Logging Trail the climb to the lookout requires skill and strength; skill and caution are needed coming down. A shortcut trail can be taken to avoid the climb.

RIDE 13   *GIANTS RIDGE SILVER TRAIL*

You might expect that a trail on Minnesota's Iron Range would be named after a mine, since the "range" is where half the ore used in World War II came from. But the kind of silver mined at Giants Ridge didn't come out of the ground. It was in silver medals fought over by some of the world's best cross-country skiers. Giants Ridge is one of the few sites in the country that has hosted a World Cup cross-country ski race.

The competition trails at Giants Ridge are as tough as they come, and the 6.2-mile (10 kilometer) Silver Trail will give any mountain biker a workout.

The Silver Trail at Giants Ridge challenges any rider.
Photo courtesy of Giants Ridge Recreation Area.

Yes, there is a Gold Trail and you don't even want to try it. The intestinal look of the Silver Trail map is no accident. Every turn seeks out another hill. Wide, mowed and grassy, it is constantly rolling with many short, steep grades. No great technical riding ability is needed, but the ever-present "dead heads," melon-sized glacial boulders, make suspension systems welcome. The trail deserves a challenging rating for the average rider. There are three possible shortcuts if you're in over your head.

It's not all grunt and groan on the Silver Trail. The way the trail flows is a dream. You'll hardly have to touch your brakes as you roll through the pine and aspen forest. Two bridges cross creeks. Deer and grouse are common, and timberwolves are sometimes seen. The trail is part of the course for the Giants Ridge Mountain Bike Festival, one of the Midwest's most popular off-road races, held each Labor Day weekend. Giants Ridge is attractive for more than just its trails. The extensive facilities that serve the downhill and cross-country skiers in winter are at the disposal of mountain bikers in summer and fall.

General location: Five miles northeast of Biwabik.

Elevation change: About 1,200′ of elevation will be gained and lost. This will be accomplished by scaling a succession of very steep 40′ to 60′ climbs.

Season: Giants Ridge Trails are open for mountain biking May 1 to October 31.

Services: Food, beverage, and bike rental are available at Giants Ridge. Lodging is available at the site's comfortable Olympic Training Center and more luxurious condos. All services are available in Biwabik and Virginia, including a full-service bicycle shop in Virginia.

Hazards: Trails are well maintained, but windfall trees and branches may be encountered. Glacial rocks are common in the trail surfaces.

Rescue index: Help is available at the trailhead.

Land status: Private Giants Ridge land and easements through the Superior National Forest.

Maps: A comprehensive trail map is available from Giants Ridge. The Biwabik quadrangle USGS 7.5 minute map shows the terrain very well, but not the trails.

Finding the trail: From Biwabik travel 1.5 miles east on MN 135 and turn north on County Road 138. Follow it three miles to Giants Ridge Recreation area on the left.

Sources of additional information:

> Giants Ridge Recreation Area
> P.O. Box 190
> Biwabik, MN 55708
> (218) 865-4143, (800) 688-7669

> Virginia Chamber of Commerce
> P.O. Box 1072
> Virginia, MN 55792
> (218) 741-2717

Notes on the trail: The trail is well marked for one-way counter-clockwise travel with green and brown mountain bike silhouette signs and cross-country ski trail signs. The trail begins to the northeast of the ski chalet. Head toward the barn-shaped timing building, the easternmost of the ski area structures. There are three possible shortcuts and a number of hill bypasses.

RIDE 14 *GIANTS RIDGE LAURENTIAN TRAIL*

The Laurentian Trail proves that there is some relatively tame riding at Giants Ridge. How this is accomplished looping around the same area as the tough Silver Trail may seem a mystery. The answer is that the Laurentian loop avoids

RIDE 13 *GIANTS RIDGE SILVER TRAIL*
RIDE 14 *GIANTS RIDGE LAURENTIAN TRAIL*

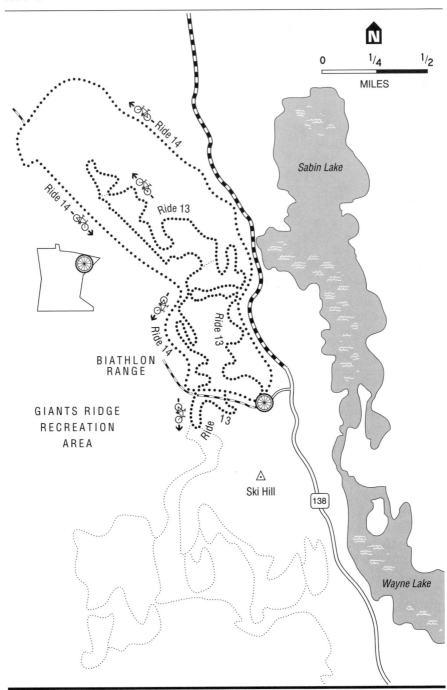

Giants Ridge stages the state's most popular fat tire festival each Labor Day weekend. *Photo courtesy of Giants Ridge Recreation Area.*

much of the tumble of rugged glacial moraine by skirting its edge. This geographical feat makes the 5.2-mile Laurentian Trail of moderate difficulty for the average rider. Bikers travel over rolling terrain on an old gravel-surfaced road and snowmobile trail for just over half the distance; the trail finishes up on a wide, mowed, grassy cross-country ski trail. You will be in the deep pine and aspen forest for nearly the entire ride.

General location: Five miles northeast of Biwabik.
Elevation change: About 800′ of elevation will be gained and lost over rolling terrain.
Season: Giants Ridge trails are open for mountain biking May 1 to October 31.
Services: Food, beverage, lodging, and bike rental are available at Giants Ridge. All services are available in Biwabik and Virginia, including a full-service bicycle shop in Virginia.
Hazards: Trails are well maintained, but windfall trees and branches may be found at any time. Glacial rocks are common in the ski trail's surface.
Rescue index: Help is available at the trailhead.
Land status: Private Giants Ridge land and easements through the Superior National Forest. A $6 daily trail fee is charged.
Maps: A comprehensive trail map is available from Giants Ridge. The Biwabik quadrangle USGS 7.5 minute map shows the terrain very well, but not the trails.

The Laurentian Trail is an easy roll through the woods.

Finding the trail: From Biwabik travel 1.5 miles east on MN 135 and turn north on County Road 138. Follow it three miles to Giants Ridge Recreation area on the left.

Sources of additional information:

Giants Ridge Recreation Area
P.O. Box 190
Biwabik, MN 55708
(218) 865-4143, (800) 688-7669

Virginia Chamber of Commerce
P.O. Box 1072
Virginia, MN 55792
(218) 741-2717

Notes on the trail: A daily trail fee is charged (see Land Status). The trail is well marked for two-way travel with green and brown mountain bike silhouette signs, orange snowmobile signs, and cross-country ski trail signs. The cues given here are for riding it counter-clockwise. The trail begins on an old, rough, paved road at the northeast corner of the paved parking lot. It soon becomes a rough gravel downhill. You will need to veer left at the bottom. This is the snowmobile trail and you will stay on it until 3 miles, where it splits off to the northeast and the Giants Ridge ski trail begins at a gated intersection. Follow the ski trail and mountain bike signs back to the trailhead.

Minnesota Arrowhead Region

You know you've gone about as far north as you can go in the lower 48 states when the daily low temperature is below freezing over half of the year. The Arrowhead region is named after its shape. Maybe it should have been called the Icicle region. Sandwiched between the Canadian border and Lake Superior, the area includes the vast Boundary Waters Canoe Area, the last great wilderness of lakes and portages in the United States, and the Sawtooth Mountains abutting the lake shore.

The Sawtooth shape of the peaks that rise one thousand feet above the lake are easily seen from the shore drive. The rugged terrain hosts many streams that tumble over the basalt (lava) rock and often from scenic waterfalls. Much of the slopes and the plateau above is part of the Superior National Forest (SNF), which has numerous signed forest road and trail routes for mountain biking.

The Timber / Frear and Pancore routes are, respectively, moderate and easy SNF rides that explore the dense woods and lakes of the plateau. The Cascade Trail features moderately difficult sections that include an 800-foot descent to the lake edge and a view, after a short hike, of the impressive flow of Cascade Falls. Lutsen Mountains, the Midwest's most prestigious downhill ski area, packages challenging mountain biking with a gondola lift ride to the top of Moose Mountain. The Mark Lake / Pike Lake Tour and Eliason Tower Trail are, respectively, moderate and challenging SNF routes that wind through the lakes, streams, and woods of the Sawtooth Mountains.

The Gunflint Trail is an ancient trade route that links Lake Superior to Canada. One ride lies at each end. The Pincushion Mountain Trails offer a moderate ride on rolling cross-country ski trails with a fantastic Lake Superior view from the peak's bedrock surface. From the Upper Gunflint Trails, you can look over Gunflint Lake to the Canadian shore and keep an eye out for magnificent moose as you skirt the bog country inland.

RIDE 15 *TIMBER / FREAR TRAIL*

This 19-mile loop takes you through the birch- and aspen-forested lake country of the Superior National Forest. There is a grand ridge view along Forest Road 390 and also access to Cross River Lake and Four Mile Lake at boat landings. The riding surface varies from maintained gravel forest roads to grassy, but firm—and sometimes rocky and stump-strewn—old logging roads. The old roads are unmowed, but there should be enough traffic to

RIDE 15 *TIMBER / FREAR TRAIL*

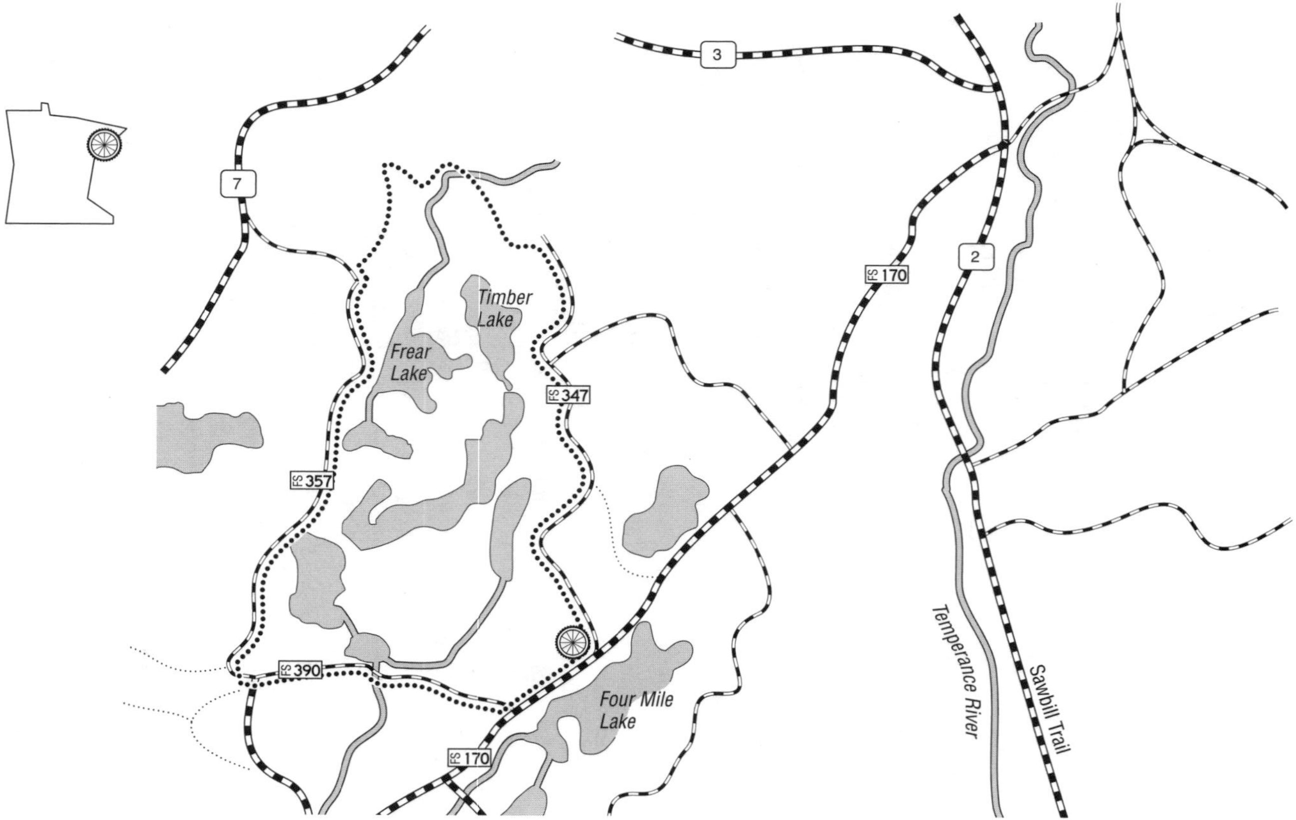

Sawbill Trail

Temperance River

2

170

3

347

Timber Lake

Frear Lake

Four Mile Lake

170

357

390

7

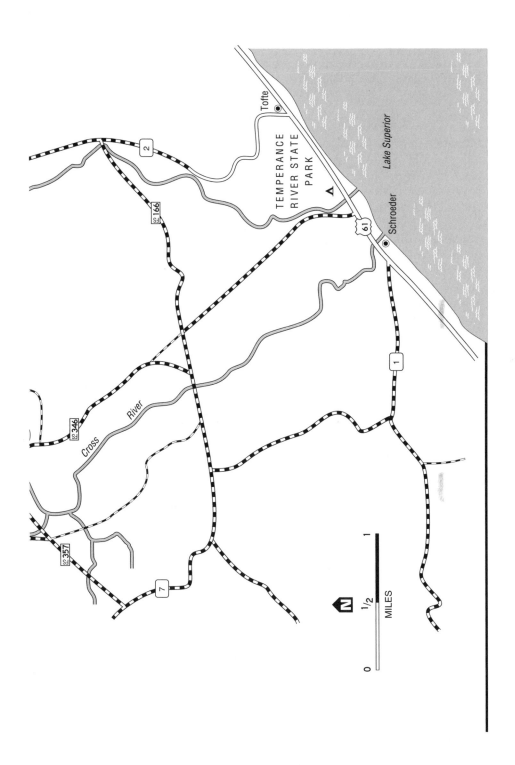

make parallel vehicle tire tracks. No technical skill is needed for this route, but the rough surface and distance rank it at the low end of the moderate scale for the average rider. FS 170 can be very muddy after a rainy spell.

General location: Sixteen miles northwest of Tofte.
Elevation change: There are two gradual climbs of about 100′ within one mile along FR 347. Otherwise the terrain is level to gently rolling.
Season: Late April through October. Insect populations are high from late May to August. Temperatures can be very cool at any time of the year in this region. The daily low temperature is below freezing for half of the year.
Services: None at all along the route. All services, except bicycle services, are available in Tofte. In Grand Marais, Superior North Outdoor Center provides outfitting and bicycle service.
Hazards: Downed trees and branches may be found at any time. The grass on FS 347 may be high late in the season, hiding old stumps and rocks. The Superior National Forest is managed for logging; logging trucks may be encountered anywhere along the route. All-terrain vehicles and four-wheel-drive vehicles may be encountered anywhere during the fall hunting season.
Rescue index: Help is available in Tofte and can be summoned at the Crooked Lake Resort on County Road 7. FS 170 is the only road with any amount of traffic.
Land status: Superior National Forest.
Maps: Excellent maps of the routes based on USGS 7.5 minute quadrangles are available for a charge from McKenzie Maps, 315 West Michigan Street, Suite 10, Duluth, MN 55802; (218) 727-2113. Map number 203 covers the Timber/Frear area. A useful regional locator map, "Mountain Biking," is available at no charge from the Lutsen-Tofte Tourism Association.
Finding the trail: From US 61 at Tofte, drive 5.4 miles north on County Road 2 (Sawbill Trail). Turn west on FS 166 and drive 5.9 miles to the junction with FS 346. Drive 5.5 miles north on FS 346 to the junction with FS 170. Turn right on FS 170 and drive 1 mile to the Four Mile Lake boat landing at the junction of FS 347. Park well off the road.

Sources of additional information:

Lutsen-Tofte Tourism Association
Tofte, MN 55615
(218) 663-7804

Superior North Outdoor Center
P.O. Box 177
Grand Marais, MN 55604
(218) 387-2186

The Superior National Forest is a land of lakes and streams.

Tip of the Arrowhead Visitor Center
Grand Marais, MN 55604
(218) 387-2524

Gunflint Ranger Station
Grand Marais, MN 55604
(218) 387-1750

Mountain Biking Adventure (group tours)
Birch Grove Foundation
P.O. Box 2242
Tofte, MN 55615
(218) 663-7977

Notes on the trail: Park at the boat landing at Four Mile Lake on FS 170. The route is well signed with red-and-white Forest Service mountain bike signs. Forest Service roads are marked with small, low brown signs with yellow lettering. Because of the possibility of vandalism and the density of the forest, a compass and a bicycle odometer are recommended. The route can be ridden in either direction.

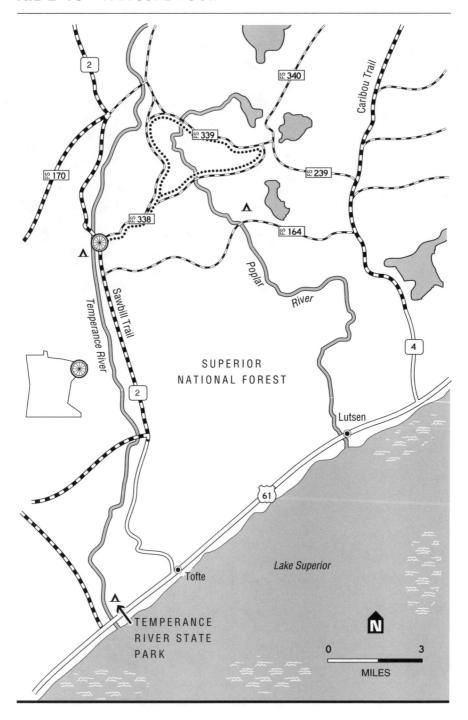

Smooth forest roads make the Pancore route an easy tour.

RIDE 16   *PANCORE TOUR*

A 16.6-mile roll on the Pancore Loop will take you through a dense forest and occasional openings in the trees created by old logging operations. It is characterized by fine north woods scenery with tall pines and a few small lakes. There is a stream crossing at Poplar River and you may find patches of wild blueberries along the route in summer. This easy route consists of Forest Service roads and logging roads. The surface varies from firm old roadbed, to sand, to grass with a firm base. For the most part trails will be double-track.

General location: Eleven miles north of Tofte.
Elevation change: The terrain is flat to rolling with no significant elevation gains.
Season: Late April through October. Insect populations are high from late May to August. Temperatures can be very cool at any time of the year in this region. The daily low temperature is below freezing for half of the year.
Services: None at all along the route. All services are available in Tofte. In Grand Marais, Superior North Outdoor Center provides outfitting and bicycle service.
Hazards: Downed trees and branches may be found at any time. The Superior National Forest is managed for logging; logging trucks may be

encountered anywhere along the route. All-terrain vehicles and four-wheel-drive vehicles may be encountered anywhere during the fall hunting season.

Rescue index: Help is available in Tofte. For the best chance of rescue, make your way to the Sawbill Trail (CR 2) or Caribou Trail (CR 4).

Land status: Superior National Forest and some private land easements.

Maps: Excellent maps of the routes based on USGS 7.5 minute quadrangles are available for a charge from McKenzie Maps, 315 West Michigan Street, Suite 10, Duluth, MN 55802; (218) 727-2113. Map number 102 covers the Pancore area. A regional map, "Mountain Biking," is available at no charge from the Lutsen-Tofte Tourism Association.

Finding the trail: From US 61 at Tofte, drive 11.5 miles north on CR 2 (Sawbill Trail) to the junction of FR 338. Park well off the road.

Sources of additional information:

Lutsen-Tofte Tourism Association
Tofte, MN 55615
(218) 663-7804

Superior North Outdoor Center
P.O. Box 177
Grand Marais, MN 55604
(218) 387-2186

Tip of the Arrowhead Visitor Center
Grand Marais, MN 55604
(218) 387-2524

Gunflint Ranger Station
Grand Marais, MN 55604
(218) 387-1750

Notes on the trail: The route should be well signed with red-and-white Forest Service mountain bike silhouette signs. Forest Service roads are marked with small, low brown signs with yellow lettering. Because of the possibility of vandalism and the density of the forest, a compass and a bicycle odometer are recommended. The route can be ridden in either direction. If you find yourself at **T** intersections when you are eastbound or northbound, you have gone too far and missed the appropriate turn.

RIDE 17   *CASCADE TRAIL*

Great overviews of Lake Superior, a downhill run that drops over 800 feet in less than four miles, and a chance to hike to one of the north shore's most scenic waterfalls are included on this 13.4-mile loop. Beginning your ride near

RIDE 17 *CASCADE TRAIL*

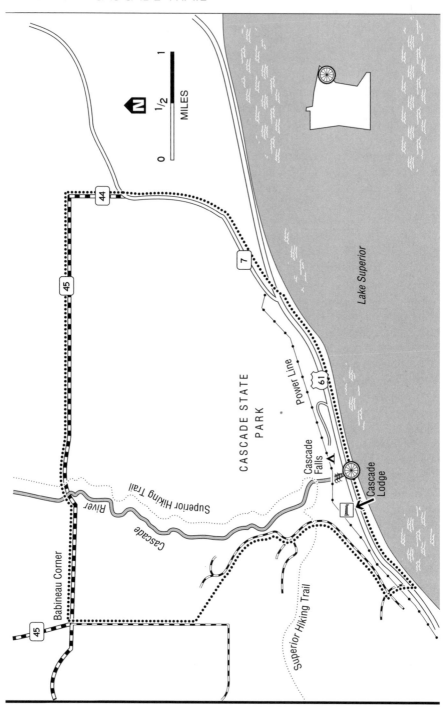

the lakeshore lets you warm up on the flat and gain altitude on a paved road. Other than the long climb, this route is not demanding, although some bike handling skill will be needed for the downhill. It is moderately difficult, a ride that provides a good variety of experiences.

Once on top of the slopes that rise out of the lake, the ride on County Road 45 is on a wide, well-maintained gravel surface over rolling terrain. The initial descent is on a steep, rutted four-wheel-drive vehicle road with periodic culverts on which you could easily get airborne. The rest of the downhill is on cross-country ski trails that vary from a soft surface initially to hardpack farther on.

Back at the lakeshore, you can warm up with a bowl of homemade soup at the Cascade Lodge and Restaurant and, if you take a short hike from the trail-head, you can view scenic Cascade Falls.

General location: At Cascade Lodge, 95 miles north of Duluth.
Elevation change: The starting point on US 61 is at 620′ and the climb to Babineau Corner takes you to 1,480′. Including the rolling section along CR 45, 1,040′ of climbing is required to cover the loop.
Season: Late April through October. Insect populations increase from late May to August. Swampy sections are worse when it has rained much, typically in the spring. Temperatures can be very cool at any time of the year in this region. The daily low temperature is below freezing for half of the year.
Services: Food, lodging, and phone are available at Cascade Lodge. Camping and phone are available at Cascade State Park. All services are available in Grand Marais, including outfitting and bicycle service at Superior North Outdoor Center. Services are also available in Tofte, and there is a country store on US 61 near Lutsen.
Hazards: Motor vehicle traffic may be significant along US 61. County Road 45 may have vehicle traffic at any time. The Superior National Forest is managed for logging; logging trucks may be encountered on federal or county roads. The steep downhill section after turning south off of CR 45 is rocky, rutted, and has serious bumps created by culverts. Braking for the turn onto the cross-country ski trail will be difficult. The initial sections of the trail are grassy and soft-surfaced, which moderates speed, but occasional spots where logs have been laid parallel to the trail direction in soft areas may be hazardous. There is a large step up to and off of a narrow wooden bridge halfway down.
Rescue index: Help can be summoned at Cascade Lodge and Cascade State Park. Rescue is available in Grand Marais, Lutsen, and Tofte. If you are injured or have a mechanical failure on the trail, make your way to the county or federal roads where your chances of rescue will be better.
Land status: Superior National Forest and Cascade Lodge property.
Maps: Excellent maps of the routes based on USGS 7.5 minute quadrangles are available for a charge from McKenzie Maps, 315 West Michigan Street, Suite 10, Duluth, MN 55802; (218) 727-2113. Map number 101 covers the

Scenic Cascade Falls is a short hike off the riding trail.
Photo courtesy of Minnesota Office of Tourism.

Cascade area. A useful regional locator map, "Mountain Biking," is available at no charge from the Lutsen-Tofte Tourism Association.
Finding the trail: Drive 16.6 miles northeast of Tofte into the Cascade Falls parking area on US 61.

Sources of additional information:

Lutsen-Tofte Tourism Association
Tofte, MN 55615
(218) 663-7804

Superior North Outdoor Center
P.O. Box 177
Grand Marais, MN 55604
(218) 387-2186

Gunflint Ranger Station
Grand Marais, MN 55604
(218) 387-1750

Mountain Biking Adventure (group tours)
Birch Grove Foundation
P.O. Box 2242
Tofte, MN 55615
(218) 663-7977

Notes on the trail: From the Cascade Falls parking area ride northeast on US 61 and turn left on County Road 7. When CR 7 turns to the northeast, continue straight onto CR 44. One-half mile later turn left on CR 45. When CR 45 turns northwest (Babineau Corner), turn south on an unnamed four-wheel-drive road. At 1.2 miles from this point turn left onto the Pioneer Loop cross-country ski trail. Begin braking well before this point and look carefully for the trail opening in the woods, since there is no on-road signage. If you make a 90-degree turn to the west, you have ridden too far. Follow ski trail signs directing you to Cascade Lodge. You have several opportunities to shorten the route and ride directly to Cascade Lodge, or you can follow the ski trail out to US 61 and enjoy a scenic cool-down ride back to the parking area. Mountain biking is not allowed on the Superior Hiking Trail.

RIDE 18 *LUTSEN MOUNTAINS TRAILS*

A 12-mile loop at Lutsen Mountains takes in about as much vertical relief as you can find on Minnesota's north shore. Lutsen (pronounced Loot-sen) is the most prestigious alpine ski area in the state and seems determined to claim the same status for mountain biking. The area offers something that no other hill in the Midwest has. The trail pass fee includes a scenic ride in an enclosed gondola from the trailhead to the top of Moose Mountain. You might think that a ride that begins with a lift will be a piece of cake. This is hardly the case at Lutsen. Even the most abbreviated route you could take from the gondola landing back to the trailhead requires 790 feet of steep climbing. The loop shown here takes in over 1,300 feet of elevation.

Besides the climbing, you'll have to handle some tough downhills as well. In places you'll ride on solid rock. Lutsen is a difficult, but extremely scenic and rewarding mountain biking experience. It demands your best in both technical bike handling ability and physical effort.

Trails on this 35-mile system vary from wide, mowed grass sections on the downhill slopes to rocky, root-crossed, and sometimes muddy single-track in the pine and maple forest, to firm, fast, hardpack graveled access roads. There

An old stressed iron bridge overlooks Poplar Falls near
Lutsen Mountains.

are great views of Lake Superior from Moose Mountain. From the Poplar
River bridge between Mystery Mountain and Ullr Mountain you can pause to
enjoy the cascade of water at Poplar Falls. You don't have to look far to find
a spot to relax and swap ride stories. The restaurant at the Village Inn is a perfect place to appreciate the view and the challenging terrain you've conquered.

General location: Lutsen Mountains is two miles off of US 61 at a point 86
miles north of Duluth.
Elevation change: This ride is punctuated by a series of steep climbs and
descents. The longest climb gains 420′ and the longest descent drops 580′.
The total elevation for the loop is over 1,300′ if the gondola is used. If not,
add another 290′.

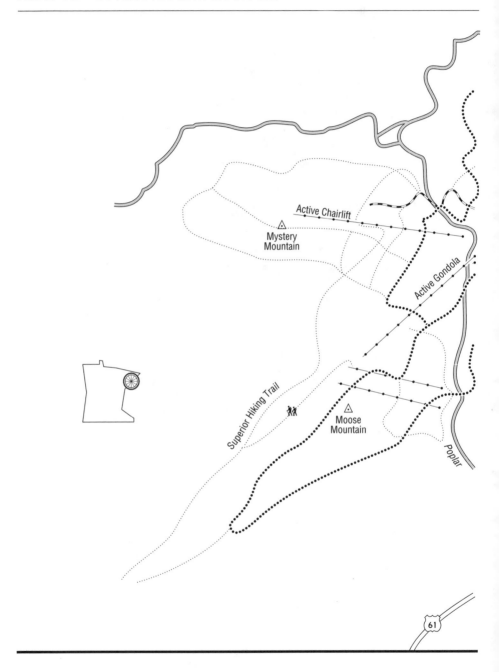

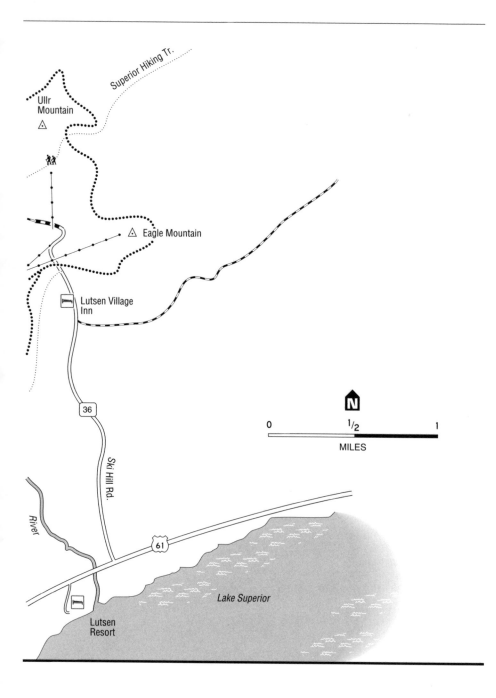

Season: June to mid-October. Insect populations increase from late May to August. Temperatures can be very cool at any time of the year in this region. The daily low temperature is below freezing for half of the year.

Services: Trail lunches and beverages are available at the Mountain Top Deli at the top end of the gondola lift. There are rest rooms, bike rentals, service, and a hose for bike cleaning at the gondola lift house/trailhead. Lodging, restaurants, and a snack shop can be found at the Village Inn. All services are available in Tofte and Grand Marais, and there is a grocery store/gas station on US 61 just north of CR 36. In Grand Marais, Superior North Outdoor Center offers outfitting and bicycle service.

Hazards: Downed trees and branches may be found at any time. Steep slopes may have loose, rough surfaces.

Rescue index: Help is available at the trailhead and the top of the gondola lift.

Land status: Private land and Superior National Forest. Trail passes are required and can be purchased at the gondola station at the trailhead. A $10 pass includes one gondola or chairlift ride and a $20 pass features unlimited gondola or chairlift access.

Maps: The USGS 7.5 minute quad for the Lutsen quadrangle shows the terrain. Excellent maps based on USGS 7.5 minute quadrangles are available for a charge from McKenzie Maps, 315 West Michigan Street, Suite 10, Duluth, MN 55802; (218) 727-2113. Map number 102 covers the Lutsen area and some of the trails. Trail maps are available at the trailhead.

Finding the trail: From Tofte, drive 7 miles north on US 61 to CR 36. Drive 2 miles north on CR 36 to the Lutsen Mountains gondola lift station/trailhead.

Sources of additional information:

Lutsen Mountains
Box 129
Lutsen, MN 55612
(218) 663-7281

Lutsen-Tofte Tourism Association
Tofte, MN 55615
(218) 663-7804

Superior North Outdoor Center
P.O. Box 177
Grand Marais, MN 55604
(218) 387-2186

Notes on the trail: Trail passes must be purchased at the gondola station at the trailhead (see Land status). Trail sections on ski slopes are mowed. Riding is allowed only on designated trails. Open ski slopes are closed to bikes, as is the Superior Hiking Trail. Trails are marked with color coded signs. Travel is

A trail pass at Lutsen Mountains includes a gondola ride
to the top of Moose Mountain. *Photo courtesy of
Minnesota Office of Tourism.*

generally one-way. From the trailhead follow the Ridgeline Trail to the southeast over Moose Mountain, then follow trails to Mystery Mountain, Ullr
Mountain, and Eagle Mountain to return to the gondola lift station.

RIDE 19   *MARK LAKE / PIKE LAKE TOUR*

This route takes you along the rolling plateau of forest, lake and marsh that
lies 1,000 feet above the level of Lake Superior. The long loop totals 21.9
miles and the short loop around Mark Lake adds up to 15.3 miles. Most of
the distance is on hardpack gravel two-wheel-drive roads that range from easy
to moderately difficult with some steep climbs. No technical riding skill is

RIDE 19 *MARK LAKE / PIKE LAKE TOUR*

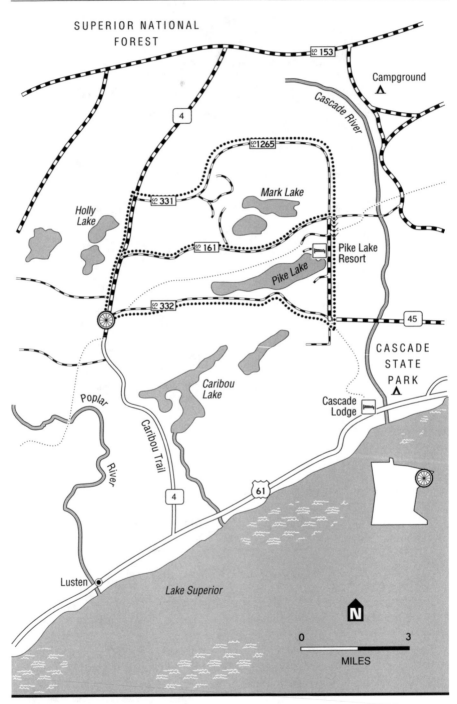

SUPERIOR NATIONAL FOREST

FS 153

Campground

Cascade River

4

FS 1265

Mark Lake

FS 331

Holly Lake

FS 161

Pike Lake Resort

Pike Lake

FS 332

45

CASCADE STATE PARK

Caribou Lake

Cascade Lodge

Poplar

Caribou Trail

River

4

61

Lusten

Lake Superior

N

0   3
MILES

needed. At times the roads are rocky. Along the northwestern section of Forest Road 331 are low, marshy sections with some remnants of old corduroy (logs laid down to make the marsh passable). Overviews of Mark Lake and of Turtle Lake with Eagle Mountain in the background are visible from high points along the central Forest Road 161.

General location: Seven miles north of US 61, 89 miles northeast of Duluth.
Elevation change: Expect moderately steep climbs of up to 200′ at most, with more common 80′ climbs. The total elevation gain on the long loop is approximately 1,000′.
Season: Late April through October. Insect populations are high from late May to August. Swampy sections are worse after heavy rain, typically in the spring. Temperatures can be very cool at any time of the year in this region. The daily low temperature is below freezing for half of the year.
Services: None at all along the route. All services are available in Grand Marais, including outfitting and bicycle service at Superior North Outdoor Center. Services are also available in Tofte, and there is a country store on US 61 near Lutsen.
Hazards: Steep downhill sections can be rocky. County Road 4 and County Road 45 will have two-wheel-drive vehicle traffic at any time. The Superior National Forest is managed for logging; logging trucks may be encountered anywhere along the route. All-terrain vehicles and four-wheel-drive vehicles may be encountered anywhere during the fall hunting season.
Rescue index: Help is available in Grand Marais, Lutsen, and Tofte. The Pike Lake Resort, at the east end of Pike Lake, can be used for summoning aid.
Land status: Superior National Forest with some private land easements.
Maps: The USGS 7.5 minute quad for Mark Lake and Tail Lake show the route. Excellent maps of the routes based on USGS 7.5 minute quadrangles are available for a charge from McKenzie Maps, 315 West Michigan Street, Suite 10, Duluth, MN 55802; (218) 727-2113. Map number 101 covers the entire area. A regional locator map, "Mountain Biking," is available at no charge from the Lutsen-Tofte Tourism Association.
Finding the trail: Drive 10.7 miles northeast of Tofte on US 61. Turn north on CR 4 (Caribou Trail) and drive 7.2 miles to the junction with FR 332. Park well off the road.

Sources of additional information:

Lutsen-Tofte Tourism Association
Tofte, MN 55615
(218) 663-7804

Superior North Outdoor Center
P.O. Box 177
Grand Marais, MN 55604
(218) 387-2186

Riders penetrate the heart of the Superior National Forest. *Photo courtesy of Minnesota Office of Tourism.*

Tip of the Arrowhead Visitor Center
Grand Marais, MN 55604
(218) 387-2524

Gunflint Ranger Station
Grand Marais, MN 55604
(218) 387-1750

Mountain Biking Adventure (group tours)
Birch Grove Foundation
P.O. Box 2242
Tofte, MN 55615
(218) 663-7977

Notes on the trail: The route should be well signed with red-and-white Forest Service mountain bike signs. Forest Service roads are marked with small, low brown signs with yellow lettering. The route can be ridden in either direction. Because of the possibility of vandalism and the density of the forest, a compass and a bicycle odometer are recommended. The route can be ridden in either direction. There is a swimming spot on Holly Lake just off CR 4 a half-mile north of FS 161.

RIDE 20   *ELIASON TOWER TRAIL*

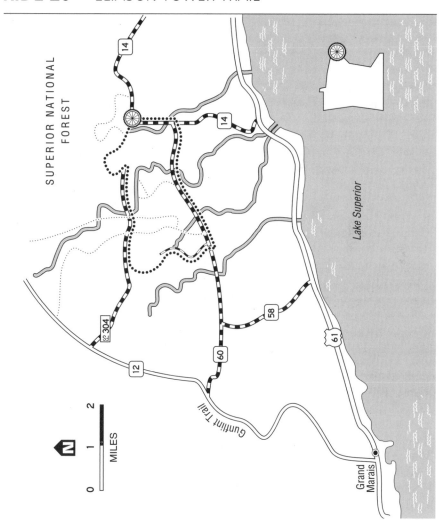

RIDE 20   *ELIASON TOWER TRAIL*

The steep slopes that rise up from Lake Superior on this 10-mile loop offer some challenging riding. Two-thirds of the route follows gravel surface four-wheel-drive county and Superior National Forest Service roads; one-third is on dirt surface or grassy logging roads. Some stretches may be soft in the wet season or after a rainy period. There is easy, gently rolling terrain along the northern and eastern legs. The southern leg features several fun stream crossings. The western leg will be a steep 300-foot climb if you are riding the route clockwise, or a very fast, twisting downhill from the opposite direction. The steep grade makes it a ride of moderate difficulty. The forest is dense, but there are several fine views of Lake Superior.

General location: Eleven miles northeast of Grand Marais.
Elevation change: This ride begins at 1,500′ and climbs as high as 1,740′. If you ride in a clockwise direction, you climb 300′ in one mile when you turn north. The total elevation gain is 740′.
Season: Late April through October. Insect populations flourish from late May to August. Swampy sections are worse after rainy spells, typically in the spring. Temperatures can be very cool at any time of the year in this region. The daily low temperature is below freezing for half of the year.
Services: None at all along the route. All services are available in Grand Marais, including outfitting and bicycle service at Superior North Outdoor Center.
Hazards: Expect rocks and washouts on steep downhill sections. Roots and rocks may be hidden in the grassy sections. The Superior National Forest is managed for logging; logging trucks may be encountered anywhere along the route. The route also may be used by all-terrain vehicles and four-wheel-drive vehicles, although all uses are typically low.
Rescue index: Help is available in Grand Marais. If you are injured or have mechanical problems, make your way to US 61 or the Gunflint Trail as best you can. Your chances of on-route rescue are slim.
Land status: Superior National Forest.
Maps: The USGS 7.5 minute quad for Kadunce River shows most of the route. Excellent maps of the routes based on USGS 7.5 minute quadrangles are available for a charge from McKenzie Maps, 315 West Michigan Street, Suite 10, Duluth, MN 55802; (218) 727-2113. Map number 99 covers the Eliason Tower area. A useful regional locator map, "Mountain Biking," is available at no charge from the Lutsen-Tofte Tourism Association.
Finding the trail: The ride begins on County Road 14 approximately 3 miles north of US 61. Follow US 61 northeast approximately 8 miles from Grand Marais. Turn north on CR 14. Park at the pull-off (wide spot for logging trucks) where CR 14 makes a 90-degree turn to the east.

Sources of additional information:

Lutsen-Tofte Tourism Association
Tofte, MN 55615
(218) 663-7804

Superior North Outdoor Center
P.O. Box 177
Grand Marais, MN 55604
(218) 387-2186

A long downhill is the payoff on the Eliason Tower route.

Tip of the Arrowhead Visitor Center
Grand Marais, MN 55604
(218) 387-2524

Gunflint Ranger Station
Grand Marais, MN 55604
(218) 387-1750

Mountain Biking Adventure (group tours)
Birch Grove Foundation
P.O. Box 2242
Tofte, MN 55615
(218) 663-7977

Notes on the trail: The route is well signed with red-and-white Forest Service mountain bike signs. Forest Service roads are marked with small, low brown signs with yellow lettering. Because of the possibility of vandalism to signs and the density of the forest, a compass and a bicycle odometer are recommended. The route can be ridden in either direction. If you ride counter-clockwise, look for the turn onto the south-bound trail at 3.4 miles from the start.

RIDE 21   PINCUSHION MOUNTAIN TRAILS

A ride up Pincushion Mountain will take you to a grand overview of Lake Superior and the Superior National Forest. Pincushion is part of the Sawtooth Mountains. Passing peak after peak as you travel up the shore on US 61, it will become obvious how they got the name. Since the trailhead and the over-look are at about the same elevation, you can enjoy the same view from Pincushion on a ride with a moderate rating.

You begin riding 500 feet above the small lake port town of Grand Marais (Grand Mar-aay), which has become somewhat of an artists' colony in recent years. It's inspiring; the same can be said for riding this 5.8-mile loop on the single- and double-track cross-country ski trails that wind through the pine, aspen, and birch forest. The trails are a mix of firm, graveled, rooted, and mowed grass with a single-track worn in. Some spots are wet in early summer. On the out-and-back run up to the Pincushion Mountain overlook you will ride on bedrock. Be careful of delicate plant communities.

General location: Northeast of Grand Marais, 105 miles north of Duluth.
Elevation change: The terrain is constantly rolling and some grades can be quite steep. From the trailhead you will gain 120′ before descending 100′. The climb to the Pincushion Mountain overlook is 60′.
Season: Late April through October. Insect populations are high from late May to August. Temperatures can be very cool at any time of the year in this region. The daily low temperature is below freezing for half of the year.
Services: The Pincushion Mountain Bed & Breakfast Inn is on the northern loop of the trail. All services are available in Grand Marais and there is outfitting and bicycle service at Superior North Outdoor Center.
Hazards: Downed trees and branches may be found at any time. Use partic-ular caution on the climb to the Pincushion Mountain overlook when it is wet. About half the route is part of the popular Superior Hiking Trail, which joins the cross-country ski trail at the trailhead. Use caution on bridges in low spots because they are not always flush with the trail. Carrying a compass is always a good idea in the deep woods.
Rescue index: Help is available in Grand Marais and can be summoned from the Pincushion Mountain Bed & Breakfast Inn. Although the trail is popular, you should make your way to the Gunflint Trail for the best chance of rescue.
Land status: Superior National Forest and some private land easements.
Maps: Excellent maps of the routes based on USGS 7.5 minute quadrangles are available for a charge from McKenzie Maps, 315 West Michigan Street,

RIDE 21 *PINCUSHION MOUNTAIN TRAILS*

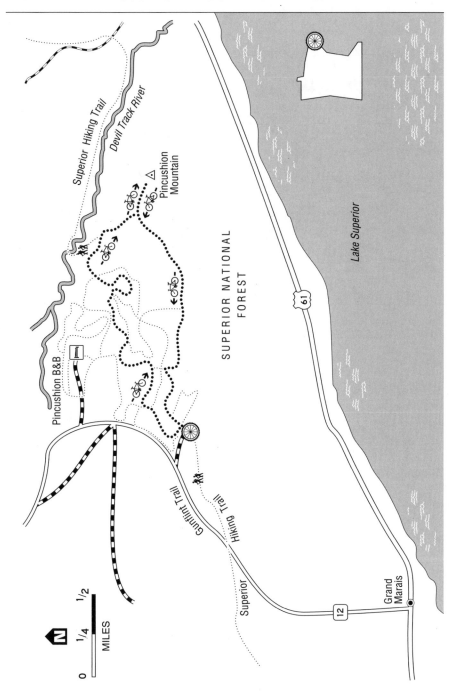

Bedrock and a great view of Lake Superior at the peak of Pincushion Mountain. *Photo by Mark Spinler.*

Suite 10, Duluth, MN 55802; (218) 727-2113. Map number 99 covers the Pincushion area. A regional map, "Mountain Biking," is available at no charge from the Lutsen-Tofte Tourism Association.

Finding the trail: From Grand Marais drive 1.7 miles north on County Road 12 (Gunflint Trail) to CR 53. Turn right on CR 53 and park in the Grand Marais Overlook parking lot.

Sources of additional information:

Lutsen-Tofte Tourism Association
Tofte, MN 55615
(218) 663-7804

Superior North Outdoor Center
P.O. Box 177
Grand Marais, MN 55604
(218) 387-2186

Tip of the Arrowhead Visitor Center
Grand Marais, MN 55604
(218) 387-2524

Gunflint Ranger Station
Grand Marais, MN 55604
(218) 387-1750

Notes on the trail: The route is well signed with frequent "you are here" maps posted at trail intersections. This is a very complex trail system with many short-cut options. Note that mountain biking is prohibited on the Superior Hiking Trail except the two-mile section that is part of the ski trail. From the trailhead follow the West Overlook, North Advanced, Hilfiker Hill, and Pincushion Mountain loops, in that order.

RIDE 22 *UPPER GUNFLINT TRAILS*

This 9.9-mile combination of ski trails, improved gravel, and old logging roads offers a moderately difficult riding experience through the deep boreal forest on the edge of the U.S. border. In fact, the rocky hills that rise up on the far side of Gunflint Lake are in Canada. More dramatic proof that you are way up north would be if you spot North America's largest mammal, the moose, along your ride. The chances are good, since King's Road runs by what are known as the moose bogs. Beaver and white-tailed deer are also commonly sighted along the route. Riding surfaces vary from gravel to grassy and forest floor to rock.

Though smoothed by the continental glacier, the resistant layers of rock in this area lay upon each other like shingles, creating parallel finger-like lakes in the low areas. The ridges between the lakes provide great scenic riding. The 4.9-mile western loop offers the best chance for sighting moose while the 5.2-mile eastern loop overlooks virgin white pines and Gunflint Lake. Gunflint Lodge is a great place to swap ride stories.

General location: Forty-seven miles northwest of Grand Marais.

Elevation change: The terrain is generally rolling. There is 280′ of elevation difference between the trailhead and the high point. Most of this elevation will be gained or lost on the Overlook Trail which connects the two loops.

Season: Early May through October. Insect populations are high from late May to August. Temperatures can be very cool at any time of the year in this region. The daily low temperature is below freezing for half of the year.

Services: Lodging, meals, water, and rental are available at Gunflint Lodge and two other lodges along Gunflint Lake. All services are available in Grand Marais, including bicycle rental, retail, and repair at Superior North Outdoor Center.

Hazards: Downed trees and branches may be found at any time. The Superior National Forest is managed for logging; logging trucks may be encountered anywhere along the route, but it would be very rare. Bull moose become unpredictable when in rut in October. Because of the density of the forest, a compass and a bicycle odometer are recommended. Hiking is allowed on all trails.

RIDE 22 UPPER GUNFLINT TRAILS

Note: *More trails exist in this area than can be shown on this map.*

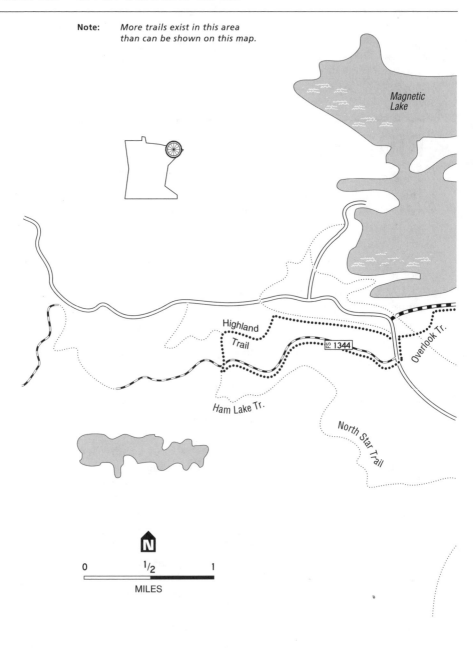

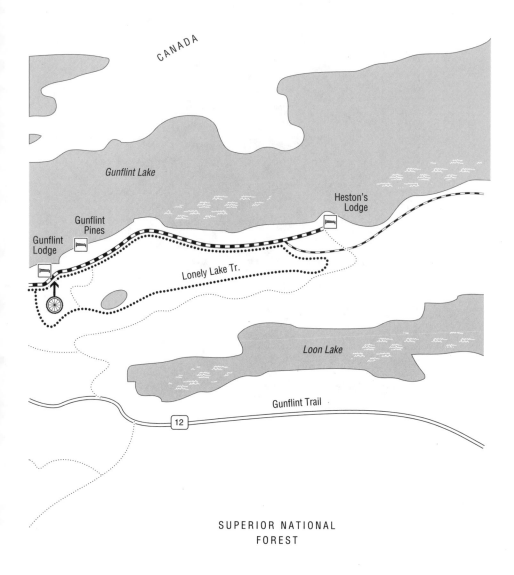

CANADA

Gunflint Lake

Gunflint
Pines

Gunflint
Lodge

Heston's
Lodge

Lonely Lake Tr.

Loon Lake

Gunflint Trail

12

SUPERIOR NATIONAL
FOREST

A ridgetop roll along the Highlands Trail.

Rescue index: Help is available at Gunflint Lodge. Your chances of on-trail rescue are slim. Make your way to the trailhead, Gunflint Trail (County Road 12), or the lake shore road (County Road 50).

Land status: Superior National Forest and some private land easements.

Maps: An excellent map of the trails and topography is available at Gunflint Lodge.

Finding the trail: Travel 105 miles north of Duluth on US 61 to Grand Marais. Turn inland on CR 12 (Gunflint Trail) for 47 miles. Turn right on a gravel road, CR 50, and drive .8 mile to Gunflint Lodge.

Sources of additional information:

Gunflint Lodge
HC 64, Box 750
Grand Marais, MN 55604
(800) 238-3325

Superior North Outdoor Center
P.O. Box 177
Grand Marais, MN 55604
(218) 382-2186

Tip of the Arrowhead Visitor Center
Grand Marais, MN 55604
(218) 387-2524

Gunflint Ranger Station
Grand Marais, MN 55604
(218) 387-1750

Notes on the trail: The route is well signed with cross-country ski and snow-mobile trail signs. Forest Service roads are marked with small, low brown signs with yellow lettering. The route can be ridden in either direction, although the directions given here are for riding each loop counter-clockwise. From the trailhead at Gunflint Lodge, cross CR 50 onto the Big Pine Trail and follow it a short distance, then take the Overlook Trail to the right. At the crossing of the Gunflint Trail (paved road) bear left onto the Highlands Trail. After 1.5 miles turn left onto the Ham Lake Trail. After one-third mile turn left on FS 1344 (King's Road), which is an old logging road and a snowmobile trail. At the junction with the Gunflint Trail turn left and pick up the connecting Overlook Trail at the Scenic Overlook. Turn right at the Big Pine Trail junction. After one-half mile turn right onto Lonely Lake Trail. Turn left onto an unimproved road at the T intersection. Turn left at the junction with a gravel road (CR 50) and follow it back to the trailhead.

WISCONSIN

Southern Wisconsin

Wisconsin is America's Dairyland, and the southern part of the state is the archetype of this moo-world. Some counties have more cows than people. Within this scenic setting are near-forgotten rural roads and towns as well as pockets where natural beauty has been preserved.

The southwestern region is a geological phenomena called the Driftless Area, so named because none of the four great continental glaciers of the last million years flowed over it. Essentially, it is an island of orderly, but rugged terrain and sculpted rock formations surrounded by the tumbled and rounded landscape that marks the path of glacial ice sheets.

In the east, the Wisconsin State Forest system preserves a glacial feature known as the kettle moraine. This is ideal mountain bike terrain made up of pits and hills that were formed by the grinding joint of two huge ice sheets, the Green Bay and Lake Michigan lobes, which buried huge blocks of ice in the till. After the ice sheet receded a mere ten thousand years ago, the ice blocks melted and the pock-marked landscape was left.

The Wyalusing Tour is an easy gravel road route in the Driftless Area that visits sleepy river towns, follows scenic side valleys, and skirts the edge of the Mississippi River. Also in the heart of the Driftless Area is the moderately difficult Hyde Mill Tour, which passes a country store, a pioneer mill, and a massive sandstone rock formation.

Two Wisconsin State Parks at the edge of the Driftless Area offer mountain bike routes. Devils Lake marks where the last continental glacier put on the brakes. Its last gasp was to plug up both ends of the 300-foot-deep gorge of the preglacial Wisconsin River Valley, forming a basin for the clear, blue lake and some terrific, moderately difficult riding terrain. Nearby Mirror Lake State Park has some easy riding trails near a finger-like lake formed by the damming of a Wisconsin River side valley near Wisconsin Dells, a popular tourist town.

Three cross-country ski trail systems in the Kettle Moraine State Forest are real treats for off-roaders. The trails at New Fane are an easy introduction to the kettle moraine experience. At Greenbush the glacial terrain will challenge any rider with steep, rough slopes. Thousands of riders gather each week to take on the challenge of the Muir and Carlin trails. The large numbers give any weekend a festival atmosphere.

RIDE 23   *WYALUSING TOUR*

Anyone with a sense of adventure and the ability to make it up one moderate 450-foot climb can take on this easy 24.5-mile tour. A combination of well-maintained, hard-packed gravel roads and paved roads will take you through narrow, winding hollows and sleepy Mississippi River settlements. There is a total of six miles of pavement, three miles of which you cover twice.

Your on-trail refreshment options have a bucolic air. In the village of Bagley there is the Bagley Bottoms Inn, Hotel Bagley Dining Room, Oswald's Tavern ("1912" it says on the store front), and Grampa's General Store. Don't count on modern financial services at the Prairie City Bank; it's been closed for years. Riding the northern loop will take you 450 feet up Ready Hollow to the open farmland on Military Ridge and to the Dew Drop Inn at the junction of County Road X and County Road C.

The out-and-back route south of Bagley leads along a narrow track called Dugway Road, which clings so closely to the towering limestone river bluffs that at one point it actually passes under the rock. The road will take you above the lush green backwater of part of the Upper Mississippi National Wildlife and Fish Refuge, the home of graceful white egrets and great blue herons. The Burlington Northern, one of the nation's busiest railroads, runs as many as 40 freight trains a day along the shore. At the village of Glen Haven the river channel holds tight to the Wisconsin shore.

One of Wisconsin's largest and most beautiful state parks is just off the northern loop. Wyalusing State Park (pronounced Y-ah-loo-sing) overlooks the confluence of the Wisconsin and Mississippi Rivers. Proliferate Indian mounds testify to the centuries-old attraction to this spot. It is a great place to camp and hike. There are several signed mountain bike trails, but they are so short or uninteresting that they could not be recommended in this book. This is very unfortunate, since the park has 500′ of scenic, challenging terrain and a great many miles of seldom-used trails. People probably would not be pleased if they traveled many hours and paid the park fee just to bounce around the edges of an open field.

General location: Seventeen miles south of Prairie du Chien.
Elevation change: Generally flat to gently rolling with one moderate 450′ climb and descent.
Season: Roads are likely to be clear of snow and ice from March through November. Cold temperatures are likely at the extremes of this season; heat and humidity can be oppressive in July and August.
Services: All services, except bicycle services, are available in the village of Bagley. There are several taverns in the village of Glen Haven and a tavern/restaurant at the junction of CR X and CR C. In Prairie du Chien there

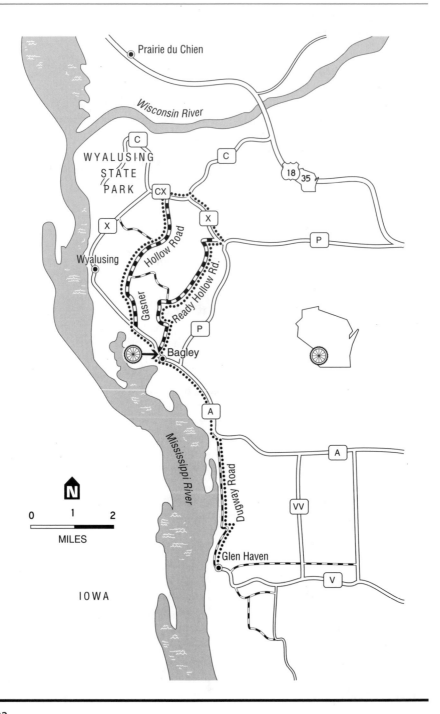

Prairie du Chien

Wisconsin River

WYALUSING
STATE
PARK

C

C

CX

X

X

18
35

P

Wyalusing

Hollow Road

Gasner

Ready Hollow Rd.

P

Bagley

A

A

Dugway Road

VV

N

0   1   2
MILES

Mississippi River

Glen Haven

V

IOWA

High above the Mississippi River at Wyalusing State Park.

are many dining and lodging choices; bicycle repair can be arranged at (608) 326-8787.

Hazards: All roads are open to two-way motor vehicle traffic. Gravel roads are periodically maintained with fresh coverings of loose gravel. Rattlesnakes are common in rocky crevasses.

Rescue index: Help is available in Bagley, Glen Haven, and Wyalusing State Park.

Land status: Public roadways through private land.

Maps: The DeLorme book, *Wisconsin Atlas & Gazetteer,* shows all roads and road names.

Finding the trail: From the junction of US 18/WI 35 and County Road C, on the south side of the Wisconsin River, turn west on CR C. After three miles, turn right at a **T** intersection (across from the Dew Drop Inn) onto County Road CX. After one mile CR C splits off to the right to Wyalusing State Park. At this point follow County Road X for six miles to the village of Bagley and park on any street.

Sources of additional information:

Prairie du Chien Tourism Council
P.O. Box 326
Prairie du Chien, WI 53821
(608) 326-8555, (800) PDC-1673

Wyalusing State Park
13342 County Highway C
Bagley, WI 53801
(608) 996-2261

Notes on the trail: The route is well signed with standard county road signs and street-type town road signs. The northern loop can be ridden in either direction, but the following cues are for riding counter-clockwise. From the village of Bagley, ride northwest on County Road X a half-mile and turn right on Ready Hollow Road (gravel). At a **T** intersection with a paved road (CR X) turn left. At the junction of CR C, at the Dew Drop Inn, proceed straight on County Road CX. After one-half mile turn left onto Gasner Hollow Road (gravel). At a **T** intersection with a paved road (CR X) turn left and follow it back to Bagley. To ride the southern route, continue southwest through Bagley where CR X becomes Country Road A. After three miles turn right onto Dugway Road (gravel) and follow it to the village of Glen Haven. If you begin to climb on CR A, you have missed Dugway Road. Return from Glen Haven by the same route.

RIDE 24   *HYDE MILL TOUR*

This 11-mile loop is a two-wheel-drive gravel road ride with a few paved road sections. It travels through valley and ridge farmland and wooded hillsides. One steep 225-foot climb makes it a moderate ride. No technical ability is needed other than braking and cornering proficiency on a gravel surface. This is a fine introductory ride for novice mountain bikers or a nice cruise for experienced riders.

The route winds through the quiet hill and valley country of rural Iowa County. A photo opportunity at Hyde Mill is one reward on this tour. This tiny mill was built in 1850, and it is well kept under private ownership. You are welcome to stop for a rest to watch the veil of water spill over the mill dam. At times the owners engage the water wheel and let it turn slowly under the weight of the water as it did in days gone by. To reach the mill you cross another remnant of America's past, an old wood-planked stressed iron bridge. Near the mill, at the intersection of County Road T, is the Hyde Chapel and Cemetery. The small, white, clapboard structure illustrates how simple the Greek Revival style can be.

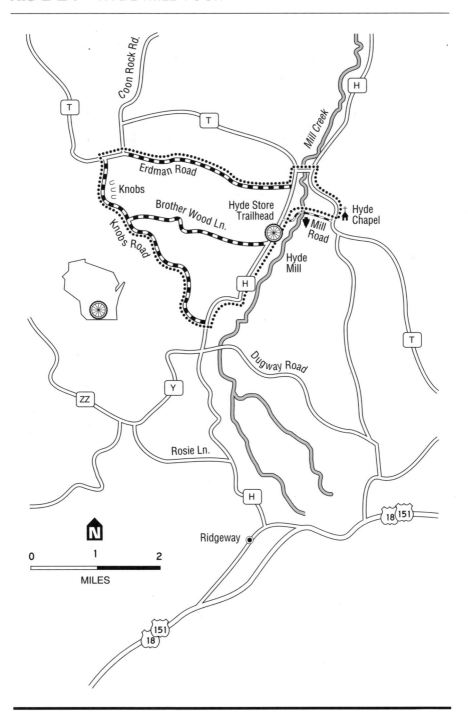

The trailhead is at the Hyde Store, another rapidly disappearing feature of rural America. Little country stores once served most of the needs of farm families. What they couldn't raise, grow, or make they could buy there. The Hyde Store is still a friendly place to stop for refreshment.

The scenery is a mix of farmland on ridge tops and valley bottoms and dense oak and maple forest on the hillsides. The view is also punctuated by the Knobs, a large sandstone outcrop that rises above the treetops and lends its name to the road that passes by. There is a fine view of it to the south as you ride near the west end of Erdman Road. Small herds of white-tailed deer are a common sight along the route.

General location: Five miles north of the village of Ridgeway, 31 miles west of Madison.

Elevation change: Over 460′ of elevation are gained and lost. There is a 225′ climb on Erdman Road and a long, steep descent on Knobs Road.

Season: The roads are open year-round, but good riding conditions can be expected March through October. Cool or cold temperatures are likely early or late in the season.

Services: Snacks and drink are available at the Hyde Store. Gas and food can be found in the village of Ridgeway.

Hazards: All roads are open to motor vehicle traffic. Loose gravel may be encountered. Be careful of scared deer crossing your path on downhill runs.

Rescue index: Help is available in Ridgeway and at the Hyde Store. Farms are plentiful along the route and farmers are usually friendly and helpful.

Land status: Public roads through private land.

Maps: All of the roads are well marked and the route depiction shown here should be adequate. For the true map freak, the roads on the USGS 15 minute maps for Spring Green and Blue Mounds are shown, but the town roads are not named. The DeLorme book, *Wisconsin Atlas & Gazetteer,* shows all roads and road names.

Finding the trail: Take CR H north from US 18/151 from the village of Ridgeway.

Sources of additional information:

An area visitor's guide entitled "Southwest Wisconsin's Uplands" is available for $1 from:

Uplands, Inc.
P.O. Box 202
Mt. Horeb, WI 53572-0202
(800) 279-9472

The historic Hyde Mill was built in 1850.

General information is available from:

Wisconsin Division of Tourism
123 West Washington Avenue
Madison, WI 53707
(800) 372-2737

Notes on the trail: Park alongside the road on CR H near the Hyde Store. Be sure to pull well off the pavement. The route can be ridden in either direction. County roads are signed with standard, on-road, white-and-black signs; town road signs are green and white. Twisting town road signs 90 degrees is a popular prank, so trust your map.

RIDE 25 *DEVILS LAKE STATE PARK TRAILS*

A five-mile loop-and-spur ride at Devils Lake State Park takes in over 400 feet of elevation and some of the finest views this side of the Rockies. Over 240 feet are gained in one steady climb, making this a ride of moderate difficulty. No great technical skill is needed. Except for a short paved stretch between the campground and park concession stand, and a short unpaved section on

RIDE 25   *DEVILS LAKE STATE PARK TRAILS*

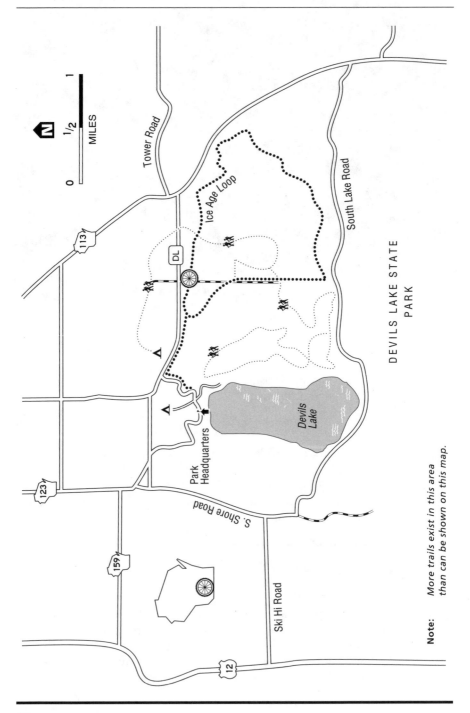

an access road, the entire distance is on wide, mowed cross-country ski trails. Mountain biking is only allowed on trails signed for it. There are many heavily used hiking trails in the park where riding is prohibited. Leaving your bike and taking a short hike on the CCC Trail or Devils Doorway Trail will lead you to a great overview of the lake gap.

Devils Lake is bottled up between steep, talus-strewn quartzite bluffs that once formed the valley of the Wisconsin River. During the last continental glacier, ice sheets pushed moraines in from either end of the valley gap, creating a basin for the clear, clean lake. If you ride down to the park concession stand, you will get a good view of the gap and a chance to check out the swimming at North Shore Beach. Although the park is one of the most popular in the state, the area used for the designated mountain bike trails is unlikely to be crowded.

General location: Eleven miles south of Interstate 90/94 Exit 92, Baraboo / Wisconsin Dells.

Elevation change: For the most part, the trails are rolling with short, moderate climbs. There is a steep 120′ climb and descent on the Ice Age Loop. The spur trail to the park concession stand covers 240′ of elevation in .6 mile.

Season: Depending on trail conditions, the park will be open for mountain biking from late March to early November. Expect cool or cold temperatures at the beginning and end of the season. The swimming beach is open from Memorial Day weekend through Labor Day.

Services: Snacks are available at the park concession stand at the North Shore Beach. There is a grocery store near the park's north entrance at WI 123 and CR DL. All services, including bicycle retail and repair, are available in Baraboo.

Hazards: Trails are regularly maintained and clear, but fallen trees and branches may be encountered at any time. Hikers may be encountered on all trails.

Rescue index: Help is available at Park Headquarters. Although Devils Lake State Park is the most popular in Wisconsin, the mountain bike trails are, for the most part, not heavily used; the chances of rescue are slim. In case of injury, making for the park headquarters, bluff edge trails, or paved roadways is recommended.

Land status: Wisconsin State Park. A daily or annual vehicle sticker ($5 daily / $18 annually for Wisconsin residents, $7 daily / $25 annually for out-of-state residents) is required to park in state forest lots. Bicycles are not charged for visiting the park, but a trail pass fee is required of bicyclists age 18 and older ($3 daily or $10 annually). The trail pass also covers activities like cross-country skiing, horseback riding, and bicycling on railroad grade bike trails.

Maps: Maps of the trails are available at Devils Lake State Park Headquarters. The USGS 7.5 minute Baraboo quad gives excellent information on the terrain, but doesn't show the mountain bike trails.

Rocky parapets line the bluffs at Devils Lake State Park. *Photo courtesy of Wisconsin Department of Natural Resources.*

Finding the trail: To locate the north entrance to Devils Lake State Park, take I-90/94 Exit 92, Baraboo/Wisconsin Dells (also known as US 12). Follow US 12 for 9 miles. Turn east at WI 159. Turn right at the T intersection with WI 123 and follow it to the junction with County Road DL. If you need to purchase a park sticker or trail pass, proceed straight across CR DL onto the park road and follow it to the park headquarters. If you already have a sticker and pass, turn left on CR DL and drive 1.5 miles to the trailhead parking lot.

Sources of additional information:

> Devils Lake State Park
> S5975 Park Road
> Baraboo, WI 53913-9299
> (608) 356-8301

> Wisconsin Department of Natural Resources
> Bureau of Parks and Recreation
> P.O. Box 7921
> Madison, WI 53707-7921
> (608) 266-2181

> Baraboo Area Chamber of Commerce
> P.O. Box 442
> Baraboo, WI 53913
> (800) 227-2266

Notes on the trail: An annual or day-use motor vehicle sticker is required to park on state land as well as an annual or daily per-person trail fee (see Land status). The trails are sometimes subject to flooding or damage and may be closed for these reasons. Be sure to call ahead to check on the status. The recommended starting point is up on the plateau formed by the bluffs of Devils Lake State Park. Before riding, you must purchase a trail pass at the park headquarters on the north shore. You may start below by the lake, but you will face a long 240′ climb before you've warmed up. All trails are two-way, but it is advisable to start on top at the parking area shown as the trailhead on the map and follow the Steinke Basin and Ice Age loops to the east. This allows you to save the out-and-back, 1.2-mile (total) spur down to the park concession stand for last. If you want to avoid the long climb back up, you can skip the spur and return to the trailhead, having already covered a total of 3.8 miles. The trails are well marked with green-and-white bicycle silhouette signs. The Ice Age Loop will turn to the south and west where you will face a steep 120′ climb. Riding is prohibited on trails not specifically marked for mountain biking, although these hiking trails are not marked to prohibit biking. Assume that riding is not allowed anywhere not specifically marked for bikers.

RIDE 26   *MIRROR LAKE STATE PARK TRAILS*

Just down the road from one of the Midwest's most popular tourist traps lies Mirror Lake State Park. The hype and clutter of the "attractions" at the nearby town of Wisconsin Dells is a mecca to some and a mishap to others. Mirror Lake is a vastly different experience. The pleasant oak and pine forests and open fields of the park boast 8.7 miles of mountain biking trails. The grassy and bare forest-floor cross-country ski trails offer an easy riding experience for the average cyclist. Three loops are pieced together to form a system that rolls gently over the terrain. The biggest challenges will be a few soft, muddy low spots and exposed sandy stretches.

General location: Three miles south of the town of Lake Delton.
Elevation change: The terrain is sometimes flat, but mostly gently rolling to rolling. Moderate climbs of 50′ will be found on the Turtleville and Fern Dell loops. There are steeper climbs on the Hastings loop with gains of 70′.
Season: Mirror Lake trails are open for mountain biking from May 1 to November 1. The trails are sometimes subject to flooding or damage and may be closed for these reasons. Be sure to call ahead to check on the status.
Services: Water is available at the campground parking lot just northeast of the park office. All services, except bicycle services, are available in the towns of Lake Delton and Wisconsin Dells. Bicycle retail and repair are available in Baraboo, eight miles south.

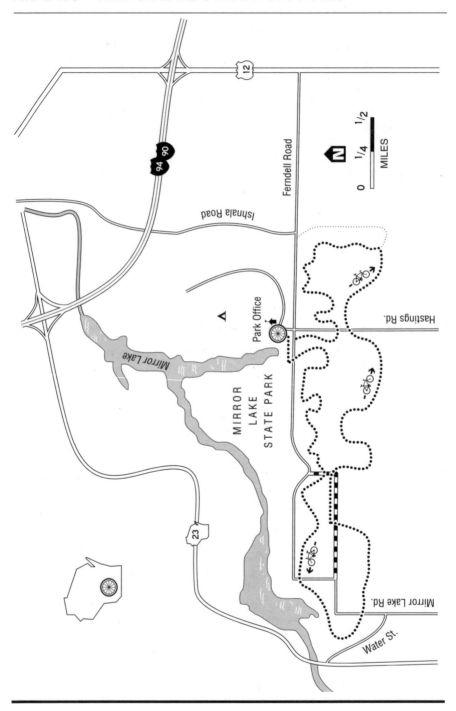

Trails at Mirror Lake State Park are wooded, well marked, and sandy.

Hazards: Although the trails receive regular maintenance, fallen trees or branches may be encountered at any time. The trails are open to hikers.

Rescue index: Help is available at the park office. Trails are not heavily used, but you are never far from a well-traveled road.

Land status: Wisconsin State Park. A daily or annual vehicle sticker ($5 daily / $18 annually for Wisconsin residents, $7 daily / $25 annually for out-of-state residents) is required to park in state parks. Bicycles are not charged for visiting the park, but a trail pass fee is required of bicyclists age 18 and older ($3 daily or $10 annually). The trail pass also covers activities like cross-country skiing, horseback riding, and bicycling on railroad grade bike trails.

Maps: A detailed trail map is available at the park office or from the DNR.

Finding the trail: Exit Interstate 90/94 onto east US 12 at the Lake Delton interchange and travel .5 mile south on US 12. Turn west at Fern Dell Road and follow it 1.5 miles to the park office parking lot on the right.

Sources of additional information:

Mirror Lake State Park
E10320 Fern Dell Road
Baraboo, WI 53913
(608) 254-2333

Wisconsin Department of Natural Resources
Bureau of Parks and Recreation
P.O. Box 7921
Madison, WI 53707-7921
(608) 266-2181

Baraboo Area Chamber of Commerce
P.O. Box 442
Baraboo, WI 53913
(800) 227-2266

Notes on the trail: An annual or day-use motor vehicle sticker is required to park on state land, as well as an annual or daily per-person trail fee (see Land status). The trails are well marked with green-and-white mountain bike silhouette signs and cross-country ski signs for mostly one-way travel. Trails where riding is not allowed have white signs with a red slash through the silhouette.

From the trailhead, ride out to Fern Dell Road and turn right. After a short distance, just before the narrow old bridge, turn left off the pavement onto a grassy cross-country ski trail that is signed for mountain biking and follow it as it loops around a beaver pond. You are on the Fern Dell Loop. At the junction with a gravel road (Turtleville Road), go straight across onto the Turtleville Loop. The loop will cross a paved road (Fern Dell Road) twice and a gravel road (Turtleville Road) once before returning to this intersection. Cross the road back onto the Fern Dell Loop and follow it to the south. At the junction with a paved road (Hastings Road), cross onto the Hastings Loop. When the loop returns to this intersection, turn right onto Hastings Road and return to the trailhead.

RIDE 27 KETTLE MORAINE MUIR AND CARLIN TRAILS

When you talk about mountain biking the Kettle Moraine, the John Muir and Emma Carlin trails are what most riders think of. Combined they are one tough trail system. Steep slopes, tight turns, and some side hill riding make it challenging. You can cover 25 miles by riding the outer loops and connector trail. Many variations are possible by combining loops. The single-track width cross-country ski trails give an intimate feel in the oak and pine forested area.

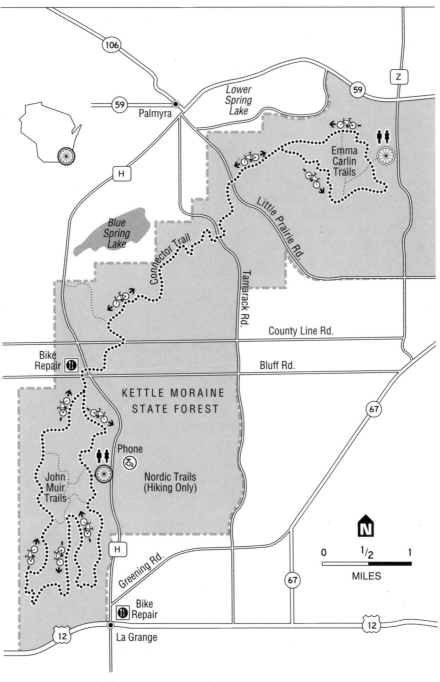

Note: More trails exist than can be shown on this map.

Lots of athletic-looking riders are also part of the scenery.

Despite heavy use, the trails remain a great place to ride for more gung-ho bikers thanks to trail hardening and a one-way system. Riding surfaces vary from grassy with a hardpack track to fine limestone gravel over Geoblock, a plastic gridwork placed to slow erosion.

The narrow trails and one-way travel direction make it an excellent riding experience without a feeling of crowding. You'll pass and get passed occasionally, but until you stop and see the constant flow, you won't believe how many bikes are on the trails. Trails are easy to follow with color coded sign posts and "you-are-here" map signs at intersections.

The trails are used for a popular late September event called the Kettle Moraine Fall Color Festival. A limited entry event featuring food, awards, and raffles, the festival allows riders to run the trails in time trial fashion.

Popularity has resulted in good privately run services in the area. The General Store at La Grange has long been a favorite for food, rental, retail, and repairs. The recent Quiet Hut Sports and Artisan Cafe offer similar services on the north end at the intersection of Bluff Road and CR H.

General location: Nine miles east of Whitewater.
Elevation change: There are many short steep climbs and several 80′ to 120′ ones.
Season: Trails should be open from April to November.
Services: Food and bike sales and repair are found at La Grange and at Bluff Road. All services are available in Palmyra. All services, including bike sales and repair, are available in Whitewater, nine miles west.
Hazards: The trails are very well maintained, but windfall trees or branches should be watched for. The plastic grid placed under the trail surface can become exposed and is very slippery when wet even from a heavy morning dew.
Rescue index: Aid can be summoned at La Grange, at the Quiet Hut Sports at Bluff Road and CR H, and by calling 911 at the pay phone in the Nordic Trails parking lot across CR H from the John Muir parking lot.
Land status: Wisconsin State Forest, Southern Kettle Moraine Unit. A daily or annual vehicle sticker ($5 daily / $18 annual for Wisconsin residents, $7 daily / $25 annual for out-of-state residents) is required to park in state forest lots. Bicycles are not charged for visiting the forest, but a trail pass fee is required of bicyclists ages 18 and older for riding the off-road trails ($3 daily or $10 annual). The trail pass also covers usages such as cross-country skiing, horseback riding, and bicycling on railroad-grade bike trails.
Maps: Sheet maps are available at the trailhead and are posted at trail intersections. The 7.5 minute series USGS quads for Whitewater and Little Prairie show the terrain very well, but do not show the trails.
Finding the trail: Trailhead parking lot on the west side of CR H 1.5 miles north of the crossroads village of La Grange and US 12. An overflow parking

Challenging terrain and beautiful forest scenery lure riders to the Muir and Carlin Trails.

lot is located across CR H. Local activist James Wamser has a map on his web
site.

Sources of additional information:

Kettle Moraine
Southern Unit
S91 W39091 Highway 59
Eagle, WI 53119
(414) 594-2135

James Wamser (SASE for map)
1511 South 98th Street
West Allis, WI 53214

(414) 774-7336
WWW. execpc. com/~jWAMSER

Whitewater Area Chamber of
Commerce
P.O. Box 34
Whitewater, WI 53190-0034
(414) 473-4005
or (414) 473-0520

Notes on the trail: Daily or annual State Park vehicle admission and daily or
annual Trail Pass for riders 18 and older are required (see Land status). There

is a self-pay station at the trailhead. There are white and red no-biking signs on hiking trails. Fines apply for riding on hiking-only trails. Always phone ahead to make sure trails are open for riding.

The trails are marked with color coded sign posts that correspond to different loops. Often there will be more than one color at a time. Frequent "you-are-here" map signs at intersections help keep everything straight.

RIDE 28   *KETTLE MORAINE NEW FANE TRAILS*

This 3.1-mile loop is a great place for a novice rider to enjoy the scenery and fun of riding in the kettle moraine. This doesn't mean that more seasoned riders will be bored here. The wide, smooth, grassy cross-country ski trails invite fast riding. There is a hardpack track worn in and, except for a few roots and cobbles on the uphills and downhills, there is nothing to slow down for. There is some rough terrain, but it's the sort that makes things a bit more exciting. The trails can be challenging if you hammer, but they're never humbling. This is an easy, nontechnical ride that can really turn a newcomer on to the sport.

Most of New Fane's trails loop through a forest that is at times hardwoods of oak, birch, and maple and, in other areas, pine. In a few spots you will break out into the open for fine overviews of the countryside. Near the end of the ride you will pass by a pond to the right of the trail that is a haven for waterfowl.

General location: Six miles northeast of Kewaskum.

Elevation change: Terrain varies from flat to rolling. One moderately steep climb and descent of 80′ will be encountered early on, followed by another more gradual 50′ hill.

Season: Trails may be open from mid-April to early November (just before hunting season). The trails are sometimes subject to flooding or damage and may be closed for these reasons. Be sure to call ahead to check on the status.

Services: There is water at the trailhead. You will only find a tavern in New Fane, but all services, except bicycle services, are available in the small town of Kewaskum.

Hazards: Trails are well maintained, but windfall trees and branches may be found. All trails are open for hiking.

Rescue index: Help can be summoned in the village of New Fane.

Land status: Wisconsin State Forest, Northern Kettle Moraine Unit. A daily or annual vehicle sticker ($5 daily / $18 annually for Wisconsin residents, $7 daily / $25 annually for out-of-state residents) is required to park in state forest lots. Bicycles are not charged for visiting the forest, but a trail pass fee is

RIDE 28   *KETTLE MORAINE / NEW FANE TRAILS*

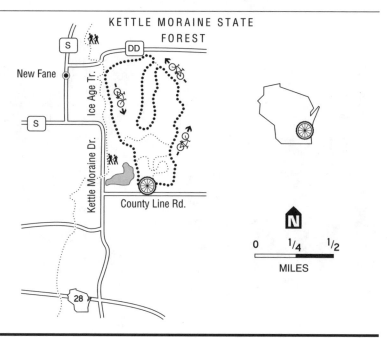

required of bicyclists age 18 and older ($3 daily or $10 annually). The trail pass also covers activities like cross-country skiing, horseback riding, and bicycling on railroad grade bike trails.

Maps: A detailed cross-country ski trail map is available from the forest headquarters or from the DNR office. The 7.5 minute series USGS quad for Kewaskum shows the terrain, but does not show the trails.

Finding the trail: From the village of Kewaskum on US 45 turn east on WI 28. After .4 mile, just after crossing the Branch River, turn north on County Road S while still in the village. Follow CR S for 3.7 miles and go straight east onto Kettle Moraine Drive (look for a street-type sign and a green Kettle Moraine Scenic Drive sign) at an intersection where CR S turns north into the village of New Fane. Kettle Moraine Drive will bend to the south. Follow it for 1.5 miles to County Line Road and turn to the east. The parking lot for New Fane Trails is .6 mile farther on the left.

Sources of additional information:

> Kettle Moraine State Forest–Northern Unit
> Box 410
> Campbellsport, WI 53010
> (414) 626-2116

A self-serve trail pass station at the New Fane trailhead.

Wisconsin Department of Natural Resources
Bureau of Parks and Recreation
P.O. Box 7921
Madison, WI 53707-7921
(608) 266-2181

Notes on the trail: An annual or day-use motor vehicle sticker is required to park on state land, as well as an annual or daily per-person trail fee (see Land status). These fees can be paid by a self service system at the trailhead. The trails are marked for one-way travel. There is a brown sign with a mountain bike silhouette at the trailhead, but beyond that point you will only see color-coded cross-country ski trail signs. Follow the markers for the yellow loop throughout. For most of the distance, this route will also be the red loop. At 1.8 miles the yellow route separates to dip south before rejoining the red loop. Keep a close watch for this sharp intersection, since it comes up suddenly along a fast-rolling section of the trail. At the point where the green trail rejoins the yellow and red loop, a connecting trail runs off to the west to the Ice Age Trail, which is not open to mountain biking and is marked accordingly. This is the only trail that is off-limits to bikers.

RIDE 29   *KETTLE MORAINE GREENBUSH TRAILS*

The 5.1-mile purple loop on the Greenbush Trails snakes through a classic oak and maple hardwood forest, skirts the edge of a marsh, and passes a pine plantation. The wide, mowed grass or forest floor cross-country ski trails cover terrain that is typical of the kettle moraine: a jumbled landscape that makes for fun mountain biking. The glacier only left the area about 10,000 years ago—not much time for nature to smooth over the mess. Cobble-sized rocks, roots, and more rocks make up the riding surface. Downhills are very rough.

Your shifters, brakes, and legs will get a workout on trails that are seldom level or even the same grade for very long. A stretch along the southwest segment of the loop, where the route runs along a marsh, gives some relief from the up and down, but it also features soft or mucky surfaces. Overall this route will be on the low end of the challenging scale for the average rider because of the rough surface.

The Greenbush Trails are just a few miles south of the historic village by the same name. Set in the green rolling hills of the kettle moraine, the tiny town looks more like a village in Vermont than one in Wisconsin. Many of the white, clapboard Greek Revival buildings are operated by the Wisconsin State Historical Society, including a carriage museum and the Wade House, a restored stage coach inn.

General location: Two and a half miles south of WI 23 at the village of Greenbush, six miles west of Plymouth.

Elevation change: Much of the terrain is rolling. Steep grades of 50′ to 60′ are common.

Season: Trails are open for mountain biking from mid-April to early November, although the yellow loop shown here will typically be closed after mid-September because of small game hunting season. The trails are sometimes subject to flooding or damage and may be closed for these reasons. Be sure to call ahead to check on the status.

Services: There is a tavern / restaurant and gas station in the village of Greenbush. All services, except bicycle services, are available in Plymouth, six miles east of Greenbush.

Hazards: Trails are well maintained, but windfall trees and branches are always possible hazards. A horseback riding trail crosses this system at several points. Hiking is allowed on all trails.

Rescue index: Help is available in Greenbush. In the case of injury or mechanical difficulty, make your way back to the trailhead.

Land status: Wisconsin State Forest, Northern Kettle Moraine Unit. A daily or annual vehicle sticker ($5 daily / $18 annually for Wisconsin residents,

RIDE 29 *KETTLE MORAINE / GREENBUSH TRAILS*

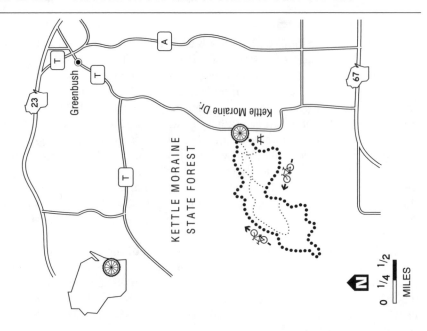

$7 daily / $25 annually for out-of-state residents) is required to park in state forest lots. Bicycles are not charged for visiting the forest, but a trail pass fee is required of bicyclists age 18 and older ($3 daily or $10 annually). The trail pass also covers activities like cross-country skiing, horseback riding, and bicycling on railroad grade bike trails. These fees can be paid by a self service system at the trailhead.

Maps: A detailed cross-country ski trail map is available from the forest headquarters or from the DNR office. The 7.5 minute series USGS quad for Cascade shows the terrain very well, but does not show the trails.

Finding the trail: From WI 23, six miles west of Plymouth, turn southeast on County Road T into the village of Greenbush. Follow CR T through the village and after 1.3 miles turn south (left) onto Kettle Moraine Drive. Travel 1.9 miles to the Greenbush Picnic Area parking lot on the right.

Sources of additional information:

Kettle Moraine State Forest–Northern Unit
Box 410
Campbellsport, WI 53010
(414) 626-2116

Color coded marker posts make the Greenbush trails easy to follow.

Wisconsin Department of Natural Resources
Bureau of Parks and Recreation
P.O. Box 7921
Madison, WI 53707-7921
(608) 266-2181

Plymouth Chamber of Commerce
P.O. Box 584
Plymouth, WI 53073
(414) 893-0079

Notes on the trail: An annual or day-use motor vehicle sticker is required to park on state land, as well as an annual or daily per-person trail fee (see Land status). More trails exist in the area than can possibly be shown on this map.

The area is marked for mountain biking at the trailhead with a green-and-white square mountain bike silhouette sign, and the trails are well marked with color-coded cross-country ski trail signposts and signs on trees. From the trailhead, follow the markers for the purple trail for the entire loop. Riding is not allowed on the Ice Age Trail, marked with blue-and-white posts, which crosses the ski trails near the trailhead.

Central Wisconsin

Central Wisconsin is a transition zone where farmland begins to give way to forest. It is a region of great variation. Along the Mississippi, the terrain is steep and rugged. In the middle, the land flattens; this central lowland is the legacy of Glacial Lake Wisconsin, which pooled the meltwater of the continental ice sheet and laid down a layer of sand. In places the area is punctuated with sculpted sandstone bluffs that were once islands. In the east Door County a spear-shaped peninsula separates Green Bay from Lake Michigan. Its flat, resistant layer of Niagara Dolomite is the western edge of a sheet of sedimentary rock that at one time stretched all the way to New York state. (Niagara Falls tumbles off the opposite edge.) During the last glacial epoch the peninsula split the ice sheet into two lobes.

Riders can enjoy the character of the Mississippi river on two unique routes. On the moderately difficult Maiden Rock tour, a network of paved and gravel roads leads riders through picturesque side valleys and along the towering limestone palisades that line the shore of scenic Lake Pepin, a lake within the course of the Mississippi. The terrain is much more challenging, but no less scenic at Perrot State Park, where a ski trail system takes riders up long, steep climbs to grand overviews of the Mississippi.

In the middle of the state, trails at Black River State Forest wind around and over remnant islands of ancient Lake Wisconsin. On the Castle Mound Trail riders can enjoy the view of the namesake mound on an easy ride that follows a scenic creek. On the challenging Wildcat and Smreaker trails, they can enjoy the view from the top of the one-time islands. On the east end of what was once Glacial Lake Wisconsin are the pock-marked rounded hills that mark the farthest extent of the Lake Michigan Lobe. Standing Rocks County Park is located there among huge granite boulders rolled there by the ice sheet. Such terrain makes for challenging riding. It is never level for more than a few yards.

All of the riding in Door County is easy, but there is more than enough variety and scenery to make it enjoyable for any off-roader. Potawatomi, Peninsula, and Newport State Parks feature trail systems that show off the wild and scenic side of this popular tourism area.

RIDE 30   *MAIDEN ROCK TOUR*

Mississippi River scenery is the big payoff on this combination paved and gravel road tour. You have a choice of 14.2-mile or 21.5-mile loops that have 5.6 or 10.5 miles of paved surface, respectively. Grades are sometimes steep on the gravel roads, but no great technical skill is needed besides braking proficiency. The short and long loop are of moderate difficulty because of the steep grades.

Starting along the Mississippi, you will have a chance to warm up before taking on the 400-foot climbs that wind up narrow side valleys. This part of the river is called Lake Pepin. The Mississippi fills up the valley from bluff to bluff for a twenty-two mile section, creating one of the most beautiful stretches along North America's greatest river. The towering 300-foot limestone bluffs were noted by early French explorers who built forts along the shore. A historical marker near the village of Stockholm notes the Dakota Sioux tale of a young woman who jumped off of a jagged cliff, known ever since as Maiden Rock, rather than marry a man she didn't love.

The gravel road sections follow narrow, wooded valleys that lead to blufftop farmland. Pine Creek Road (signed as 20th Avenue) has been protected from development because of its designation as a Wisconsin Rustic Road. There are several small stream fords to splash through as you follow its one-lane gravel surface. All gravel roads are open to traffic and can be traveled by two-wheel-drive vehicles.

Along County Highway CC you will pass the Little House Wayside Park, which is the birthplace of children's author Laura Ingalls Wilder and the site of the homestead she wrote about in "Little House in the Big Woods." Stockholm is an artists' community with several cafes and a great bakery. A few miles off-route, in the village of Pepin, is an excellent restaurant called The Harbor View Cafe. Be prepared and be patient. A posted sign states, "No reservations, no credit cards, no whining."

General location: Between the villages of Maiden Rock and Stockholm, 79 miles north of LaCrosse.

Elevation change: On the short loop you will gain and lose 480´. Riding the long loop involves 700´ of climbing and descending. Each loop has a moderately steep 400´ climb.

Season: Late March to early November, although the temperatures will be cool or cold at the beginning and end of this period.

Services: Food, lodging, and gas are available in Stockholm, Maiden Rock, and Pepin. There is a water pump at the trailhead. A soft drink machine is all you will find in Lund. All services are available in Red Wing, Minnesota, 25 miles northwest, and Wabasha, Minnesota, 21 miles southeast of the trailhead.

Wooded side valleys lead to the Mississippi River on the Maiden Rock Tour.

Bicycle rental, retail, and repair service are available in Red Wing at The Outdoor Store.

Hazards: Loose gravel may be present on any of the unpaved roads. Stream fords can be deep in the spring or during rainy periods. Washouts may be encountered on gravel roads. Two-wheel-drive vehicle traffic may be significant on all roads during the summer months and the fall color period in mid-October.

Rescue index: Help can be summoned at Stockholm. The blufftop sections of the route are lined with farms; farmers are usually friendly and willing to help.

Land status: Public roadways through private land.

Maps: Good signage on all roads make additional maps unnecessary unless you love topo maps. If so, the short route can be found on the Maiden Rock and Nerike Hill USGS 7.5 minute quads. The long route appears on these and the Stockholm and Pepin quads. The DeLorme book, *Wisconsin Atlas & Gazetteer,* still shows the old road names in Pierce County instead of the current numbering system.

Finding the trail: The scenic overlook wayside starting point is located on WI 35, 3.5 miles south of Maiden Rock and 2.8 miles north of Stockholm.

Sources of additional information:

Red Wing Area Chamber of Commerce
420 Levee Street
Red Wing, MN 55066
(612) 388-4719

RIDE 30 MAIDEN ROCK TOUR

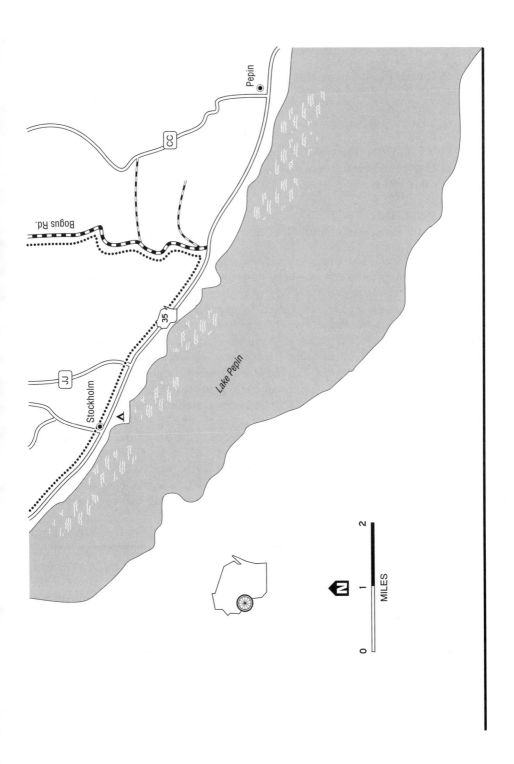

Pepin

CC

Bogus Rd.

35

JJ

Stockholm

Lake Pepin

N

0   1   2
        MILES

Mississippi Valley Partners
c/o John Hall, Anderson House
333 West Main Street
Wabasha, MN 55981
(612) 565-4524

Wisconsin Department of Transportation
Rustic Roads Board, Room 901
P.O. Box 7913
Madison, WI 53707
(608) 266-3661
Request "Wisconsin's Rustic Roads: A Positive Step Backward."

Notes on the trail: The routes are easy to follow due to good highway and town road signage. You can ride both loops in either direction. On the short route you begin riding north on WI 35 to County Road AA and return by the same roads. There is a wide paved shoulder along WI 35. Other roads should be lightly traveled. In Pierce County, the town road names were recently changed to a numerical system, but the locals continue to know them by the old names. Pine Creek Road (20th Avenue) and Willow Road (50th Avenue) are Wisconsin Rustic Road R-51. The town roads are signed with standard green-and-white street signs. A common rural prank is to twist these signposts 90 degrees, so check your map closely. Someone even made the extra effort of unbolting the arrow for the Rustic Road sign and turning it 180 degrees. In Pepin County, at the intersection of Bogus Road and CR CC, the street-type sign still indicates that CR CC is State Highway 183, its former designation.

Your choice of travel direction will determine whether you climb or descend Pine Creek Road (20th Avenue). It is hard to say which way of covering this lovely road you would enjoy most, but splashing through the fords on a downhill run is always fun.

RIDE 31 *PERROT STATE PARK TRAILS*

If you like flat land, don't ride at Perrot State Park. On the other hand, if challenging riding and some great scenic views interest you, Perrot is the place for you. Besides, thanks to a maverick presidential candidate (who spells his name with one "r") you can even pronounce the park's name correctly and sound like a local. The village of Trempealeau is pronounced Tremp-ah-low, so now you're really ready.

A historical marker in the park will tell you that trader and explorer Nicholas Perrot wintered there in 1685–86, around the time he claimed all of the lands of the Mississippi and its tributaries for the King of France. A look

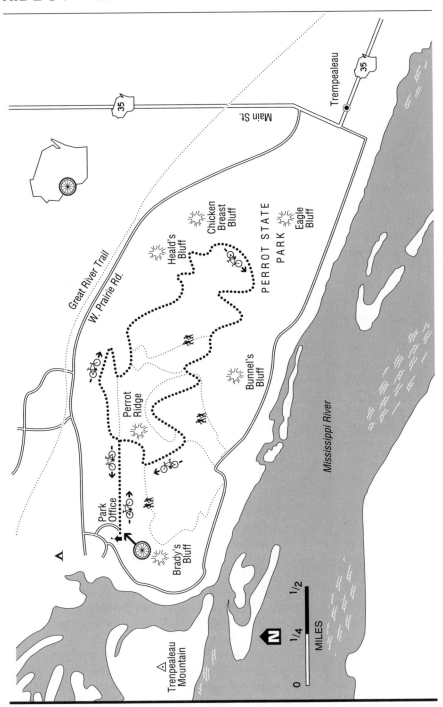

at the Indian mounds around the corner might have given him a clue that, if it belonged to anyone, it belonged to the people who had been there for thousands of years. That's not how the exploring game worked, though. He claimed the land for the king, and eventually, the park name for himself.

At the west end of the park a solitary peak stands in the Mississippi backwater. This is Trempealeau Mountain, and it is the only geological feature like it in the entire course of North America's longest river. The French named it *La Montagne qui trempe a l'eau*, or, the mountain which soaks in the water. It was a natural landmark that anyone could find and a perfect place to build a trading post.

The 5.1-mile spur-and-loop route shown here will give you a good idea why people wanted to possess this land. The hardwood forest is glorious, and white-tailed deer abound. The views of the Mississippi are unforgettable. The river valley is narrow here because the channel, less than a mile wide, is relatively new. It was formed when the last continental glacier melted and the river was forced away from its old course in the four-mile-wide valley north of the park.

Such grandeur has its price. There are no flat sections at all on the Perrot trails. Steep sections test your ability to keep moving and keep the front wheel on the ground at the same time. The downhills require different, although no less important, technical skills. On the positive side, the single-track cross-country ski trails are fairly wide and the surfaces are mostly smooth with a few rocks and roots. You will find some soft sand on the bluff trails that makes climbing impossible and descending tricky.

General location: Just west of the village of Trempealeau, 23 miles north of LaCrosse.

Elevation change: The terrain varies from constantly rolling to extremely steep. There is a 250′ variation between the trailhead and high point. There are two steady 200′ climbs and many 50′ to 80′ climbs.

Season: May through October. Park management is very sensitive to potential erosion and trails may be closed at any time due to wet conditions. Be sure to call ahead to check on trail status.

Services: Water is available near the trailhead. Some services, including bicycle rental, gas, lodging, food, and beverage are available in Trempealeau. All services are available in LaCrosse.

Hazards: Expect to find extremely steep slopes and some rough surface. Soft sand can make bike handling difficult. Deep, narrow washout gullies will be found on steep sections. On these sections, log water bars have been laid across the trails at angles to prevent erosion. Try to cross them at close to a right angle. Hiking is allowed on all trails.

Rescue index: Help is available at the park office. You will encounter few people on the trails, so if you are injured or have mechanical trouble you should return to the trailhead or follow a hiking trail to the paved park road.

A great view of the Mississippi River from the blufftop at Perrot State Park. *Photo courtesy of Wisconsin Department of Natural Resources.*

Land status: Wisconsin State Park. A daily or annual vehicle sticker ($5 daily / $18 annually for Wisconsin residents, $7 daily / $25 annually for out-of-state residents) is required to park in state forest lots. Bicycles are not charged for visiting the forest, but a trail pass fee is required of bicyclists age 18 and older ($3 daily or $10 annually). The trail pass also covers activities like cross-country skiing, horseback riding, and bicycling on railroad grade bike trails like the Great River Trail, which skirts the northern boundary of the park.

Maps: A cross-country ski trail map is available at the park office. The 7.5 minute USGS Trempealeau quad map does an excellent job of showing the terrain, but does not show any of the trails.

Finding the trail: From the Interstate 90, WI 35 / 53 interchange just north of Lacrosse, follow WI 35 northwest 16 miles to Trempealeau. Turn left on Main Street and after several blocks turn right on First Street (unmarked) just before the railroad tracks. Follow this road 3.2 miles to the Perrot State Park office.

Sources of additional information:

Perrot State Park
Route 1, Box 407
Trempealeau, WI 54661
(608) 534-6409

Wisconsin Department of Natural Resources
Bureau of Parks and Recreation
P.O. Box 7921
Madison, WI 53707-7921
(608) 266-2181

Trempealeau County Clerk's Office
1720 Main Street
Whitehall, WI 54773
(715) 538-2311

Notes on the trail: The trails are sometimes damaged during periods of wet weather and may be closed for this reason. Be sure to call ahead to check on the status. A daily or annual Wisconsin Trail Pass fee is required to ride on the off-road park trails (see Land Status). The trails are mostly one-way with some two-way connectors. They are well signed with green-and-white square mountain bike silhouette signs, trail name signs, and "you are here" sign maps at trail intersections. Trail signs prohibiting riding are white squares with red slashes through the mountain bike silhouette.

From the trailhead at the park office, follow the two-way trail signed as Brady's Bluff Trail. After a short distance, Brady's Bluff Trail turns to the right and is signed for hiking only. At this point, continue straight on the unmarked trail. After a similar distance turn left on the Wilber Trail, which will lead you through a meadow and the White Pine Run, a mini-forest of majestic pines. At the next signed trail intersection, turn left up Tow Rope Hill (black diamond rated) to Cedar Glade Trail and Prairie Trail. At around 3.5 miles you will climb to a trail junction where the trail to the right falls away sharply. Turn left to complete the route shown here and follow Perrot Ridge around. If you turn right you can return to the trailhead by a slightly shorter route that will save a considerable amount of climbing.

RIDE 32 *CASTLE MOUND TRAIL*

This easy route offers even the most inexperienced rider a chance to enjoy the wooded scenery of the Black River State Forest on an almost entirely flat, nine-mile (total distance) out-and-back trail. The surface is mostly hard, sandy soil with a grassy cover. Some soft sand will be found near the north end, and there are a few swampy, muddy spots in the pine and aspen forest between Castle Mound Road and Cranberry Road. The trail is always wide enough for a four-wheel-drive vehicle.

The trailhead is at the Black River State Forest Campground near the east end of the trail's namesake, Castle Mound. The view of this half-mile-long,

RIDE 32 *CASTLE MOUND TRAIL*

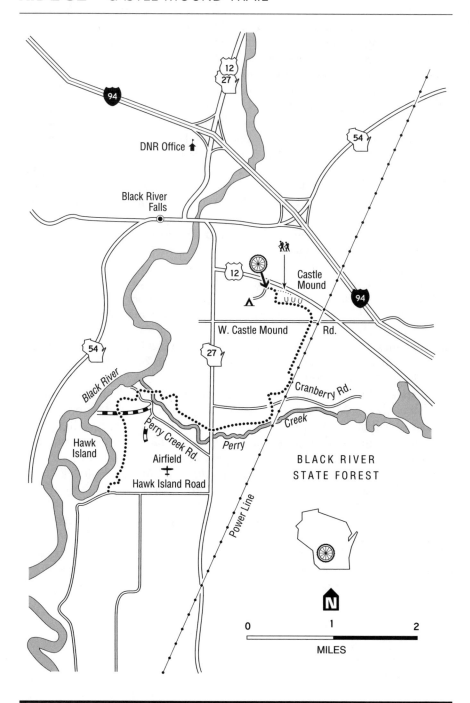

parapet-like, 200-foot-high sandstone rock is shrouded by trees along most of the trail. There is one fine view after the leaves fall as you ride north just before crossing Castle Mound Road. From this spot you can see the mound's famous balancing rock, which seems to defy gravity. A hiking trail that also starts at the campground will lead to a closer look.

The trail's most scenic section, and the only one with any significant elevation change, is along Perry Creek. The trail is rolling as the stream winds along with numerous rapids in a narrow gorge through a pine, birch, and oak forest. You cross the stream at a scenic spot on a wooden bridge. Deer and numerous birds of prey are common throughout the forest.

General location: Two miles south of the I-94 exit for WI 54/Black River Falls.
Elevation change: Generally flat with two stream crossings that involve a 50′ and an 80′ descent and climb.
Season: Trails are open for mountain biking from May 1 to November 1.
Services: All services including bicycle retail and repair are available in the town of Black River Falls.
Hazards: Although the trails receive regular maintenance, fallen trees or branches may be encountered at any time. The trail is open to hikers, although it is seldom used for hiking. For a short distance near Cranberry Road the trail is shared with ATVs.
Rescue index: Help is available at the Castle Mound Campground office, at the main Black River State Forest office just south of the I-94 and WI 54 interchange, or in the town of Black River Falls.
Land status: Wisconsin State Forest. A daily or annual vehicle sticker ($5 daily / $18 annually for Wisconsin residents, $7 daily / $25 annually for out-of-state residents) is required to park in state forest lots. Bicycles are not charged for visiting the forest, but a trail pass fee is required of bicyclists age 18 and older ($3 daily or $10 annually). The trail pass also covers activities like cross-country skiing, horseback riding, and bicycling on railroad grade bike trails.
Maps: A detailed map is available at the Black River State Forest Campground office.
Finding the trail: Exit I-94 at the WI 54, Black River Falls Exit. Proceed west one mile and turn left on US 12/WI 27 as you enter the town of Black River Falls. Turn left on US 12 after one-half mile where WI 27 continues straight. Follow US 12 for .7 mile to the entrance of Castle Mound Area State Forest Campground on the right. Follow "Picnic Area" and "Parking" signs .2 mile to the "Perry Creek Mountain Bike Trail."

Sources of additional information:

Black River State Forest
Route 4, Box 18
Black River Falls, WI 54615
(715) 284-1400

Wooded trails lead to Perry Creek at Castle Mound.

Wisconsin Department of Natural Resources
Bureau of Parks and Recreation
P.O. Box 7921
Madison, WI 53707-7921
(608) 266-2181

Black River Falls Chamber of Commerce
336 North Water Street
Black River Falls, WI 54615
(715) 284-4658

Notes on the trail: An annual or day-use motor vehicle sticker is required to park on state land, as well as an annual or daily per-person trail fee (see Land status). These can be paid at the Black River State Forest Campground office seven days a week from Memorial Day weekend to Labor Day weekend and on weekends until November 1. At other times, the fees must be paid at the main Black River State Forest office just south of the interchange of I-94 and WI 54.

From the Perry Creek Mountain Bike Trail trailhead at the Black River State Forest Campground picnic area parking lot, you will follow a route that is well marked in both directions by small brown-and-white mountain bike silhouette signs. The only spot that might be at all confusing is a short jog on Perry Creek Road, where you will ride on the pavement for approximately one-tenth of a mile. Keep a sharp lookout for trail openings back into the woods since there is no on-road signage. The end of Perry Creek Road is only a short distance from this point. A parking lot at the end is another possible place to start your ride.

RIDE 33 *BLACK RIVER STATE FOREST TRAILS*

The Smreaker, Red Oak, and Wildcat trail systems in the Black River State Forest are great routes for riders looking for challenging climbing. Once you are on top of the 200-foot mounds you can view the vast, flat expanse of the forest. On a windy day the tops of the pine trees look like waves. Ten thousand years ago the scene really would have been waves of water. The mounds were once islands in a vast inland sea formed from melted ice as the continental glacier receded to the north.

There are many shortcut options on this 19.4-mile ride. With the exception of the 6.4-mile (total) out-and-back run from the trailhead on the Pigeon Creek Trail, all trails will challenge the average rider. It's not just the steep climbs on the 6.4-mile Smreaker, 3.2-mile Red Oak, and 3.4-mile Wildcat trail loops that make it difficult; it's the technical skill needed to handle loose surfaces and soft sand on the fast downhills. The route is entirely in the woods; pines predominate in the low areas and oaks on the ridges.

The route is on grassy or forest floor cross-country ski trails except for the Pigeon Creek Trail, which was created for mountain bikes to connect the campground with the mound trails. The Pigeon Creek Trail runs through a boggy lowland. It will be soft at any time and impassable during wet periods. All of the mound trails are well drained, thanks to a sandy base that also creates a fair amount of rolling resistance in low areas.

General location: Two miles northeast of the Interstate 94/County Road O Exit at the village of Millston.
Elevation change: The terrain is flat to gently rolling in the low land and very steep to rolling on the mounds. There are seven climbs and descents in the 120′ to 200′ range on one complete circuit.
Season: Black River State Forest trails are open for mountain biking from May 1 to November 1.

RIDE 33   *BLACK RIVER STATE FOREST TRAILS*

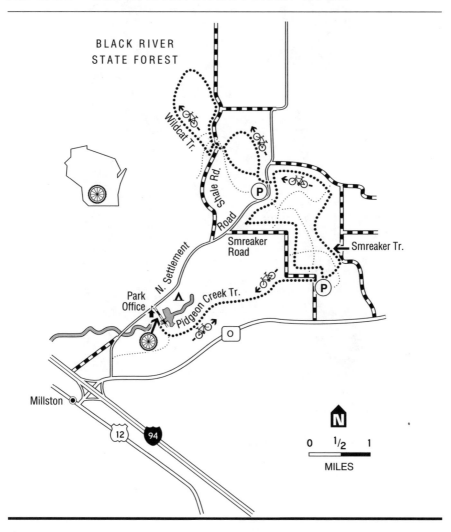

Services: Water is available at the trailhead and at the Smreaker and Red Oak trail parking lots. Food, lodging, and gas are available in the small village of Millston. All services, including bicycle retail and repair, are available in the town of Black River Falls 12 miles to the northwest on I-94.

Hazards: Although the trails receive regular maintenance, fallen trees or branches may be encountered at any time. The trails are open to hikers and are heavily used during the fall. Rough, loose surface downhills and soft sand washouts at the bottoms of them can be hazardous to the unskilled.

Riders love the challenge at Black River Falls State Park.

Rescue index: Help is available at the Pigeon Creek Campground office or in the village of Millston. To increase your chance of rescue, make your way to one of the more heavily traveled paved or gravel roads.

Land status: Wisconsin State Forest. A daily or annual vehicle sticker ($5 daily / $18 annually for Wisconsin residents, $7 daily / $25 annually for out-of-state residents) is required to park in state parks. Bicyclists are not charged for visiting the park, but an off-road trail pass fee is required of bicyclists age 18 and older ($3 daily or $10 annually). The trail pass also covers other activities like cross-country skiing, horseback riding, and bicycling on railroad grade bike trails.

Maps: A detailed map is available at the Pigeon Creek Campground office. The 7.5 series USGS quads for Millston and Hartfield SE show the terrain very well, but do not show the trails.

Finding the trail: Exit I-94 at the CR O/ Millston Exit. Travel northeast .1 mile and turn left on North Settlement Road. Travel two miles to the Pigeon Creek Campground entrance on the right. Park in the picnic area parking lot.

Sources of additional information:

> Black River State Forest
> Route 4, Box 18
> Black River Falls, WI 54615
> (715) 284-1400

> Wisconsin Department of Natural Resources
> Bureau of Parks and Recreation
> P.O. Box 7921
> Madison, WI 53707-7921
> (608) 266-2181

> Black River Falls Chamber of Commerce
> 336 North Water Street
> Black River Falls, WI 54615
> (715) 284-4658

Notes on the trail: The trails are sometimes subject to flooding or damage and may be closed for these reasons. Be sure to call ahead to check on the status. An annual or day-use motor vehicle sticker is required on state land, as well as an annual or daily trail fee (see Land status). These can be paid at the Pigeon Creek Campground office seven days a week from Memorial Day weekend to Labor Day weekend and on weekends until November 1. At other times, the fees must be paid at the main Black River State Forest office just south of the I-94/WI 54 interchange.

The mainly one-way trails are well marked with brown-and-white mountain bike silhouette signs and cross-country ski trail signs. From the trailhead at the Pigeon Creek Campground picnic area, follow the unimproved road on top of the earthen dam along the swimming pond. After .3 mile, turn left (east) on Pigeon Creek Trail and follow it to the junction with an improved gravel road (Smreaker Road). Bear right and follow it one-half mile east to the Smreaker Trail parking lot. From the south side of the parking lot follow the East, Ridge, and North trails to the two-way link trail that crosses a paved road (North Settlement Road) to the Red Oak Trail, which you will pick up at the northwest side of the parking lot. Partway around the Red Oak Trail you will junction with another two-way link trail that will take you across an improved gravel road (Shale Road) to the Wildcat Trail. Link trails are gated at road crossings. Return by the same links and follow the North, Central, and West loops on the Smreaker Trail to the trailhead.

RIDE 34   *STANDING ROCKS TRAILS*

In the winter they sell T-shirts that say "Home of the Skiing Fanatic and the Glacial Erratic." Since Standing Rocks County Park is an alpine and cross-country ski area, anyone can understand the skiing fanatic part of the slogan. You have to know a little about geological history to understand the second part. Standing Rocks got its name from the abundance of rounded granite stones that dot the area. Technically, they are glacial erratics, meaning they were pushed there by an ice sheet of the continental glacier. Evidently there used to be a granite mountain somewhere northeast of the park before the relentless ice pancaked it. Some erratics are huge—the height of a man—and some are just nasty watermelon-sized buggers poking up out of the trail. In light snow winters skiers call the place "Constant Rocks." In summer mountain bikers appreciate suspension forks.

The 6.3-mile outer loop at Standing Rocks is a workout, and a fun one. With the exception of a short stretch of Tower Road's graveled surface, the route runs entirely on a one-way, grassy and hardpacked, double-track cross-country ski trail system through a dense forest of pine, oak, and aspen. Wildlife thrives here, particularly white-tailed deer. There is only about 100 feet of relief at the park, but you will climb that amount of elevation twice in two separate, steady climbs; you can overlook Bear Lake from the ski hill. Otherwise, the terrain is seldom the same grade for more than a few yards and there are some real hero slopes that, although short, will test anyone's ability to stay on the bike. All of this makes Standing Rocks a moderately difficult ride that requires no great technical ability.

General location: Sixteen miles southeast of the city of Stevens Point.

Elevation change: Generally rolling with two steady 100′ climbs.

Season: Officially open for mountain biking May through October, but may be closed due to excessively wet conditions.

Services: Food and gas are available in Amherst. All services including bicycle repair and retail are available in Stevens Point.

Hazards: Downed trees and branches may be found at any time. Some trail sections are steep and rough.

Rescue index: The trails are patrolled at times, but if you are injured or have mechanical trouble, you should make your way back to the trailhead and Standing Rocks Road. There is a pay telephone outside the ski lodge, which is closed during mountain bike season.

Land status: Portage County Park. A trail pass must be purchased before riding. These are available as a $25 season pass or a $4 daily pass. There is a self-pay system at the trailhead, or passes can be purchased at the Portage County Parks

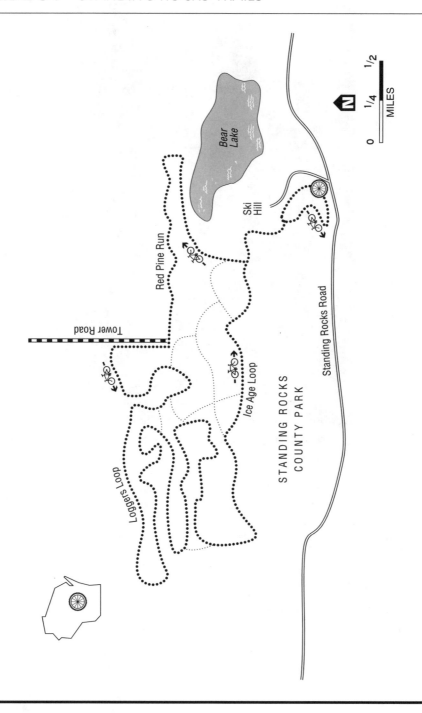

Steep cross-country ski trails are the norm at Standing Rocks County Park.

Department on weekdays (see below), at several bicycle shops in Stevens Point, or at O.K. Hardware in Amherst.

Maps: A detailed map of the trails is available at trail pass purchase locations. "You are here" sign maps are posted frequently along trails.

Finding the trail: From US 10, at Amherst, drive 4.5 miles west on County Road B. At County Road K turn south and drive one mile to Standing Rocks Road and turn west. Drive one mile to Standing Rocks County Park entrance.

Sources of additional information:

Portage County Parks Department
Portage County Courthouse
1516 Church Street
Stevens Point, WI 54481
(715) 346-1433 or (715) 824-3175

Stevens Point Chamber of Commerce
600 Main Street
Stevens Point, WI 54481
(715) 344-1940

Waupaca Area Chamber of Commerce
221 South Main Street
Waupaca, WI 54981
(715) 258-7343

Notes on the trail: A trail pass must be purchased before riding (see Land status). Be sure to phone ahead to the Parks Department to make sure the trails are open, because they may be closed to prevent damage due to excessive rainfall. A recorded trail condition message will play on weekends and evenings. From the roadside parking lot/trailhead, ride the mainly one-way route shown on the map by following the blue route on the frequent "you are here" cross-country ski trail signs. Mountain bikers are required to ride on the fine, crushed red granite surface in the sections where it has been laid down. Deer and other wildlife are seen often, and there is a fine overview of Bear Lake from the ski hill.

RIDE 35 *POTAWATOMI STATE PARK TRAILS*

The 5.7-mile spur-and-loop of easy-riding mountain bike trails at Potawatomi State Park wind through a spellbinding woods of birch, maple, and hemlock. The Door Peninsula has always been an appealing place. The Potawatomi tribe defended it against the Iroquois who had canoed all the way from what is now New York. Every French explorer of any repute passed through. Today it is a popular tourist destination. Fortunately, despite the beautiful views of the bay, Potawatomi State Park is a bit off the beaten path and is seldom overcrowded.

The park is easily accessible from the interesting town of Sturgeon Bay, or vice versa, via a short bike trail at the southeast corner of the park that connects to Duluth Avenue. Sturgeon Bay has a maritime flavor. Shipyards once built huge lake freighters in the bay and they still repair them. Only yachts and smaller ships are still constructed along its shore.

The single-track cross-country ski trails that make up the off-road route have a grassy or forest floor surface that is mostly smooth with some rocks and roots. This provides a good introduction to off-roading for the novice and a nice tour for the more advanced rider. Complete newcomers might question how much they would enjoy the sport judging by the first off-road section that runs next to the park road. It is littered with angular chunks of limestone and makes for a very rough ride. This is temporary though; the surface smoothes

RIDE 35   *POTAWATOMI STATE PARK TRAILS*

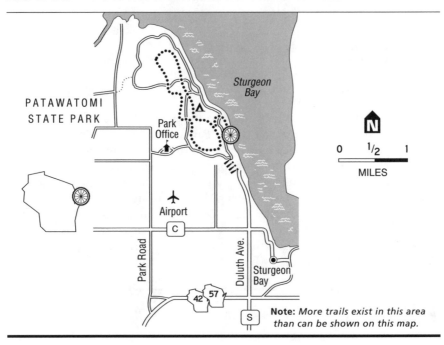

Note: *More trails exist in this area than can be shown on this map.*

out as soon as you climb up on the bluff. Any other doubts about the appeal of off-roading should be dispelled with the first sight of white-tailed deer or wild turkey.

General location: Three miles northwest of Sturgeon Bay.
Elevation change: The terrain is mostly flat. There is a moderately steep climb or descent of 50′ on the out-and-back section near the trailhead and an even more moderate climb and descent of 30′ near the north end of the loop.
Season: Trails are open for mountain biking from mid-April to early November. The trails may be closed due to wet conditions. Be sure to call ahead to check on the status.
Services: There is water near the trailhead. All services, including bicycle retail and repair, are available in Sturgeon Bay.
Hazards: Windfall trees and branches can litter the trail at any time. Hiking is allowed on all trails.
Rescue index: Help is available at the park office and in Sturgeon Bay. There is a telephone at the shelter on the shore road. A bike trail connection to Duluth Avenue at the southeast corner of the park is a shortcut into Sturgeon Bay.
Land status: Wisconsin State Park. A daily or annual vehicle sticker ($5 daily / $18 annually for Wisconsin residents, $7 daily / $25 annually for

Birch and pine line the Potawatomi State Park Trails.

out-of-state residents) is required to park in state parks. Bicycles are not charged a trail pass fee at Potawatomi.

Maps: A mountain bike trail map is available at the park office or from the DNR.

Finding the trail: From WI 42 / 57, go 1.5 miles east of Sturgeon Bay and turn north on Park Road. A large brown sign will direct you to the park. After 2.5 miles turn right into the park. At a **T** intersection turn right on Norway Road and follow it to the picnic areas near the bay shore. Park at the lot for Picnic Area #2 and ride down to the bay, where you will find a trail map for the Hemlock Trail.

Sources of additional information:

Potawatomi State Park
3740 Park Drive
Sturgeon Bay, WI 54235
(920) 746-2890

Wisconsin Department of Natural Resources
Bureau of Parks and Recreation
P.O. Box 7921
Madison, WI 53707-7921
(608) 266-2181

Door County Chamber of Commerce
P.O. Box 40
Sturgeon Bay, WI 54235
(920) 743-4456

Notes on the trail: An annual or day-use motor vehicle sticker is required to park on state land (see Land status). Begin at the trail map for the Hemlock Trail between the Picnic Area #2 parking lot and the bay shore. Follow the old paved road north along the shore (Hemlock Trail markers are small gray squares with the silhouette of a hemlock branch) and ride around a gate just before the old road junctions with the park drive. Ride onto the unpaved Hemlock Trail directly across the road from the junction. Almost immediately turn left onto an unnamed trail that is signed with a square green-and-white mountain bike silhouette. The Hemlock Trail veers to the right and a red slash through the mountain bike silhouette indicates that riding is no longer allowed. From this point the route is well marked with green mountain bike signs, blue cross-country ski trail signs, and periodic "you are here" map signs. Ignore "do not enter" signs; these are for one-way ski travel.

After a short distance the trail swings to the right and climbs a moderately steep slope. Near the top you will cross a trail that marks the beginning of the loop. Two-way riding is allowed on the loop, but these directions are for counter-clockwise travel. The trail to the right at this intersection is the trail you will return on. The trail to the left is the Hemlock Trail, signed to prohibit mountain biking. Take the trail ahead, which is also the Hemlock Trail. Riding is allowed on this stretch and after a short distance the Hemlock Trail will split off as the mountain bike route turns left. After another short stretch, look for a trail running to the right that is signed for mountain biking. This is not obvious, and you have to look down the trail to see the sign. If you make a mistake and continue straight at this point, you will reach the paved road after a short distance.

At 1.9 miles you will reach a split where both trails are signed for mountain biking. Take the trail to the left and, after a short distance, cross the paved road. The trail to the right connects with the return loop and offers a shortcut that will save two miles of riding. The signage is a bit confusing when you return to the intersection where you first began riding the loop. An arrow below the green mountain bike sign points to the right, which would send you off on another loop. To return to the trailhead turn to the left.

RIDE 36 *PENINSULA STATE PARK TRAILS*

Peninsula State Park is one of the most popular parks in Wisconsin, and on your first visit you'll find out why. It is the essence of the Door County experience—a place of great natural beauty. The wooded bluffs of the peninsula jut out into Green Bay above the small towns of Fish Creek and Ephraim. Norwegian and Icelandic fishermen settled in this area and made their livings from the lake. The "fish boil," a mix of fish, potatoes, and onions thrown in a cauldron, remains a popular "all you can eat" traditional dinner in the old fishing villages.

This 13.8-mile spur-and-loop route is a mix of crushed limestone surface, near-flat bike trail, gently rolling, rough surface, cross-country ski trails, and about four miles of paved roads. The ride warrants an easy rating despite the roughness of the ski trails. These rocky and root-covered trails should only be difficult if ridden fast. But hard riding isn't what mountain biking is all about. Sometimes it's good to just take it easy and let nature's beauty soak in. Peninsula State Park is the perfect place for some serious beauty absorption.

The ski trails are almost entirely in a deep woods of pine, hemlock, birch, and maple. When you rejoin the Sunset Trail, you will roll through strands of fragrant cedar with views through the trees of the bay and islands. There are many beautiful scenes in the park. A four-mile side trip will take you to Eagle Tower for a great view of the bay and the village of Ephraim. Just off of the Sunset Trail stands the Eagle Lighthouse, a historic beacon that is now a museum.

General location: Just north of the village of Fish Creek, which is 22 miles northeast of Sturgeon Bay.

Elevation change: The terrain is mostly flat or gently rolling. There are several moderately steep climbs gaining 50′ to 80′. The difference between the lowest and highest points on the route is 130′.

Season: The trails should be open for mountain biking from mid-April to early November. The trails may be closed due to wet conditions. Be sure to call ahead to check on the status.

Services: There is water at the trailhead and a concession stand at the Nicolet Bay beach that rents bikes. All services including bicycle retail, rental, and repair are available in Fish Creek. One-speed bicycles can be rented just outside the park entrance.

Hazards: Windfall trees and branches may be present. In low spots, rough rock has been laid down, making bike handling difficult. All trails are open for hiking.

RIDE 36 *PENINSULA STATE PARK TRAILS*

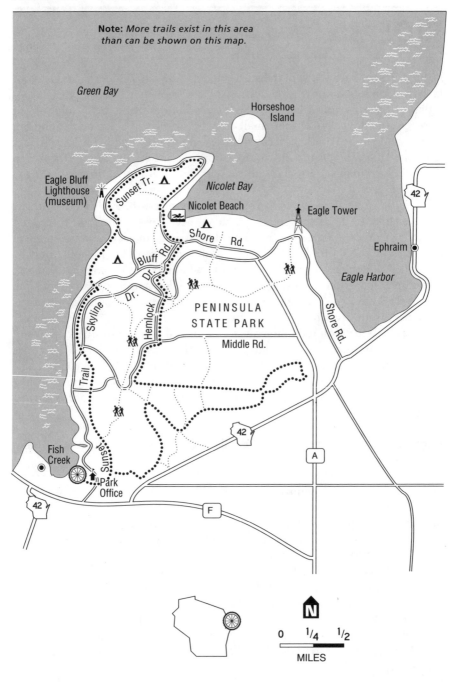

Note: *More trails exist in this area than can be shown on this map.*

Green Bay

Horseshoe Island

Eagle Bluff Lighthouse (museum)

Sunset Tr.

Nicolet Bay

Nicolet Beach

Eagle Tower

Shore Rd.

Bluff Dr.

Ephraim

Eagle Harbor

Skyline Dr.

Hemlock

Trail

PENINSULA STATE PARK

Middle Rd.

Shore Rd.

42

A

Fish Creek

Sunset

Park Office

42

F

N

0   1/4   1/2
MILES

Rescue index: Help is available at the park office and at the Nicolet Bay beach concession stand.

Land status: Wisconsin State Park. A daily or annual vehicle sticker ($5 daily / $18 annually for Wisconsin residents, $7 daily / $25 annually for out-of-state residents) is required to park in state parks. Bicyclists are not charged for visiting the park, but a trail pass fee is required of bicyclists age 18 and older ($3 daily or $10 annually). This does not include the Sunset Trail, where no trail pass is required. The trail pass also covers activities like cross-country skiing, horseback riding, and bicycling on railroad grade bike trails.

Maps: A mountain bike trail map is available at the park office or from the DNR.

Finding the trail: Follow WI 42 through the village of Fish Creek and turn north into the park at the eastern village limits. Just past the park office, where the inbound drive rejoins the outbound drive, turn left into the Sunset Bike Trail parking lot. The trail begins on the south side of the parking lot.

Sources of additional information:

Peninsula State Park
Box 218
Fish Creek, WI 54212
(920) 854-5791

Wisconsin Department of Natural Resources
Bureau of Parks and Recreation
P.O. Box 7921
Madison, WI 53707-7921
(608) 266-2181

Door County Chamber of Commerce
P.O. Box 40
Sturgeon Bay, WI 54235
(920) 743-4456

Notes on the trail: An annual or day-use motor vehicle sticker is required to park on state land, as well as an annual or daily per-person trail fee for riding the off-road trails (see Land status) except for the Sunset Trail, where no trail pass is required. The trails are well marked with small, square green-and-white mountain bike silhouette signs, blue cross-country ski trail markers, and periodic "you are here" sign maps. Trails where mountain biking is not allowed are marked with a red slash through the mountain bike silhouette.

From the south side of the trailhead parking lot, follow the crushed limestone–surfaced Sunset Trail to the southeast across the park road and around to the north. Trails can be ridden in either direction, but these cues describe counter-clockwise travel. Watch very carefully for the right-angle

The deep woods are only a short ride from the lakeshore.

turn off the Sunset Trail onto the unsurfaced cross-country ski trail that is marked "difficult trail." After a fairly steep climb you will come to an intersection where both the left and right trails are signed for mountain biking. Go left here; the right trail will take you out to the highway.

At the next intersection turn right onto the remnants of an abandoned paved road. This section is also signed with orange snowmobile diamonds. Watch closely for the next turn to the left one-half mile farther. If you reach the highway you have gone too far. The rest of the cross-country trail section is easy to follow. There are "you are here" signs at each intersection. Eventually you will junction with Hemlock Road, a paved road that you will take north. Follow it until you reach Bluff Road. Turn right on Bluff Road and, a short distance later, turn left (west) on Shore Road. For an interesting side trip you can follow Shore Road to the east to Eagle Tower, an observation platform with a great view of the bay and neighboring towns.

Just beyond the Nicolet Bay beach on Shore Road, a sign will direct you to the Sunset Trail on the east side of the road. Follow the Sunset Trail back to the trailhead.

RIDE 37 *NEWPORT STATE PARK TRAILS*

Although Door County is a very popular tourist destination, it gets a lot quieter the farther north you go. And you can't get much farther north than Newport State Park, which is near the tip of the peninsula where Porte des Morts Passage (Death's Door) separates the mainland from Washington Island. The passage was named for the havoc it wreaked on sailing ships; the county was named after the channel. The highest concentration of wrecks in the country lie beneath its waters. A small maritime museum in the nearby village of Gills Rock (where you can take a ferry to Washington Island) displays artifacts from many wrecks.

Your 10.9-mile loop and out-and-back ride at Newport will be much less menacing. The easy, quiet hiking and cross-country ski trails can be handled by even the most inexperienced rider. The terrain is almost dead flat, and the grassy and forest floor surfaces of the cross-country ski trails offer little rolling resistance, save some swampy sections on the southwest loops. But riding is hardly the whole story at Newport. There are many opportunities to get off your bike and walk out to the more than 11 miles of lakeshore to enjoy the tranquillity of this unique park.

General location: Four miles east of the village of Ellison Bay, which is 36 miles northeast of Sturgeon Bay.
Elevation change: No significant change.
Season: Trails should be rideable from mid-April to November.
Services: Water is available along the trail at Newport Bay. All services, except bicycle services, are available in the small villages of Gills Rock and Ellison Bay. Bicycle retail and repair are available in Fish Creek, 17 miles south on WI 42
Hazards: Windfall trees and branches are always possible hazards. All trails are open for hiking.
Rescue index: Help is available at the park office.
Land status: Wisconsin State Park. A daily or annual vehicle sticker ($5 daily / $18 annually for Wisconsin residents, $7 daily / $25 annually for out-of-state residents) is required to park in state parks. A bicycle trail pass fee is not charged in Newport.
Maps: A cross-country ski trail map is available at the park office or from the DNR.

RIDE 37 *NEWPORT STATE PARK TRAILS*

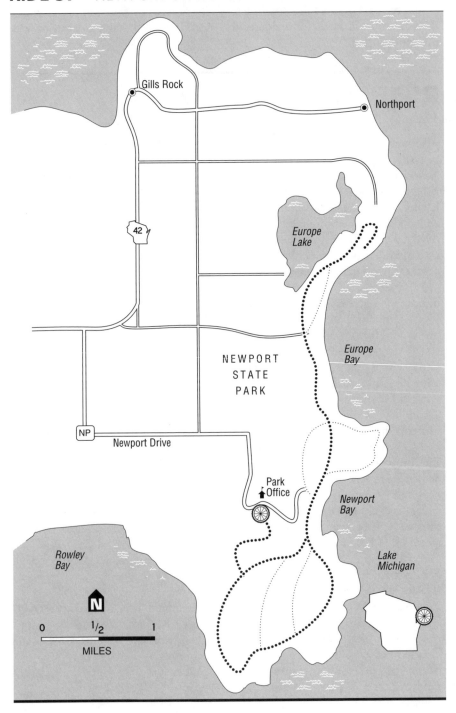

Gills Rock

Northport

42

Europe
Lake

Europe
Bay

NEWPORT
STATE
PARK

NP

Newport Drive

Park
Office

Newport
Bay

Rowley
Bay

Lake
Michigan

N

0   1/2   1
MILES

The influence of Lake Michigan makes a perfect climate for white paper birch trees.

Finding the trail: From the village of Ellison Bay, travel two miles east on WI 42 and turn south on County Road NP (Newport Drive). Follow it three miles to the park office.

Sources of additional information:

Newport State Park
475 County Highway NP
Ellison Bay, WI 54210
(920) 854-2500

Wisconsin Department of Natural Resources
Bureau of Parks and Recreation
P.O. Box 7921
Madison, WI 53707-7921
(608) 266-2181

Door County Chamber of Commerce
P.O. Box 40
Sturgeon Bay, WI 54235
(414) 743-4456

Notes on the trail: An annual or day-use motor vehicle sticker is required to park on state land (see Land status). There is no special signage for mountain biking, but the trails are well marked for cross-country skiing with frequent "you are here" sign maps. The small confines of the park make getting lost unlikely. This route features a loop and an out-and-back section. Trails can be ridden in either direction, but these cues apply to riding counter-clockwise. Begin riding at Parking Lot #1 near the park office and head south on the blue trail. At a **T** intersection turn right on the blue trail. Make right turns at all trail intersections, blue to red, red to yellow, and yellow to white. Once on the white trail, you are on the out-and-back stretch.

Chequamegon Region

Chequamegon (pronounced Sha-wa-ma-gun) means "place of the beaver" in the language of the native Ojibwe. It was the wealth of the fur trade that drew the first white men to this region of lakes, rivers, and dense forest. Renegade Frenchmen Pierre Radisson and Menard Groseilliers wintered on nearby Lac Court Orielles (pronounced La-coo-der-aay) in 1660 at the site of the present reservation of the same name. In his account of the journey, Radisson claimed they marched like "Caesars of the wilderness" to their destination, but the local Ojibwe tradition recounts that the first two white men, found starving on the shore of Lake Superior, were sheltered and nursed back to health. Interestingly, the Native American version was accounted before Radisson's journal turned up in the mid-nineteenth century.

The Chequamegon has become legendary among off-roaders, thanks to a pioneering off-road event called the Chequamegon Fat Tire Festival. This weekend of mountain bike races and games was the first off-road competition in the Midwest when it began in 1983. Today it features the largest off-road race in the nation, attracting 2,500 riders to the Chequamegon 40 and the 16-mile Short & Fat, which runs concurrently.

There are many more reasons than a weekend of racing to pay a visit to the Chequamegon. The people who live there and ride there knew this and several years ago formed the Chequamegon Area Mountain Bike Association (CAMBA), which in a remarkably short time mapped and marked over 200 miles of mountain bike routes. The area's wild terrain is mostly interlobate glacial moraine, formed between the Superior and Chippewa lobes. It is similar to the kettle moraine of southern Wisconsin. It simply can't be beat for fun mountain biking. And the Ojibwe reservation at Lac Court Oreilles has the best listener-sponsored radio station in the Midwest, WOJB. From blues to country, you'll hear music on 88.9 FM that most stations ignore or have forgotten.

The CAMBA routes, seven of which are included here, are favorites among the active local community. Good signage makes them accessible to visitors who need not fear getting lost in the vast forest. There are no fees for riding the trails, but CAMBA sells packets of detailed maps and encourages riders to join the organization. All the off-roading activity has resulted in another benefit. The area undoubtedly has more bike shops per capita than any place in the Midwest. CAMBA has strong support from many other mountain biker–friendly businesses throughout the area.

The Frost Pocket Tour is an easy paved road, forest road, and snowmobile trail route in and out of the small sport- and lumber-oriented community of Seeley. The Lake Helane Tour is a moderately difficult ride on forest roads that starts at the halfway rest cabin on the famous American Birkebeiner cross-country ski trail. The Short & Fat is a challenging route that follows the Chequamegon Fat Tire Festival race course. A challenging glacial feature is the highlight of a ride on the Esker Trail. At Rock Lake, riders can take on a challenging route punctuated by pristine lakes that has been popular with off-roaders for years. The Drummond Trails offer a moderate ride that follows some single-track on the North Country Trail and leads to a scenic swimming beach. The Delta Hills Trails are a challenging slice of deep woods beauty through a land of lakes and white paper birch.

RIDE 38 *FROST POCKET TOUR*

This easy 10.5-mile loop takes you deep into the north woods and past the strange feature that gave the route its name. The frost pocket is unique terrain formed between two lobes of the continental glacier in northern latitudes. Melting blocks of ice formed pockets, or kettles. In an area where night temperatures are almost always cool, these pits fill with cold air so many nights that little besides tough grasses and lichens can grow in them. They are also called sun bowls because they offer openings to the sky in the dense woods.

The route follows paved and improved gravel roads as well as several unimproved roads that serve as snowmobile trails in winter. All roads would be negotiable by a four-wheel-drive vehicle. No technical riding skill is necessary other than braking ability on a short, steep section with a loose surface on snowmobile trail #5. This ride is rated as easy and is good for riders of any ability. It is also a nice introduction to the Chequamegon Area Mountain Bike Association trail system.

Silverthorn Park is a pleasant spot for the trailhead. The local baseball team, the Seeley Loggers, plays there, and the small, clean lake has a nice swimming beach. The village of Seeley has become a mix of cross-country skiers, bicyclists, and local color of the rough and ready chainsaw type. The Sawmill Saloon caters to all with food and drink. Just beyond Seeley on County Road OO and Old OO you'll pass by the Uhrenholt Memorial State Forest, which preserves a majestic stand of white pine and offers a glimpse of what the area was like before commercial logging began a hundred years ago.

General location: Silverthorn Park, one mile north of the village of Seeley.
Elevation change: The route begins and ends with a flat stretch in the Namekagon River Valley. The rest of the terrain tends to roll with about 180′ of total elevation difference, which includes one steep 120′ climb on Old OO.
Season: Late April to early November depending on remnant or early snow. From late May to late July insect populations are significant. Routes tend to

RIDE 38   *FROST POCKET TOUR*

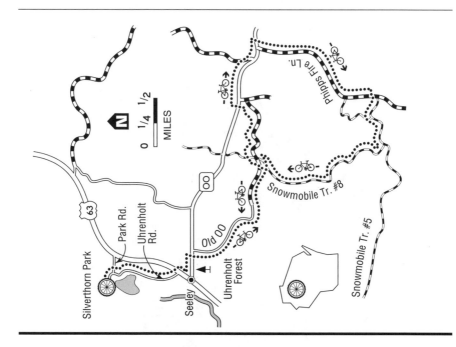

be wetter in the spring, but the glacial moraine that comprises the terrain drains very poorly and standing water may be found at nearly any time of the year.

Services: All services are available in Cable and Hayward, including bicycle rental, repair, and retail. Food and drink are available in Seeley as well as bicycle rental, repair, and retail at Seeley Hills Ski and Bike.

Hazards: Roads are kept clear, but downed trees and branches may be encountered at any time. Sandpit washouts at the bottoms of steep hills on trails and roads are common. County and forest roads, and even snowmobile trails, are used by local two-wheel-drive vehicles and logging trucks. Hunting season begins in mid-September.

Rescue index: Help is available in Seeley. While the forest road and the snowmobile trails are traveled, you should make your way back to CR OO.

Land status: Public roads through private and public land; snowmobile trails through Sawyer County Forest.

Maps: The CAMBA maps include detailed route and topographical information. The map for this route is available at the Telemark trailhead. A complete set of detailed maps for all CAMBA trails and an overview map are available for $5 by writing CAMBA at the address listed below. The overview map locates the trail clusters and mountain bike–friendly businesses in the area.

Well-marked forest roads wind through deep woods on
the Frost Pocket Tour.

CAMBA memberships include a map set, voting privileges, and a frame
sticker for a mere $20.
Finding the trail: From the village of Seeley on US 63 drive one-half mile
north and turn west on Park Road to Silverthorn Town Park. Several other
CAMBA trails can be accessed from this trailhead.

Sources of additional information:

Chequamegon Area Mountain Bike Association (CAMBA)
P.O. Box 141
Cable, WI 54821
(715) 798-3833, (800) 533-7454

Cable Area Chamber of Commerce
P.O. Box 217
Cable, WI 54821
(800) 533-7454

Seeley Hills Ski and Bike
Route 3
Seeley, WI 54843
(715) 634-3539

Notes on the trail: The route signs and these cues are for riding the loop portion of the route in a clockwise direction. It is well marked with blue and white CAMBA trail markers and "you are here" signs. From the Silverthorn trailhead follow the CAMBA signs that lead you toward US 63 on the remnant of an old road. After a short distance you will pass through a vehicle barricade. This places you on Grandis Road, which turns into Uhrenholt Road as you ride south. Turn right at a **T** intersection onto US 63, which has a paved shoulder.

At the village of Seeley turn left on CR OO. Ride .3 mile and turn right on Old OO (where CAMBA markers begin), which begins as a paved road and becomes a gravel road. Near the top of the hill the pavement begins again and Frint Road goes off to the right.   At a **T** intersection turn right on CR OO. Ride .6 mile and turn right on the Phipps Fire Lane (note that a short loop veers off to the left at this point and returns to CR OO). After riding 1.5 miles turn right on snowmobile trail #5 and use caution on the steep, loose-surfaced downhill (snowmobile trails are marked with orange diamonds and arrows). Ride .5 mile and turn right on snowmobile trail #8 (the frost pockets are along this section). At a **T** intersection turn left, which will put you on Old OO. Retrace your route to the trailhead.

RIDE 39 *LAKE HELANE TOUR*

This 14.5-mile spur-and-loop ride to Lake Helane will take you through the Sawyer County Forest on scenic two-wheel-drive forest roads and four-wheel-drive logging roads. En route, you will pass two pristine north woods lakes. It is a moderately difficult ride due to steep, rocky downhill sections on Smith Lake Road and Lake Helane Road that require technical riding skill.

The ride's namesake, Lake Helane, is an example of nature's pure poetry. It is a fine spot to stop, rest, and watch for an eagle plummeting to catch a fish; you may even hear the call of a loon if you listen. Smith Lake is a much

RIDE 39   *LAKE HELANE TOUR*

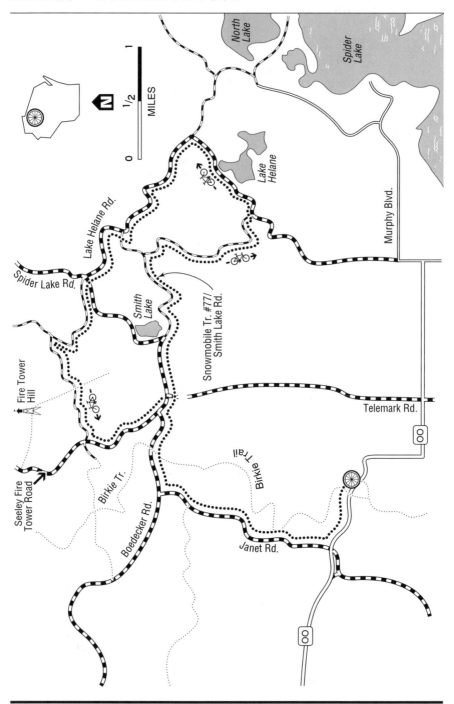

smaller sister and a scenic surprise after the tense, rocky downhill on snow-mobile trail #77. You'll skirt the tip of Smith Lake and you may find yourself splashing through shallow water on the firm road surface when the lake level is high. This is another gorgeous forest spot ringed with pine trees.

In the 1930s, Smith Lake was the site of a Civilian Conservation Corps (CCC) camp. The Roosevelt administration created the CCC program during the Great Depression to help ease overwhelming unemployment rates among young men. It put them to work on useful public projects. In this area, the CCC men reforested a landscape that lumber barons had left as barren as the face of the moon. They also created the excellent system of forest roads that riders enjoy today.

An interesting alternative route on the way back to the trailhead is to ride the section of the Birkebeiner Ski Trail parallel to Janet Road. This wide, grassy trail, known as the Birkie, is the route followed by over 6,000 cross-country skiers in the annual American Birkebeiner and Kortelopet races on the last weekend of February. It is also often used as part of the route for the Chequamegon 40, the nation's largest mountain bike race, held in mid-September.

General location: Three miles east of US 63 and the village of Seeley.

Elevation change: You will only find about 100′ of elevation difference along the route. However, there are several very steep uphill and downhill pitches of around 80′.

Season: Late April to early November, depending on remnant or early snow. From late May to late July insect populations flourish. Routes tend to be wet-ter in the spring, but the glacial moraine that comprises the terrain drains very poorly; standing water may be found at nearly any time of the year.

Services: Shelter, water, and pay telephone are available at the OO trailhead. No services whatsoever will be found on the trail. All services are available in Cable and Hayward, including bicycle retail, rental, and repair. Food and drink are available in Seeley, along with bicycle retail, rental, and repair at Seeley Hills Ski and Bike.

Hazards: Trails and roads are kept clear, but downed trees and branches may be encountered at any time. On steep slopes, loose stones and large embedded rocks may require technical riding skill. Some downhills are extremely steep and rocky. Sandpit washouts at the bottoms of steep hills on trails and roads are common. Forest roads are used by local two-wheel-drive vehicles and logging trucks. Hunting season begins in mid-September. Using a compass is recommended.

Rescue index: Help is available at Seeley or can be summoned by phone from the OO trailhead (Great Divide Ambulance: 1-798-3200; Sawyer County Sheriff: 634-4858). If you are unable to get back to the trailhead, you should make your way to Spider Lake Road or south off the route to Murphy Boulevard.

Thousands ride the Birkie Trail in the Chequamegon 40, the nation's largest mountain bike event.

Land status: Public forest roads and logging trails through private land and Sawyer County Forest.

Maps: The CAMBA maps include detailed route and topographical information. The map for this route is available at the OO trailhead. A complete set of detailed CAMBA trail maps and an overview map are available for $5 (write to CAMBA at the address listed below). The overview map locates the trail clusters and mountain bike–friendly businesses in the area. CAMBA memberships, which include a map set, voting privileges, and a frame sticker, are available for $20.

Finding the trail: Drive three miles east of US 63 from the village of Seeley on County Road OO to the CAMBA OO trailhead at the Birkebeiner cross-country ski trail rest cabin. Several other CAMBA trails also use this trailhead.

Sources of additional information:

Chequamegon Area Mountain Bike Association (CAMBA)
P.O. Box 141
Cable, WI 54821
(715) 798-3833, (800) 533-7454

Cable Area Chamber of Commerce
P.O. Box 217
Cable, WI 54821
(800) 533-7454

Placid Lake Helane invites riders to stop and enjoy the scenery.

Chequamegon Fat Tire Festival
P.O. Box 267
Cable, WI 54821
(715) 798-3811

Seeley Hills Ski and Bike
Route 3
Seeley, WI 54843
(715) 634-3539

Notes on the trail: From the CAMBA trailhead at the Birkebeiner Ski Trail rest cabin, ride west on CR OO one-half mile toward Seeley and turn right on Janet Road. The route is marked for two-way travel with blue-and-white CAMBA trail markers on Janet and Boedecker roads and for counterclockwise travel on the loop section. At a **T** intersection, turn right on Boedecker Road. Go straight at a stop sign (unmarked intersection of Spider Lake Road).

After one-half mile, as the road swings to the left, use extreme caution as you follow the CAMBA arrow to the right onto steep, rocky snowmobile trail #77. Slow down for this one, although you may be lulled into complacency by the fast, easy ride on the gravel roads. A sand washout at the bottom of the hill along Smith Lake may be difficult to negotiate. This section is followed by a steep, rocky uphill and a steep, rocky, and often rutted downhill just before a **T** intersection, at which you will turn right. There is one more rocky downhill just before Lake Helane.

At a **T** intersection a short distance past Lake Helane, turn left onto Lake Helane Road. After 1.4 miles turn right and in a half mile you will reach a junction with Spider Lake Road. Turn left and after .2 mile turn right onto Horseshoe Bend Road (unmarked). After about a half mile, turn left at a trail intersection at the horseshoe.

A half mile farther you are at the intersection of the Seeley Firetower climb, the infamous one-third mile grind in the Chequamegon 40 mountain bike race. The route goes straight here, but if you want to take on the challenge, you can climb to a fine overview of the forest. After another half mile turn left at the junction of a slightly better road (unmarked Seeley Firetower Road). At a stop sign, turn right on an improved gravel road (unmarked Boedecker Road) and return to the trailhead by retracing the route or take the American Birkebeiner Trail.

RIDE 40   *SHORT & FAT TRAILS*

When the Chequamegon Fat Tire Festival considered adding a shorter-distance race to complement their annual premier Chequamegon 40 event, the name they chose was a real no-brainer. Short & Fat describes this course well. It gives people a chance to enjoy fat-tired competition that is more achievable than the 40-mile main event. About a thousand riders annually compete in the Short & Fat. Its course has varied over the history of the Chequamegon Fat Tire Festival, but the current course has been so popular that the Chequamegon Area Mountain Bike Association (CAMBA) has signed it for recreational use.

The 16-mile route offers a fine sampling of riding experiences. You begin with an easy roll out of town on a paved and gravel forest road before following a snowmobile trail and more gravel forest roads to the American Birkebeiner (Birkie) Ski Trail. Things get serious here as you take on the steep grades that challenge thousands of skiers each winter. The very wide grassy trail gives way to narrower double-track cross-country ski trails on the Telemark Lodge property. The route merits a challenging rating because of the toughness of the Birkie Trail, but, unless washouts are encountered, no real technical skill is needed other than the ability to handle a bike on steep uphills and downhills.

The Short & Fat course is a one-way route through Bayfield and Sawyer County forests and Telemark property. The deep woods are a mix of pine, maple, aspen, birch, and oak. You won't see any sign of civilization between the start and finish. There are two options for riding back to the Cable trailhead. You can follow the pavement on Telemark Road and County Road M (which has a paved shoulder) or take the shorter, but sandy McNaught Road.

The view is fantastic from the top of Mt. Telemark.

There are other riding possibilities. For more adventure, deviate from the route: continue south on Randysek Road and take the side road up to the Seeley Firetower Hill for a grand overview of the forest. You can also pick up more Birkie trail off of Randysek or Camp #38 Road. If you want to bail out, Spider Lake Road is an easy way back to Telemark. Another bailout option entails hopping back on Randysek Road where the power line crosses the Birkie Trail, and taking the road back to Cable.

General location: The village of Cable.
Elevation change: The route is generally rolling, but will climb steadily 270′ to Camp #38 Road. On the Birkie Trail there are extremely steep grades of 50′ to 100′.
Season: Late April to early November, depending on remnant or early snow. From late May to late July insect populations flourish. Routes tend to be wetter in the spring, but the glacial moraine that comprises the terrain drains very poorly and standing water may be found at nearly any time of the year.
Services: All services are available in Cable. Lodging and dining are available at Telemark Lodge. Also at the lodge is the full-service New Moon Mountain Biking Shop, which offers repair, retail, and rental.
Hazards: Trails and roads are kept clear, but downed trees and branches may be encountered at any time. Winter frost continually heaves large glacial stones out of the ground. These rocky surfaces may be encountered anywhere and may be hidden by grass. Washouts may be found on forest roads. Forest

RIDE 40 SHORT AND FAT TRAILS
RIDE 41 ESKER TRAIL

Note: *More trails exist in this area than can be shown on this map.*

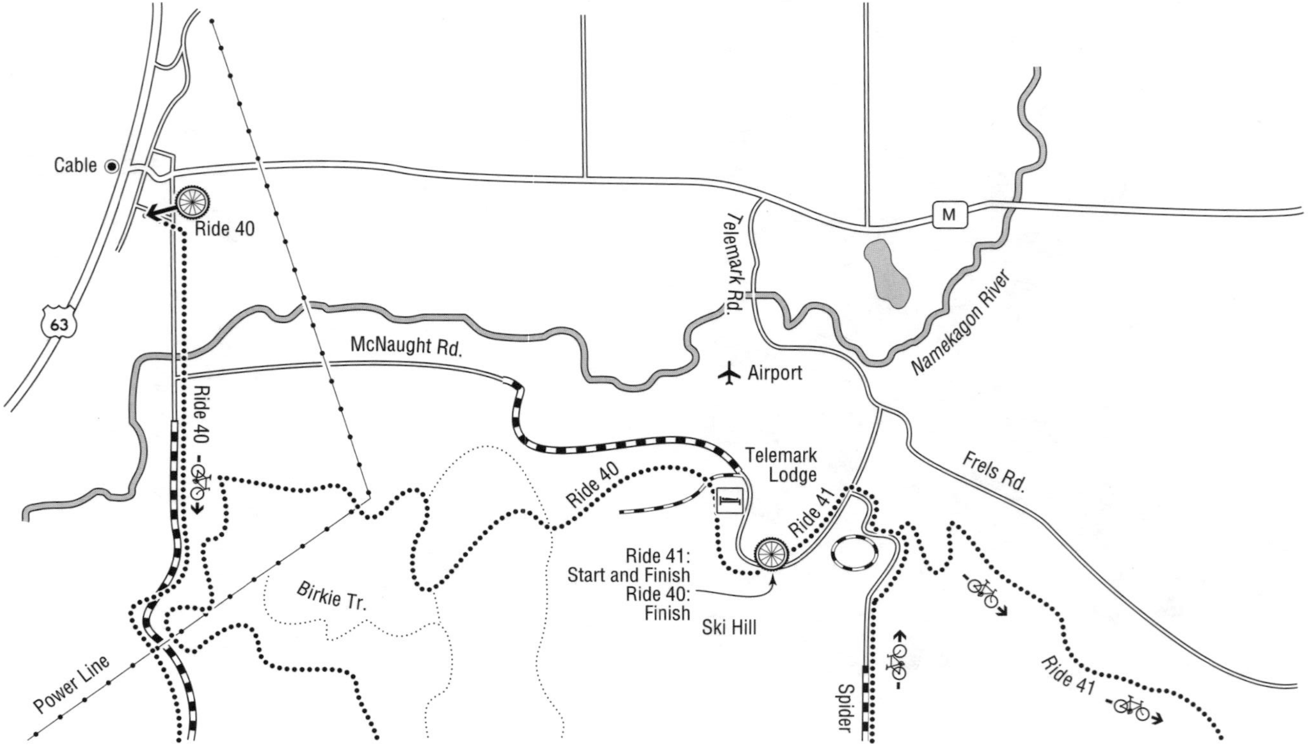

Cable

63

Ride 40

McNaught Rd.

Ride 40 -🚲→

Birkie Tr.

Power Line

Ride 40

Telemark Rd.

Airport

Namekagon River

M

Telemark Lodge

Ride 41

Frels Rd.

Ride 41 -🚲→

-🚲→

←🚲-

Spider

Ski Hill

Ride 41:
Start and Finish
Ride 40:
Finish

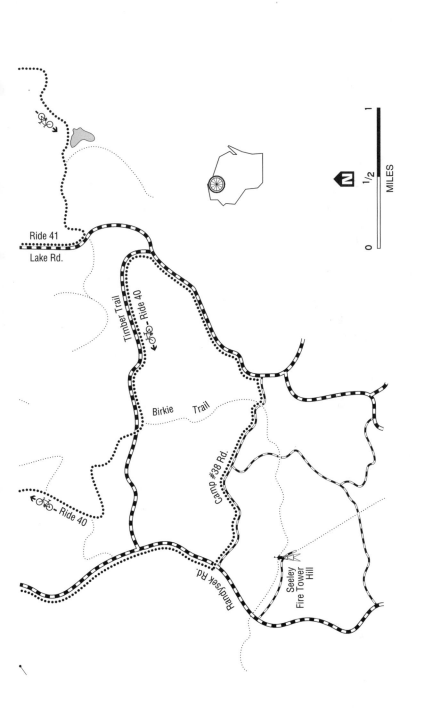

Ride 41

Lake Rd.

Timber Trail

Ride 40

Ride 40

Birkie Trail

Camp #38 Rd.

Randysek Rd.

Seeley
Fire Tower
Hill

N

0   1/2   1
MILES

roads are used by local vehicles and logging trucks. Hunting season begins in mid-September. Hikers may be encountered on ski trails, and horseback riders use some ski trails on Telemark property. CAMBA trail marking is excellent, but signage vandalism does happen; it is a good idea to carry a compass.

Rescue index: Help is available at Telemark Lodge and in Cable. If you are injured or have mechanical problems, make your way to Randysek, Spider Lake, Timber Trail, or McNaught Road for the best chance of rescue.

Land status: Public roads and ski trails through Bayfield or Sawyer County forests and private ski trails on Telemark Lodge property.

Maps: The CAMBA maps include detailed route and topographical information. The map for this route is available at the Telemark trailhead. A complete set of detailed CAMBA trail maps and an overview map are available for $5 (write to CAMBA at the address listed below). The overview map locates the trail clusters and mountain bike–friendly businesses in the area. CAMBA memberships, which include a map set, voting privileges, and a frame sticker, are available for $20.

Finding the trail: From US 63 turn east on County Highway M in the village of Cable. After one block turn right on First Street (unsigned); travel past the post office and take the first left onto First Avenue (unsigned). Travel a half block to the CAMBA trailhead in the old grade school parking lot on the left.

Sources of additional information:

Chequamegon Area Mountain Bike Association (CAMBA)
P.O. Box 141
Cable, WI 54821
(715) 798-3833, (800) 533-7454

Cable Area Chamber of Commerce
P.O. Box 217
Cable, WI 54821
(800) 533-7454

Telemark Lodge and New Moon Mountain Biking Shop
Cable, WI 54821
(715) 798-3811

Chequamegon Fat Tire Festival
P.O. Box 267
Cable, WI 54821
(715) 798-3811

Notes on the trail: The route is well marked with blue-and-white CAMBA trail signs and periodic "you are here" maps, as well as some street-type road signs and cross-country ski trail signs. From the Cable trailhead, turn east on

First Avenue and turn right (south) after a half-block on Randysek Road. At about four miles, turn left onto Camp #38 Road (unmarked). Follow it to a **T** intersection and turn left onto Spider Lake Road (unmarked). As the road finally levels out after a long downhill run, turn left onto Timber Trail. Turn right after about 1.5 miles onto the American Birkebeiner Ski Trail, the only extremely wide, grassy trail in the forest. At the power line, take a sharp left, following the CAMBA arrows onto a narrower forest trail. At a **T** intersection, turn right onto the Nature Trail Loop. A short distance later it junctions with the wide Birkebeiner race trail, where you will turn left. Follow it to Telemark Lodge.

RIDE 41 *ESKER TRAIL*

An esker is a narrow, sinuous ridge that traces the course of a river that once flowed inside a glacier. Rocks and gravel that had built up in the river bed were left behind as a ridge when the ice melted. When Olympic silver medalist Bill Koch designed a cross-country ski trail for Telemark Lodge, he chose to run it along this scenic natural landmark. It also serves as a challenging mountain biking ride.

This 6.7-mile spur-and-loop route gives you a mile to warm up on pavement before you tackle the steep, firm, single-track ski trail. Initially, you will ride a steep downhill before a long grind up the spine of the 1.5-mile–long esker. On top the trail rolls along and there are several panoramic views. Mount Telemark lies to the right. The forest is a dense mix of oak and maple along the esker and tall pines after the descent.

As the trail turns west, the route passes Island Lake, which has a large beaver dam on the far side. Farther on you pass the abandoned fields and buildings of a farmstead. Don't get spooked if you hear voices coming from the crumbling buildings. Porcupines live in the foundation. You wouldn't be the first person to be fooled by this animal's strange mumbling sounds. Past the farm the trail junctions with Spider Lake Road, which is a wide, often-traveled gravel road and an easy roll back to the paved road.

General location: Telemark Lodge, three miles east of the village of Cable and US 63.
Elevation change: The climb up the esker will be about 150′ in a half mile with some extremely steep sections. About 100′ feet of elevation is lost on the descent. The remainder of the trail is rolling with short climbs in the 20′ to 40′ range. Spider Lake Road and Telemark Road are basically flat.
Season: Late April to early November, depending on remnant or early snow. From late May to late July insect populations flourish. Routes tend to be

wetter in the spring, but the glacial moraine that comprises the terrain drains very poorly; standing water may be found at nearly any time of the year.

Services: All services are available in Cable. Lodging and dining are available at Telemark Lodge. The New Moon Mountain Biking Shop is also located at the lodge and offers repair, retail, and rental.

Hazards: Trails and roads are kept clear, but downed trees and branches may be encountered at any time. Winter frost continually heaves large glacial stones out of the ground. These rocky surfaces may be encountered anywhere and may be hidden by grass. On bare and open slopes, small, rounded stones make control difficult. It's like trying to brake on ball bearings. Some downhills are extremely steep and require technical ability. Sandpit washouts at the bottoms of steep hills on trails and roads are common. Forest roads are used by local two-wheel-drive vehicles and logging trucks. Hikers and horseback riders may be encountered.

Rescue index: Help is available at Telemark Lodge and in Cable. Although the CAMBA trails are popular by north woods standards, don't expect other riders to come along. If you are injured or have a mechanical failure, you should make your way to the trailhead, or at least out to Spider Lake or Telemark Roads, as best you can.

Land status: Private.

Maps: CAMBA maps include detailed route and topographical information. The map for this route is available at the Telemark trailhead. A complete set of detailed CAMBA trail maps and an overview map are available for $5 (write to CAMBA at the address listed below). The overview map locates the trail clusters and mountain bike–friendly businesses in the area. CAMBA memberships, which include a map set, voting privileges, and a frame sticker, are available for $20.

Finding the trail: From US 63 turn east on County Road M in the village of Cable. Proceed east two miles to Telemark Road and turn south. This takes you to Telemark Lodge. You can park in the lower parking lot on the right side of the road between the lodge and the alpine ski hill. The Telemark trailhead is directly across Telemark Road from the parking lot. Several other CAMBA trails also use this trailhead.

Sources of additional information:

Chequamegon Area Mountain Bike Association (CAMBA)
P.O. Box 141
Cable, WI 54821
(715) 798-3833, (800) 533-7454

Cable Area Chamber of Commerce
P.O. Box 217
Cable, WI 54821
(800) 533-7454

Forests and fields line the route on the Esker Trail.

Telemark Lodge and New Moon Mountain Biking Shop
Cable, WI 54821
(715) 798-3811

Notes on the trail: From the lower parking lot, ride the pavement of Telemark Road back toward CR M for .6 mile and turn right on Spider Lake Road. Ride .3 mile south on this paved road and turn left onto a narrow single-track trail just before you reach the Telemark golf course. Follow this trail past the golf course. The route is well marked for one-way travel with CAMBA signs that feature a white mountain bike silhouette on a blue background. There are many other trails and logging roads in the area, some of which are signed for snowmobiling, cross-country skiing, and horseback riding, so be sure only to follow the CAMBA signs. Trails not marked as CAMBA routes are closed to biking. Because of the possibility of vandalism, you should ride with a compass and bicycle odometer. When the trail returns to Spider Lake Road, turn right. It is a heavily traveled gravel road at this point.

RIDE 42 *ROCK LAKE TRAIL*

Once you've ridden the Rock Lake Trail, you'll have a common bond with hundreds of other mountain bikers who have enjoyed this 9.9-mile single-track, cross-country ski trail system. This is the kind of loop trail where indelible mountain bike memories are made. You'll ride through the deep woods of the Chequamegon National Forest for the entire distance. This characteristic made the Rock Lake area an ideal location for the Chequamegon Fat Tire Festival's mountain bike orienteering contests during the event's early years. There's no better place to chase through the woods with a map and compass.

The Rock Lake Trail is a good ride for people interested in a challenging route. It's a nice transition trail for riders who want to move up from moderate trails. Trail surfaces are mainly grassy with a hardpack track. On steep slopes you will find some loose rock, but no sharp turns. Technical ability is required to stay on the bike on many steep upgrades and to handle the bike on rough descents. The loop follows a cross-country ski trail that is wide enough for an all-terrain vehicle and occasionally follows sections of four-wheel-drive roads. The terrain is almost constantly rolling, and you will rarely ride the same grade for more than a few yards.

Because the forest is so dense, the trail often seems like a tunnel through the trees. When you come upon Rock Lake it is a wonderful scenic surprise. Several other small lakes also can be accessed or seen from the trail. The abundant wildlife is not easily spotted unless on the trail itself or on a lake. Look for bald eagles and loons on Rock Lake and broad-winged hawks on the trails.

General location: Seven miles east of US 63 and the village of Cable.

Elevation change: The terrain is almost constantly rolling and steep grades of 30′ to 60′ are common. A few climbs and descents of 80′ to 100′ will be encountered.

Season: Late April to early November, depending on remnant or early snow. Early in the season the snowmelt may pool at the bottoms of the many small hills. From late May to late July insect populations flourish.

Services: Snacks and beverages and bicycle retail, repair, and rental are available at Glacier Pines Outfitters a few yards from the trailhead. Food and lodging are available a short distance from the trailhead at Lakewoods Resort. Gasoline, groceries, and lodging can be found in Cable.

Hazards: The trails are regularly maintained by the U.S. Forest Service, but windfall trees and branches may be encountered at any time. Washout ruts may be found on steep slopes. Trails are open to hikers, but beyond Rock Lake encounters will be rare. Although closed to motor vehicle traffic and

RIDE 42 *ROCK LAKE TRAIL*

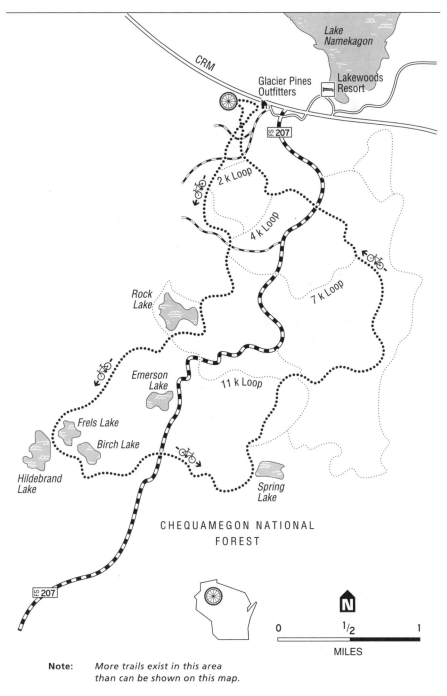

Note: More trails exist in this area
than can be shown on this map.

Riders skirt the edge of scenic Rock Lake.

signed for one-way riding, people may ride in the opposite direction. The trail crosses Forest Service Road 207 (known as Rock Lake Road) several times; caution must be exercised at this heavily traveled road.

Rescue index: Help can be summoned from Glacier Pines Outfitters or Lakewoods Resort. Although the trail is popular with off-road riders, the chances of on-trail rescue are slim. If you are injured or mechanically disabled, your best option is to make your way to FS 207 or CR M.

Land status: Chequamegon National Forest.

Maps: CAMBA maps include detailed route and topographical information. The map for this route is available at the Telemark trailhead. A complete set of detailed CAMBA trail maps and an overview map are available for $5 (write to CAMBA at the address listed below). The overview map locates the trail clusters and mountain bike–friendly businesses in the area. CAMBA memberships, which include a map set, voting privileges, and a frame sticker, are available for $20.

Finding the trail: The CAMBA Rock Lake trailhead is located on CR M seven miles east of the village of Cable and US 63. Several other CAMBA trails also use this trailhead.

Sources of additional information:

> Chequamegon Area Mountain Bike Association (CAMBA)
> P.O. Box 141
> Cable, WI 54821
> (715) 798-3833, (800) 533-7454
>
> Glacier Pines Outfitters
> P.O. Box 413
> County Highway M
> Cable, WI 54821
> (715) 794-2055
>
> Cable Area Chamber of Commerce
> P.O. Box 217
> Cable, WI 54821
> (800) 533-7454
>
> National Forest Service
> Route 10, Box 508
> Hayward, WI 54843
> (715) 634-4821

Notes on the trail: From the CAMBA Rock Lake trailhead, follow the blue-and-white CAMBA trail signs. Forest Service roads are marked with small, low brown signs with yellow lettering. The trail is signed for one-way mountain biking and cross-country skiing. Light blue diamond signs are cross-country trail markers. Frequent "you are here" signs for skiing and mountain biking will reassure you of your location. Be sure to follow the CAMBA signs for the Rock Lake Trail since the route also intersects with CAMBA's Glacier Loop Trail. The ski trail system features four shortcut loops that may be used as bailout options or to access FS 207. Although the signage is excellent, you should still carry a compass.

RIDE 43 *DRUMMOND TRAILS*

Covering this 12.9-mile loop-and-spur route will give you a fine taste of the beauty and history of the Chequamegon National Forest. The trailhead itself is in a beautiful setting on the shore of Lake Drummond. The slap of a beaver's tail may be the most startling noise at this peaceful spot. There are 2.8 miles of paved roads, roughly divided into warm up and cool down

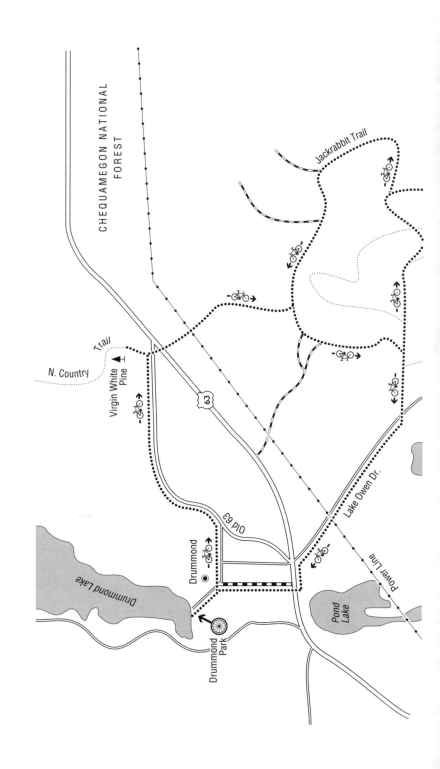

CHEQUAMEGON NATIONAL FOREST

Jackrabbit Trail

N. Country Trail

Virgin White Pine

63

Old 63

Drummond

Drummond Lake

Lake Owen Dr.

Power Line

Pond Lake

Drummond Park

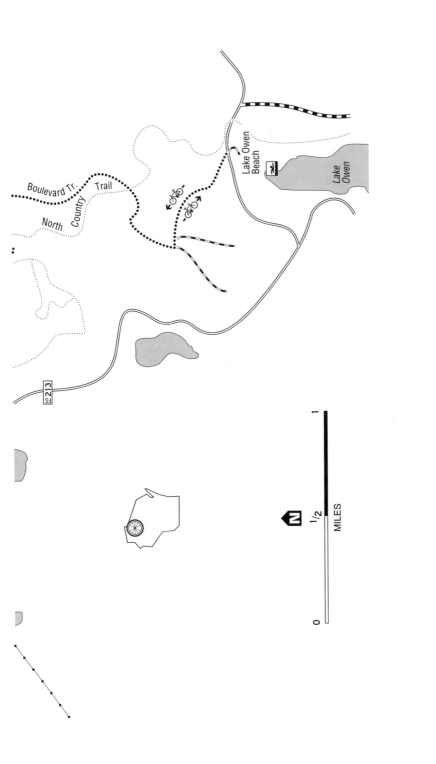

Boulevard Tr.
Trail
North Country
FS 213

Lake Owen Beach
Lake Owen

N
0 ½ 1
MILES

stretches. In between, you'll be treated to a manageable section of the North Country Hiking Trail, the easy riding Jackrabbit cross-country ski trails, and the more demanding Boulevard Ski Trail, giving this ride an overall rating of moderate difficulty.

A short .2 mile excursion north on the North Country Trail at the start of your off-pavement ride will take you past a virgin basswood tree, a living virgin white pine, and the stump of monstrous white pine that died in the late 1970s. White pines were valuable back when the appetite of the big Drummond mill left these hills completely barren in the early 1900s. Despite the tree's value, they choose to spare a few for our benefit. This part of the North Country Trail, and the section south of US 63, give a good introduction to north woods single-track riding. Rocks and roots abound on the firm trail, but none of the grades are very long, and they don't include tight downhill corners.

The Jackrabbit loop is an easy roll on wide, grassy ski trails that were once logging roads. A hardpack track is well worn in on the Jackrabbit and (to a lesser degree) on the slightly narrower Boulevard Trail. Both run under a deep forest canopy of birch, aspen, pine, hemlock, and maple trees. The perfume of the deep woods may make you dizzy. The big difference between the two cross-country ski trails is the more severe terrain on the Boulevard, which will necessitate use of low gears for most riders. Still, the trail shows how fun riding these old logging roads can be. And there is nothing to scare you unless you happen upon one of the area's residents, the black bear. Once they hear you, these fascinating creatures will take off with more speed than you would imagine they would be capable of. Just don't get caught between a mother bear and her cubs.

Your destination on this ride is the Lake Owen beach and picnic area, an idyllic spot that is a great place to take a break or a dip. This ride presents many options. You could cruise back to the trailhead on the smooth pavement of Lake Owen Drive, or if you liked the North Country Trail, you might want to ride more of it. I'll warn you, however, that it gets rougher the farther south you get off the Jackrabbit loop and the fun factor starts to wear off. If you really want to take it easy, just cruise down Lake Owen Drive to the entrance road to the Drummond Ski Trail and make the Jackrabbit loop your entire ride.

General location: In the village of Drummond off of US 63.
Elevation change: Almost constantly rolling with changes of 25′ to 50′ on the northern section and 75′ to 100′ on the southern section.
Season: Late April to early November, depending on remnant or early snow. From late May to late July insect populations flourish.
Services: Limited food and lodging are available in the village of Drummond. The Chequamegon Saloon is a gathering place for the local bike club. There is a water pump at the Lake Owen Picnic Area. The nearest bicycle retail,

Roots, rocks, twists, and turns are the norm on the
North Country Trail.

rental, and repair are available at the New Moon Mountain Biking Shop at
Telemark Lodge, three miles east of the village of Cable, which is ten miles
south on US 63.

Hazards: Trails and roads are kept clear, but downed trees and branches may
be encountered at any time. Due to the density of the forest cover and the ser-
pentine character of the trails, a compass is an important safety asset. Forest
roads are used by local two-wheel-drive vehicles and logging trucks. Hikers
may be encountered on any of the trails, particularly the North Country Trail.

Rescue index: Help is available in Drummond. If you are injured or have
mechanical failure, make your way to US 63 or to Lake Owen Drive for the
best chance of rescue.

Land status: Public roads and trails in the Chequamegon National Forest.

Maps: CAMBA maps include detailed route and topographical information.
The map for this route is available at the Drummond trailhead. A complete

set of detailed CAMBA trail maps and an overview map are available for $5 (write to CAMBA at the address listed below). The overview map locates the trail clusters and mountain bike–friendly businesses in the area. CAMBA memberships, which include a map set, voting privileges, and a frame sticker, are available for $20.

Finding the trail: From US 63 turn north on Wisconsin Avenue (at the junction of Lake Owen Drive at the Black Bear Inn) into the village of Drummond. At a **T** intersection, turn left onto Superior Street and follow it downhill to Drummond Park, site of the CAMBA trailhead. Several other CAMBA trails also can be accessed from this trailhead.

Sources of additional information:

Chequamegon Area Mountain Bike Association (CAMBA)
P.O. Box 141
Cable, WI 54821
(715) 798-3833, (800) 533-7454

Cable Area Chamber of Commerce
P.O. Box 217
Cable, WI 54821
(800) 533-7454

National Forest Service
Route 10, Box 508
Hayward, WI 54843
(715) 634-4821

Notes on the trail: From the CAMBA trailhead in Drummond Park, retrace your route up the hill and follow Superior Street (not signed as a CAMBA route in this direction) east through the village of Drummond. At Old 63 turn left and follow it to the North Country Trail crossing just before the junction with US 63. Turn left on the North Country Trail, being careful to negotiate or dismount and walk the short flight of steps. Turn right at the bottom of the steps. Ride in .2 mile to the giant white pine stump and return by the same route.

From the trailhead, cross US 63 south and follow the North Country Trail (marked with blue symbols) .8 mile to a wide, grassy trail and turn right. You will be on the Jackrabbit cross-country ski trail loop and can follow the blue and white CAMBA trail signs in a counter-clockwise direction to the Boulevard Trail. Follow the Boulevard Trail to the paved road (Lake Owen Drive) and cross it, following the CAMBA arrows to the Lake Owen Picnic Area and swimming beach.

Follow the Boulevard Trail back to the Jackrabbit loop and turn right (east) onto it. Follow the Jackrabbit loop counter-clockwise to a **T** intersection and turn right following the directions to the parking lot. At the paved road (Lake

Owen Drive, FS 213) turn right. Forest Service roads are marked with small, low brown signs with yellow lettering. At US 63 turn left, taking care to watch for traffic. Ride on the paved shoulder .2 mile and turn right on an unmarked gravel road following the CAMBA markers. At a **T** intersection, turn left and follow the paved street (Superior Avenue) downhill to Drummond Park.

RIDE 44   *DELTA HILLS TRAILS*

If you are up to taking on as much as the north woods can dish out, the 23.6-mile Delta Hills Trails loop is what you're looking for. The term "hills" implies that it's not flat and, while the climbs and descents are only in the 40 to 100 foot range, they will be constant. There is only about one mile of relatively flat off-roading on the route. This is a very challenging ride for the average bicyclist. Many grades are extremely steep and some are subject to rutting from heavy rain. There are several options that would allow you to shorten the route to 14 miles or 19.7 miles, but the very challenging rating would still apply because of the technical ability needed to handle the grades. Several forest roads also provide bailout options.

The southbound portion of the route is on the Delta Trail. Don't worry about the signs on the forest road gates that say: "Trail closed April 1 to December 1." You can ignore them. They're for the snowmobilers who use the trail in winter, the only time of year when the white paper birch forest may be even more striking than it is in summer and fall. The southern section of the loop has large stands of the stunning birch mixed with pine, oak, and maple. The birch throughout the region have been dying in recent years because of a period of drought that left them vulnerable to certain insects and a virus. This has been true in the Delta Hills area, but the stands are so vast that the decimation doesn't seem as great. On the northern parts of the loop where the soil is sandier the birch give way to Norway pine and jack pine.

There are more rewards to taking on the Delta Hills. Frequent lakes and bogs are a feast for the eyes. The route includes some sections of paved roads near the trailhead and portions of gravel forest roads on the northbound section. The trails are wide with firm, sandy soil covered with light grass and often moss. Given a choice between riding on a suspension bike or on a mossy trail, take the moss. It's like rolling over a velveteen cushion.

The Wanoka Lake campground near the north end invites you to make this ride a two-day trip or, at least, to take a swim break. You'll be far from civilization on most of this route, but the Delta Lodge near the trailhead offers the kind of end-of-ride north woods hospitality that off-roaders love.

General location: Twelve miles north of the village of Drummond.

RIDE 44 *DELTA HILLS TRAILS*

Note: *More trails exist in this area*
than can be shown on this map.

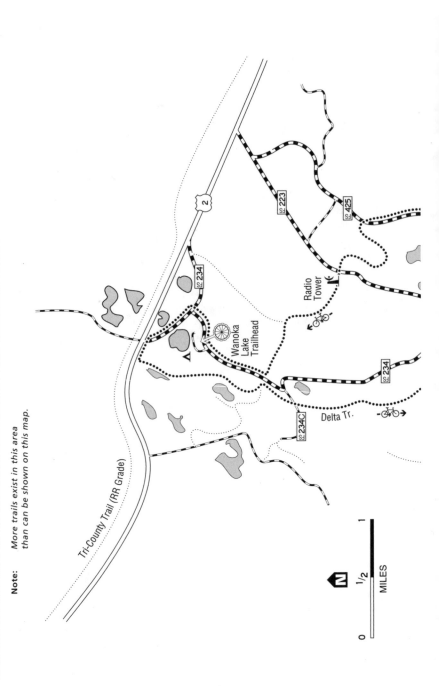

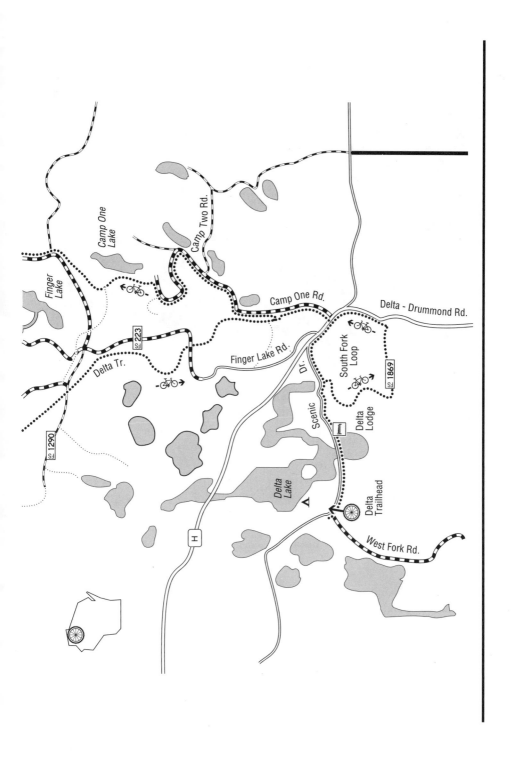

Camp One Lake

Camp Two Rd.

Camp One Rd.

Delta - Drummond Rd.

Finger Lake

FS 223

Finger Lake Rd.

Delta Tr.

South Fork Loop

FS 1869

Scenic Dr.

Delta Lodge

FS 1290

Delta Lake

Delta Trailhead

West Fork Rd.

H

A scenic trailside bog on the Delta Hills route.

Elevation change: The terrain is constantly rolling. Steep grades in the 40′ range are common and some are 70′ to 100′.

Season: Late April to early November, depending on remnant or early snow. From late May to late July insect populations flourish.

Services: Food, drink, and lodging are available at Delta Lodge. There is a water pump at the Delta Campground near the Delta trailhead. Other pumps can be found just west of the Scout Camp Cutoff intersection and at the Wanoka Lake trailhead. All services, except bicycle services, are available in the small village of Drummond or the town of Iron River, which is seven miles west of the Wanoka Lake trailhead on US 2. Bicycle rental, retail, and repair are available at White River Cyclery three miles west of the Delta trailhead on Scenic Drive.

Hazards: Trails and roads are kept clear, but downed trees and branches may be encountered at any time. Rocky surfaces may be encountered anywhere and may be hidden by grass. Some downhills are extremely steep and have sandy, rocky washouts. Forest roads are used by local two-wheel-drive vehicles and logging trucks. Hunting season begins in mid-September. Hikers may be encountered.

Rescue index: Help is available at Delta Lodge. Your chances of on-trail rescue are slim. You should make your way to one of the forest roads or paved highways.

Land status: Chequamegon National Forest.

Maps: The CAMBA maps include detailed route and topographical information. The map for this route is available at the Delta and Wanoka Lake trailheads. A complete set of detailed CAMBA trail maps and an overview map are available for $5 (write to CAMBA at the address listed below). The overview map locates the trail clusters and mountain bike–friendly businesses in the area. CAMBA memberships, which include a map set, voting privileges, and a frame sticker, are available for $20.

Finding the trail: From US 63 at the village of Drummond, travel ten miles north on Delta-Drummond Road. At CR H turn northwest and after a half mile turn west on Scenic Drive. The Delta trailhead will be on the right at 1.5 miles. There is a second trailhead on this loop at Wanoka Lake, but these trail notes are for riding from Delta. Several other CAMBA routes also begin at the Delta trailhead.

Sources of additional information:

Chequamegon Area Mountain Bike Association (CAMBA)
P.O. Box 141
Cable, WI 54821
(715) 798-3833, (800) 533-7454

White River Cyclery
Route 2, Box 133
#81 Scenic Drive
Iron River, WI 54847
(715) 372-4077, (800) 791-2171

National Forest Service
Route 10, Box 508
Hayward, WI 54843
(715) 634-4821

Cable Area Chamber of Commerce
P.O. Box 217
Cable, WI 54821
(800) 533-7454

Notes on the trail: Off the paved roads, the route is well marked for one-way travel with blue-and-white CAMBA trail signs and arrows and periodic "you are here" map signs. Forest Service roads are marked with small, low brown signs with yellow lettering. From the Delta trailhead travel east for 1.3 miles and turn south on a forest road that is marked with CAMBA signs for the South Fork Loop. Follow it to a **T** intersection with a paved road (Delta-Drummond Road) and turn north. At CR H turn left and make an immediate right onto Camp One Road.

At 6.5 miles, just beyond Camp Northwoods Girl Scout Camp, follow the CAMBA signs off the gravel road and onto a forest trail. A half mile later, shortly after turning west from Camp One Lake, you can either turn north and complete the route or continue west on the CAMBA signed Scout Camp Cut-off and eliminate 10 miles. Another shortcut option on the long route presents itself beyond the radio tower when you junction with FS 234. If you continue west on FS 234C, after a short distance when FS 234 turns north, you can pick up the Delta Trail heading south (ride around trail gate) and cut off four miles. After returning to CR H via Camp One Road, turn northwest on CR H and after a half mile turn west on Scenic Drive to return to the trailhead.

Northern Wisconsin

The highlands of northern Wisconsin are part of a vast peneplain that (except for the sunken basin of Lake Superior) stretches north to Hudsons Bay. The peneplain is actually the basement, the leveled core of ancient mountain ranges that once towered as high as the Rockies or Alps. This is known from the angles of the tilted rock and the types of metamorphic rock that can only be formed under the extreme pressure caused by the folding of mountain building.

Hundreds of millions of years of erosion wore the mountains down. Inland seas covered the remains with sedimentary rock, and four huge continental glaciers scraped it bare in places over the course of a million years . Most of the terrain is of glacial origin. The ground moraine left behind drains poorly, creating a myriad of lakes. The highlands continue to rebound from the tremendous weight of the mile-thick ice sheet at the rate of several inches per century.

The highlands are home to vast stands of mixed hardwoods and evergreens that include the Nicollet National Forest. It is a region of rivers, including the headwaters of the Wisconsin River, and areas with an incredible density of lakes. It's vacationland Midwest style. A place to bring a rod and reel, or a mountain bike, and enjoy the scenery. The services, amenities, and hospitality that support the tourism industry make it a great area to visit. You can enjoy the wilderness and follow it up with a good meal and lodging.

At Copper Falls State Park, riders can explore some fine moderately difficult single-track trails and, with a short hike, check out two impressive waterfalls. On the challenging Raven Trails, the route passes several crystal-clear lakes. The Razorback Ridges Trails are popular with north woods riders who like moderately difficult riding in a setting of a pine and birch forest. The Nicollet National Forest Anvil Trails offer riders moderately difficult riding in a beautiful mixed pine and maple forest.

RIDE 45 *COPPER FALLS STATE PARK TRAILS*

Will riders travel all the way up north just to ride less than three miles of trails? That question came up when the Copper Falls trails were considered for this book. But Copper Falls is a pretty extraordinary state park, and the Takesin Ski Trail features some fine single-track riding despite its 2.3-mile length. Add another .5-mile out-and-back on pavement from the lower parking lot trailhead and you have a total of 3.3 miles. Your reward on the outer part

RIDE 45   *COPPER FALLS STATE PARK TRAILS*

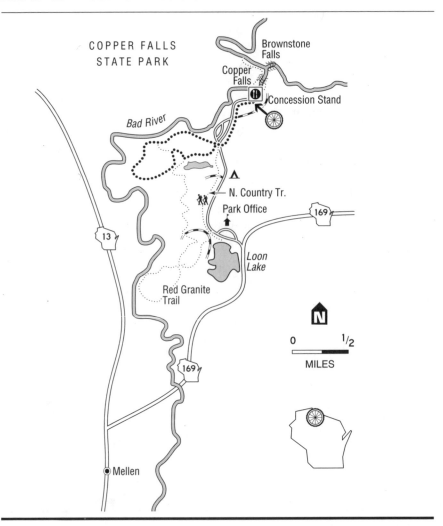

of the off-road loop is a fantastic overview of a radical bend in the Bad River 80 feet below as it courses toward Copper Falls.

The loop trail is constantly rolling, and the surface varies from rough but firm grass and earthen surface with frequent roots and occasional rocks to hardpack through clover and moss. The technical skill needed to negotiate the rough trail surface and some short, steep grades make this a ride of moderate difficulty. It is a good introduction for those with some off-road experience who want to take on some single-track under a dense canopy of a maple forest.

There is currently more off-road riding at Copper Falls than the officially signed route shown here. A 1.3-mile (each way) connecting cross-country ski trail will take you to the 1.8-mile figure eight loop, the Red Granite Ski Trail. These trails are in off-road limbo, and riding is being allowed on an experimental basis.

The Red Granite Trail is designated as a hiking trail, but is seldom used as such and the connector trail is also seldom hiked because it parallels the North Country Hiking Trail (where riding is absolutely not allowed). Since state land rules specify riding on trails signed for that activity only, a policy backed up by fines, you should check on the status of the connector and Red Granite Trail at the park office before riding them. It is hoped the experiment will be successful and the trails will be officially signed in the future. If so, it will make for a total of 7.7 miles of off-road riding trails.

The park's main attraction is the waterfalls, which are easily accessible via a foot bridge and trails created in the 1930s by the Civilian Conservation Corps. The park's namesake, Copper Falls, splits into two cascades and drops 29 feet over black lava rock. A short distance farther, where Tylers Fork joins the Bad River, Brownstone Falls plunges 30 feet over red lava. The fractured lava is called trap rock, meaning it flowed up from fissures in the earth's crust. As the rivers eroded their courses, they met these walls of solid rock, and the falls were created.

General location: Two miles north of Mellen.
Elevation change: The Takesin Ski Trail is rolling and there is one steady, steep 70′ climb. The Red Granite Ski Trail is on higher ground; the high point lies 180′ above the trailhead elevation.
Season: May through October. Trails may be closed at any time due to wet conditions.
Services: Snacks are available at the park concession stand at the trailhead parking lot. All services, except bicycle retail and repair, are available in the small town of Mellen.
Hazards: Trails are regularly maintained and clear, but fallen trees and branches may be encountered at any time. Hikers may be encountered on all trails. Despite the signage and small confines of the riding area, using a compass is a good idea.
Rescue index: Help is available at the Park Headquarters. In case of injury, head toward the park headquarters concession stand or paved roadways.
Land status: Wisconsin State Park and public roads. A daily or annual vehicle sticker ($5 daily / $18 annually for Wisconsin residents, $7 daily / $25 annually for out-of-state residents) is required to park in state parks. Bicyclists are not charged for visiting the forest, but a trail pass fee is required of bicyclists age 18 and older ($3 daily or $10 annually). The trail pass also covers activities like cross-country skiing, horseback riding, and bicycling on railroad grade bike trails.

The Bad River spills over black lava rock at Copper Falls.

Maps: Maps of the trails are available at Copper Falls State Park Headquarters. The USGS 7.5 minute Mellen quad gives excellent information on the terrain, but doesn't show the mountain bike trails.

Finding the trail: Turn east on WI 169 off of WI 13 at the north edge of Mellen. Travel 1.5 miles to the entrance road of Copper Falls State Park and follow it all the way to the parking lot at the end.

Sources of additional information:

Copper Falls State Park
Box 438
Mellen, WI 54546
(715) 274-5123

Wisconsin Department of Natural Resources
Bureau of Parks and Recreation
P.O. Box 7921
Madison, WI 53707-7921
(608) 266-2181

Mellen Area Chamber of Commerce
P.O. Box 793
Mellen, WI 54546
(715) 274-2330

Notes on the trail: The trails are sometimes subject to flooding or damage and may be closed for these reasons. Be sure to call ahead to check on the status. A daily or annual Wisconsin Trail Pass fee is required to ride on the park's off-road trails (see Land status). From the trailhead ride south back toward the park entrance. After .5 mile you will pass the exit road for the north campground on the right (marked Do Not Enter). Immediately beyond the road on the right is Takesin Ski Trail, the beginning of the off-road portion of the route.

The one-way mountain bike route is signed with green-and-white bike silhouette markers as well as blue cross-country ski trail markers. A trail that splits off to the left is marked with the blue North Country Hiking Trail symbol, and biking is not allowed on it. At .7 mile you may choose to turn left on a shortcut, but if you take it you will miss the Bad River overview.

At 1.9 miles, just before a small lake on the right, you can turn right on a cross-country ski trail that connects the Takesin Trail with the Red Granite Trail. The connector and the Red Granite Trail are not signed for mountain biking, but riding has been allowed on them on an experimental basis. Be sure to check on their status at the park office. To exit the Takesin Trail, follow the arrow directing you to the parking lot.

RIDE 46 *RAVEN TRAILS*

Lakes. They're what the Minocqua/Woodruff area vacation experience is all about. There are more lakes here per square mile than almost anywhere in the world. Only parts of Minnesota, Ontario, and Finland compare. This 4.9-mile loop on the Raven Ski Trail in the Northern Highlands American Legion State Forest takes you past two fine ones. Clear Lake is just what the name implies. Look closely at it to remind yourself how water should look. Little Inkpot Lake, on the other hand, is no less clear. It must have gotten its name from its tiny size.

This loop is only mildly challenging and a great place for an introduction to steep, technical single-track riding. Over half the distance is single-track, characterized by short, steep plunges and climbs, in the 20- to 30-foot height range, on a surface made rough by roots and rounded cobbles. The run outs (flattened areas at the base of a downhill run that allow you to control your speed) are nearly all straight and, particularly if you have suspension, you can really bomb them. On the less radical scale, the single-track is a good place to learn weight shift, proper braking, and uphill techniques for weaving through rocks and keeping momentum going. It's fun for riders and there is nothing that makes you scream, "My God, I'm gonna die!" Less experienced riders may want to lower the saddle a bit to make weight shift

RIDE 46   *RAVEN TRAILS*

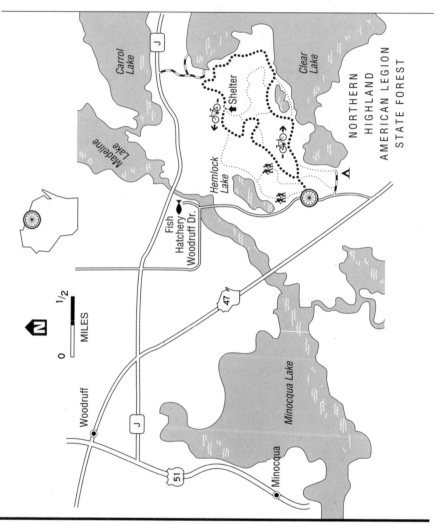

easier. The single-track is broken up by gently rolling sections on grassy, double-track cross-country ski trails. There are a number of places where you can get airborne on the single-track, including a 70-foot downhill that seems to head straight for the lake; there's a whoop-de-doo at the end where you can catch some major air—if you want to.

Too much talk about the biking might make you think that radical riding is what the Raven Trail experience is all about. Really though, the aesthetic component is at least as strong. The north woods magic begins at the trailhead where a stand of tall white pines has cushioned the rooted trail with copper-colored needles. The white pines soon give way to a dense canopy of birch, maple, and Norway pine. The trees grow close to the trail, and glimpses of the lakes through the trees are frequent. Several short side trails run down to their shores. As you turn away from Clear Lake, you'll climb a remnant sand dune and a steep hogback ridge on your way to the cross-country ski shelter. The open shelter faces south to catch the sun and the heat from an elevated stone fire ring. You can ignore the "Expert loop closed due to lack of snow" sign for now, but you may want to consider coming back when the skiing is good.

General location: The Raven Trail is six miles east of Minocqua.

Elevation change: The terrain is almost constantly rolling. Short, steep pitches of 20′ to 30′ are common. The greatest elevation difference is 70′, and there are several climbs and descents in that range.

Season: May through October.

Services: There is a water pump at the trailhead. All services are available in Woodruff and Minocqua, including bicycle retail, rental, and repair at BJ's Sport Shop in Minocqua.

Hazards: The trails are very well maintained, but downed trees and branches may be found at anytime. Single-track trails are very rough from rocks and roots. If speed is not moderated, it is possible to get airborne. All trails are open to hiking.

Rescue index: Help can be summoned at the State Fish Hatchery, one mile north of the trailhead on Woodruff Drive. Although the trail is popular with hikers and riders, you should make your way to Woodruff Drive or County Road J if you need help.

Land status: Northern Highland–American Legion State Forest. Wisconsin trail pass fees do not apply.

Maps: A basic trail map is available from the Wisconsin Department of Natural Resources. A topographical map titled "Minocqua and Tomahawk Chain" based on 7.5 minute USGS maps is available from the Art Dorwin Map Store, 8630 A Highway 51 North, Minocqua, WI 54548; (715) 356-6851. It shows most of the Raven trails.

Finding the trail: From US 51 at the Minocqua / Woodruff border, turn east on Country Road J. After 1.9 miles turn south on Woodruff Drive. After 3.9 miles turn left into the parking area for the State Forest Nature Trail and Hiking Trail.

Sources of additional information:

Northern Highland–American Legion State Forest Headquarters
4125 Highway M
Boulder Junction, WI 54512

Take some time to rest by the shore of Clear Lake.

Wisconsin Department of Natural Resources
Bureau of Parks and Recreation
P.O. Box 7921
Madison, WI 53707-7921
(608) 266-2181

Greater Minocqua Chamber of Commerce
P.O. Box 1006
Minocqua, WI 54548
(800) 44-NORTH

Notes on the trail: The Raven Ski Trail is well marked with frequent "you are here" maps and cross-country ski trail signs. The Nature Trail is marked with white-and-red "no biking" signs. From the trailhead follow the red (expert) outer loop trail. Many of the trails are marked for one-way travel. Most of the red trail is on rough single-track, but at points it will merge with wider, grassy, less steep double-track trails. After 3.4 miles at the ski shelter, you will be on wider trails to the end. A short distance beyond, the red trail splits off to the right and is marked with a "no biking" sign (it would lead you onto the Nature Trail). Ignore the "do not enter" sign and follow the wider trail to the left, which will lead you back to the trailhead.

RIDE 47 *RAZORBACK RIDGES TRAILS*

Any rider can enjoy a cruise through the deep maple, pine, and birch forest on the Razorback Ridges cross-country ski trails. The 7.7-mile Long Rider Loop garners a moderate difficulty rating because of its length and some very steep pitches. However, with numerous shortcut options and a smooth, wide, grassy or bare ground surface, it is recommended for even novice off-roaders.

A more seasoned rider can enjoy Razorback, too. There are more trails here than can possibly be depicted on this map. The trail network looks like an explosion in a spaghetti factory. The person who recommended the area said that there was some fine single-track here. This is true. But signage is very spotty on the single-track. We tried three loops and found that the riding was terrific, but even with a compass, confusion reigned about directions. Many small intersecting trails could be confused for the correct route.

The trail map was drawn freehand and the "you are here" signs on the main trails were routed into boards with even greater artistic freedom. This trail system could either use good marking or a good map and has neither. In the winter this is not as much of a problem. If a trail has tracks on it, it's a ski trail. If it doesn't, it's not.

This trail confusion doesn't mean that Razorback isn't a fine place to ride. It is and it's popular. The trails are the site of the annual Ridge Runner Off-Road Race in late August. You can have a great ride on the main trails and if you have a compass and enough time, you can take on some of the single-track loops.

General location: Two miles west of Sayner.
Elevation change: Most of the terrain is constantly rolling with the exception of a short, flat warm up and cool down stretch and a longer section about halfway around the Long Rider Loop. Elevation changes will be in the range of 30′ to 60′.
Season: April through October. Insect populations are heavy from mid-May through July.
Services: There is a water pump and ice cream stand at the trailhead. Food, drink, and gasoline are available at McKay's Corner Store. All services are

RIDE 47   *RAZORBACK RIDGES TRAILS*

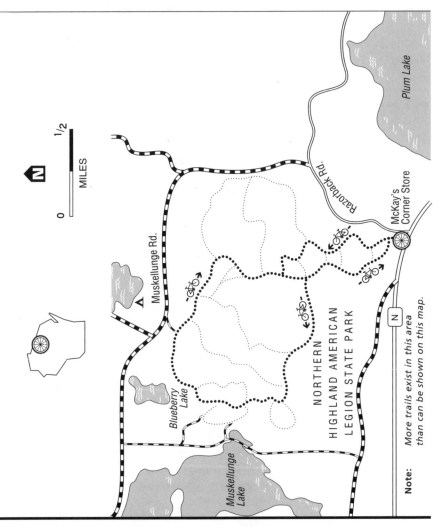

available in Sayner and the Woodruff / Minocqua area, including bicycle retail, rental, and repair at BJ's Sport Shop in Minocqua.

Hazards: The trails are very well maintained, but downed trees and branches may be found at any time. Single-track trails are rough from rocks and roots. It is a good idea to carry a compass. All trails open to hiking.

Rescue index: Help can be summoned at McKay's Corner Store at the trail-head. Although the trails are very popular, your chance of on-trail rescue is not great, and you should seek the shortest route to the trailhead.

In places the trail becomes a tunnel through the trees.

Land status: Northern Highland–American Legion State Forest. Wisconsin trail pass fees do not apply, but donations are welcomed. Trails are maintained by the Sayner-Star Lake Lions Club.

Maps: A trail map is available at McKay's Corner Store or the Sayner-Star Lake Chamber of Commerce. A topographical map titled "Boulder Junction," which is based on 7.5 minute USGS maps, is available from the Art Dorwin Map Store, 8630 A Highway 51 N, Minocqua, WI 54548; (715) 356-6851. It shows the terrain in the Razorback area, but not the trails.

Finding the trail: From the Woodruff / Minocqua town line on US 51 at County Road J, travel 5.7 miles north and turn northeast on County Road M. After 2.4 miles turn east on County Road N. After 6.7 miles turn left onto Razorback Road at McKay's Corner Store. Watch for the sign "Razorback Ridges Trails XC Parking."

Sources of additional information:

Northern Highland–American Legion State Forest Headquarters
4125 Highway M
Boulder Junction, WI 54512

Wisconsin Department of Natural Resources
Bureau of Parks and Recreation
P.O. Box 7921
Madison, WI 53707-7921
(608) 266-2181

Sayner-Star Lake Chamber of Commerce
V.M. 92
Sayner, WI 54560
(715) 542-3789

Notes on the trail: Wisconsin trail pass fees do not apply, but donations are welcomed. The main trail loops are marked with frequent "you are here" signs and arrows for specific trail loops. Single-track loops running off of the main loops are not well signed and are not shown on this map. Follow signs for the green line–coded Long Rider loop.

RIDE 48 *ANVIL TRAILS*

The Nicolet National Forest Anvil Trails are a perennial favorite among cross-country skiers. The deep maple forest and varied trail system make for fun mountain biking, too. The 7.1-mile loop shown here ranks near the upper end of the moderate difficulty category for the average rider. Several options exist to make it shorter or easier. Trails vary from firm, double-track, grassy and hardpack surface on the West Trail and North Trail, to a narrower cross-country ski trail with a bare forest floor and a rougher surface on the Ninemile Run and Lake Loop, to true single-track, rough with rocks and roots, with some very steep sections on the Devil's Run.

No matter where you ride, the grade is never constant for more than a few yards. About halfway around you will find a small log cabin shelter with a fireplace and wood supply, a nice spot for a break on a damp or chilly day. There is an overview of grassy Ninemile Lake near the end of the Lake Loop. No real technical skill is required except on Devil's Run, where you need the ability to weave among rocks and roots while climbing and bounce over the same going down. You can make the Anvil Trail experience easier by taking the West Trail from the shelter to the trailhead, cutting out the more difficult Devil's Run, or skipping the Lake Loop, which eliminates 1.8 miles of riding.

RIDE 48 *ANVIL TRAILS*

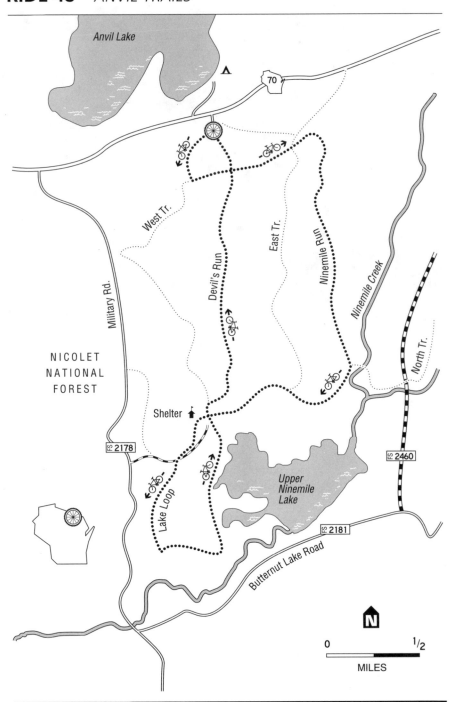

Anvil Lake

70

West Tr.

East Tr.

Ninemile Run

Devil's Run

Ninemile Creek

North Tr.

Military Rd.

NICOLET
NATIONAL
FOREST

FS 2178

Shelter

FS 2460

Upper
Ninemile
Lake

Lake Loop

FS 2181

Butternut Lake Road

N

0   1/2

MILES

The Anvil Trails are among the most popular in the Nicollet National Forest.

General location: Nine miles east of the town of Eagle River.

Elevation change: Terrain is nearly constantly rolling. Many steep pitches in the 20′ to 40′ range will be encountered as well as several in the 70′ range. The elevation difference between the high and low points on the trails is 120′.

Season: April through October. Insect populations are heavy from mid-May through July.

Services: There is a water pump at the trailhead. All services are available nine miles west on WI 70 in the town of Eagle River, including bicycle retail and repair.

Hazards: The trails are very well maintained, but downed trees and branches may be found at anytime. Single-track trails are rough from rocks and roots. All trails open to hiking.

Rescue index: Help is available in Eagle River. If you are injured or have mechanical problems, you should make your way to WI 70 or FS 2178 (Military Road).

Land status: Nicollet National Forest.

Maps: A detailed trail map is available from the Nicollet National Forest office.

Finding the trail: From the junction of US 45 and WI 70, just east of the town of Eagle River, travel eight miles and turn south at the Anvil Lake Trail sign.

Sources of additional information:

Nicollet National Forest
68 South Stevens Street
Rhinelander, WI 54501
(715) 362-1373

Eagle River Information Bureau
Box 218
Eagle River, WI 54521
(715) 479-8575, (800) 359-6315

Notes on the trail: The trails are well marked with frequent "you are here" and trail name signs. Most of the trails are one-way. From the trailhead, follow the West Trail to the right. After .3 mile at a **T** intersection, turn left on a connecting trail that runs to the east. Use caution at .9 mile, where the Ninemile Run trail begins. Brown-and-yellow Forest Service trail signs are set at a low height and are hard to spot in the deep, dark forest. The natural inclination at the Ninemile Run intersection is to go straight, which would take you to a gate out at WI 70. However, you should turn right onto the Ninemile Run that is signed off to the right. At 2.5 miles turn right on the North Trail, a wider, grassy, rolling double-track ski trail. Around mid-way you will arrive at a log cabin shelter and the intersection of the Devil's Run and West Trail. Follow the North Trail, which is a wide, unimproved road at this point, to the left. After .3 mile turn left on the Lake Loop. This will take you back to the shelter intersection, where you will pick up the Devil's Run trail and ride it back to the trailhead.

MICHIGAN

Southern Lower Peninsula
of Michigan

People commonly think of industry when southern Michigan comes to mind. The great centers of automobile manufacturing are there including Detroit, a city that has become synonymous with motor vehicle production—Motown. This is only part of the southern Michigan picture.

Thanks in large part to the creation of State Recreation Areas, large tracts of wild country have been preserved in close proximity to population centers. Much of southern Michigan is devoted to agriculture, and these recreation areas are usually interspersed among the farmland. In character, they have more services and improvements than state forests, but less than state parks.

The entire lower peninsula of Michigan was once covered by the massive ice sheet of the last continental glacier. However, this doesn't make homogenous terrain. The glacier didn't retreat (a euphemism for melting) in an even, steady manner. It would melt for a while, then mount an offensive and push southward again. This process eventually left roughly parallel ridges of tumbled debris known as terminal moraines. The Kalamazoo and Defiance moraines affect the southern part of the state. They created areas of lakes, marshes, and rocky, sandy hills that were worthless for farming—but are now great for off-road riding.

On the Fort Custer Trails, riders can enjoy an easy ride past prairies and through an oak and beech forest. Moderately difficult riding with lots of single-track will be found on the Yankee Springs Trails. The challenging Potawatomi Trails are legendary among southern Michigan riders. Island Lake and Pontiac Lake, two recreation areas just beyond the auto industry area, offer riders moderate and challenging experiences, respectively.

RIDE 49 *FORT CUSTER TRAILS*

Fast, hard, and fun, this extensive network of unmarked trails in the Battle Creek / Kalamazoo area is the place to enthuse mountain bike neophytes. A 20-mile loop can be accessed at several points, and shorter rides are easy to chart. The entire trail can be ridden in the middle chainring, since there is no sand and only small hills in the slightly rolling terrain. This will be an easy ride for anyone.

In the western part of Fort Custer, narrow single-tracks wind around a series of lakes, streams, and ponds which are an important sanctuary to

RIDE 49   *FORT CUSTER TRAILS*

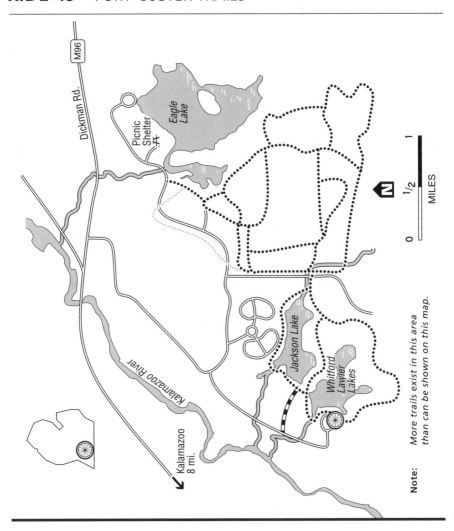

migrating wildlife. In the southern and eastern sections, old double-tracks crisscross natural-appearing areas, dotted with the remains of long-abandoned clusters of civilization.

Vegetation consists of oak and beech forests, with park-like prairies and meadows reminiscent of southern Michigan in an earlier epoch. Aside from the traffic noise drifting in, there are places on this trail where it seems implausible that a significant population concentration lies just beyond the park boundaries.

General location: Between the towns of Battle Creek and Kalamazoo.

Elevation change: Minimal.

Season: Any time the ground is not covered with snow. This is usually mid-April through mid-November.

Services: All services, including several bike shops, are located in nearby Kalamazoo and Battle Creek.

Hazards: Sunburn, crowds, and traffic on the way to and from the park. Also, the trail crosses a number of roads open to motorized vehicles.

Rescue index: Help is available at the Area Headquarters or in the suburban sprawl surrounding the Recreation Area. It is possible to get pretty thoroughly lost in the tangle of trails and double-tracks away from the more heavily populated beach areas. Bring a map and compass!

Land status: State Recreation Area managed by Michigan Department of Natural Resources. A park fee is required per motor vehicle ($4 daily, $20 annually).

Maps: Fort Custer Trail Map available at Park Headquarters.

Finding the trail: Enter the Recreation Area from Highway M–96, a.k.a. Dickman Road. Veer right after the Contact Station and proceed to the parking lot at Whitford and Lawlor Lakes. The trail starts at the far end of the lot. Alternatively, one can access the trails near the beach area at Eagle Lake.

Sources of additional information:

Fort Custer Recreation Area
5163 West Fort Custer Drive
Augusta, MI 49012
(616) 731-4200

Greater Battle Creek–Calhoun County CVB
172 West Van Buren
Battle Creek, MI 49017
(616) 962-2240

Notes on the trail: There are more trails at Fort Custer than can possibly be shown on this map. The trail is not marked, and there are no confidence markers at intersections. If you do not have the Fort Custer map or fail to pay attention to the various intersections, you may end up riding many extra miles, especially once you're away from the more heavily used hiking / biking trails near Whitford and Jackson Lakes. If time or mileage constraints are a factor, try to remain near these lakes, or restrict yourself to out-and-back tours.

On the other hand, if you have all afternoon and don't mind a few extra miles of fast double-track riding, head on into the extensive trail network that lies between Jackson and Eagle Lakes. Road riders who are transitioning to off-road riding, or who just want to rack up some miles in a more natural setting, will appreciate the long stretches of exhilarating fat tire riding.

RIDE 50   *YANKEE SPRINGS TRAILS*

At Yankee Springs Recreation Area, your idea of fun will be revealed by how fast and how far you go on this 11-mile loop. There is a lot of genuine single-track on the route, some designed especially by local mountain bikers Steve Miller, Mark Cramer, and Bob Lawson. The fun starts soon enough. Less than a mile from the trailhead you will snake through Miller's Bypass Trail. If you haven't sawed an inch off of each end of your handlebar yet, you might want to do it before coming to Yankee Springs. There isn't much space between the hardwoods (consider the word *hard*woods).

Don't be put off. This is a great place for a first taste of tight single-track. And you can learn about the oak leaf buzz—the sound of knobby tires slapping against leaves caught in your frame or brakes. The terrain in the Miller's section is flat to gently rolling on a bare hardpack forest floor with occasional roots and rocks that make things interesting. At 8 miles per hour it's just a cruise, although you wouldn't want to do any gawking. At 12 miles per hour the ride becomes a bike handling contest.

The tight single-track doesn't last forever, and after about a mile you will gradually and steeply make your way up to some high ground before you ride roller coaster–style over several miles on the Cramer Lawson Trail, the route's toughest terrain. On the way back as you again climb to high ground, you will suddenly find that the terrain drops away precipitously on the right. This is the Devil's Soup Bowl, a glacial kettle over 100 feet deep.

There are several shortcut options. You can make Yankee Springs as tough as you want, but for the prudent, average rider, it is of moderate difficulty. A swim in Gun Lake, near the main campground, is something anyone can handle. The trails at Yankee Springs are very popular, so if having the woods to yourself is your goal, visit during the week.

General location: Ten miles east of US 131 or 9 miles west of Hastings.
Elevation change: The terrain varies greatly. In the southeast it is flat to gently rolling with occasional short, steep dips at streams and ravines. The northeast section is constantly rolling with very steep grades of 50′ to 70′ common and 100′ plus occasionally.
Season: Trails may be rideable year-round depending on the snowfall. The best riding will be from May (when the ground has dried) through October.
Services: Water is available at the trailhead, and there is a concession stand at the beach on Gun Lake. All services, including bicycle retail and repair, are available in Hastings.
Hazards: Soft sand, glacial rocks, and roots will be found on parts of the trail. The trees are tight on the single-track, and eye protection is a good idea.

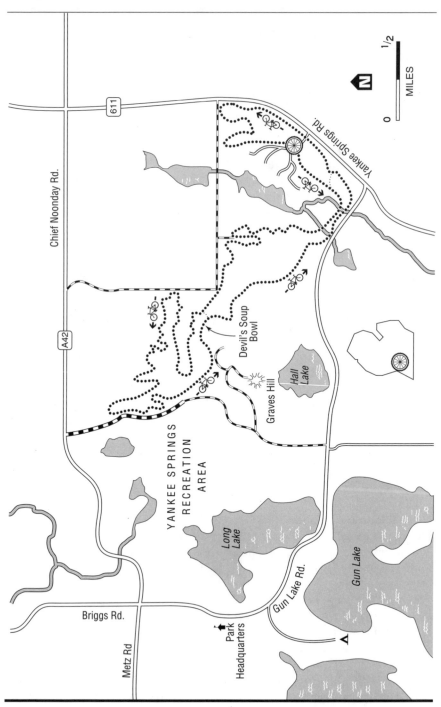

Twisting single-track draws riders to the trails at
Yankee Springs.

Rescue index: Help is available at the park headquarters. All of the paved
roads are well traveled and accessible from the trail at many points.

Land status: State Recreation Area. A park fee is required per motor vehicle
($4 daily, $20 annually).

Maps: A simple, but very usable, mountain bike trail map is available at the
park headquarters.

Finding the trail: From US 131, take Exit 61 and travel east on County Road
A 42. After 7.7 miles turn south onto Gun Lake Road (County Road 430) and
travel .7 mile to the park headquarters on the right (where park sticker and
map can be obtained). Continue on Gun Lake Road to a T intersection with
Yankee Springs Road (County Road 611) and turn left. Travel .7 mile and
turn left into the Deep Lake Rustic Campground.

Sources of additional information:

Yankee Springs Recreation Area
2140 Gun Lake Road
Middleville, MI 49333
(616) 795-9081

Hastings Area Chamber of Commerce
P.O. Box 151
Hastings, MI 49058
(616) 945-2454

Notes on the trail: A park fee is required per motor vehicle (see Land status). The one-way system is well signed by blue squares with white arrows. Begin where the trails cross the park road just before the road splits into the campground area. Start by riding to the southwest and follow the Miller's Bypass Trail, the Cramer Trail, Cramer Lawson Trail, McDonald Lake Trail, Ski Trail, Old Trail, Shotgun Shell Trail, and Campground Trail. The Campground Trail is an easy 1.8-mile loop that you begin after returning across the campground road. The trails are very close together in many places and at 2.8 miles from the start (by the Devil's Soup Bowl) you could easily pick up the return trail and eliminate the toughest section of the route and 4.3 miles of riding.

RIDE 51   *POTAWATOMI TRAIL*

This is the famous "Poto" trail. Mention it to Michigan mountain bikers and they'll know you're talking about some great riding. The 17.9-mile Potawatomi Trail and interconnecting 5.8-mile Crooked Lake Loop are among the most popular off-road trails in the state. The terrain is rolling with short, steep uphill and downhill sections. Single-track prevails throughout. Mountain bikers ride one-way in a clockwise direction and hikers walk counter-clockwise. The Crooked Lake Loop is a good introduction to the area and a great choice for novice riders. Both trails feature technical climbs and descents, but on the "Poto" they are more frequent. On the slopes you will have to deal with loose surface, small rocks, tree roots, and even widely spaced steps. Overall, the surface is hardpack, although some sandy areas will be encountered.

The trails wind through a hardwood forest interrupted by lakes and marshes. In places boardwalk bridges cross streams. There is a fine view of Crooked Lake from a picnic area not far from the trailhead.

You can expect the trails to be crowded on weekends and holidays, but most weekdays will be pretty quiet. Footraces are occasionally held on the

RIDE 51   *POTAWATOMI TRAIL*

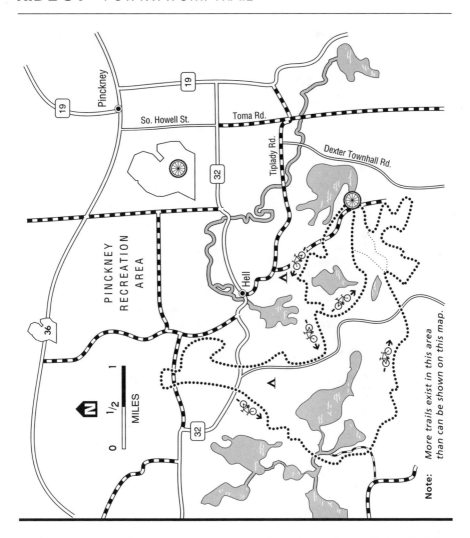

trails. It is extremely important to stay exclusively on the trails marked for mountain biking. In an area as heavily used as the "Poto," deviation by even a fraction of the trail users creates a major management problem. There is also a fine for riding off of the marked trails.

Although Pinckney is the locator town for the trail, you actually go to Hell on the "Poto." The crossroads village of Hell is worth a stop just to buy an "I've been to Hell and back" bumper sticker. It is also your only nearby option for food and drink. There is a grocery in Hell, and the Dam Site Inn is

The "Poto" is southern Michigan's most popular
mountain bike trail.

a popular gathering spot for mountain bikers. The Potawatomi Chapter of the
Michigan Mountain Bike Association holds an annual recreational ride called
the Friends of the Potawatomi Festival in late October.

General location: Pinckney State Recreation Area, 5 miles southwest of
Pinckney.

Elevation change: You'll find rolling terrain about one-third flat, one-third
uphill, and one-third downhill. Most climbs and descents are in the 30′ range,
but some will reach the 70′ to 100′ range.

Season: The trail is open through most of the year. Typically, it will be closed
in March and early April while the ground thaws. The best riding will be
from late April through November. The spring is likely to be wet, and flies
and mosquitoes will be out May through September. Be sure to call ahead for
trail conditions.

Services: There is no drinking water on the trail itself. Water and snacks are available at the concession stand at the Silver Lake parking area. Riding is prohibited on sidewalks and on the beach near the concession stand. There is a grocery store and a tavern with a short order menu in Hell. All services are available in Pinckney, including bicycle parts and service.

Hazards: Normal erosion of the glacial till that comprises the steep hills exposes rocks and roots, and sometimes creates ruts and loose surface with deep, soft sand washed to the bottom. Wind-downed trees should be removed by the park staff, but always keep an eye out for the newly fallen trees. Expect hikers to be traveling the trail in the opposite direction.

Rescue index: Help can be found at the Pinckney State Recreation Area headquarters one-quarter mile south of the Silver Lake parking lot on Silverhill Road.

Land status: State Recreation Area. A park fee is required per motor vehicle ($4 daily, $20 annually).

Maps: Pinckney State Recreation Area maps are available at the headquarters building. They don't show the trails in great detail, but they are useful and show all crossroads.

Finding the trail: If you are approaching from the north, turn south off of MI 36 onto South Howell Street (changes to Toma Road when it becomes gravel) in Pinckney. After 2 miles, turn west on Tiplady Road, go a quarter mile and turn left on Dexter Town Hall Road. Travel south 1.5 miles and turn right at the Pinckney Recreation Area entrance. Follow the park road about .75 mile to the Silver Lake parking lot.

Sources of additional information:

John Labossiere
Park Manager
Pinckney State Recreation Area
8555 Silverhill Road
Pinckney, MI 48169
(734) 426-4913

Jeff Buerman
Potawatomi Chapter
Michigan Mountain Bike Association
1625 Patterson Lake Road
Pinckney, MI 48169
(734) 878-6026

Howell Area Chamber of Commerce
404 East Grand River Avenue
Howell, MI 48843
(517) 546-3920

Notes on the trail: Begin riding from the southwest corner of the Silver Lake parking lot for the Potawatomi Trail or the northwest corner for the Crooked Lake Loop. Both trails must be ridden in a clockwise direction (hikers walk counter-clockwise). Signage is good. Both blue Potawatomi Trail hiking arrows and mountain bike signs are present. The mountain bike signs feature a bike silhouette on a green background for the riding trails and a red slash variation of it for the trails where riding is prohibited. Riding is prohibited on sidewalks and on the beach near the concession stand.

RIDE 52 *ISLAND LAKE TRAILS*

This is one of the places where Detroit metro area couch potatoes are converted into avid mountain bike fans. An easy ten-mile loop seems like a fun, roller coaster–type ride as it roughly parallels the scenic Huron River. Away from the river, the single-track trail winds through hardwood stands, in which the tall oaks characteristic of southern Michigan predominate, alternating with undisturbed meadows.

The recreation area is more highly developed than most committed mountain bikers would prefer, with picnic areas, grills, and tables scattered around, but hey, this *is* just half an hour from downtown Detroit. It's a treat to be able to enjoy this much nature so close to a metropolis.

General location: The town of Brighton, within the angle formed by Interstate 96 and US 23.
Elevation change: Very minimal. The entire trail is gently rolling, traversing a number of small ravines and ridges, but there are no exceptionally long or steep hills.
Season: Trails should be rideable from mid-March to mid-November, or whenever the ground is not covered with snow.
Services: All services including bike shops are available in Brighton or other towns in the immediate vicinity.
Hazards: Urban crime? Improperly discarded charcoal briquets? In other words, this is a pretty tame environment in terms of natural hazards. Do be careful at road crossings, especially the Huron River crossing on Kensington Road.
Rescue index: Help is available at Park Headquarters or in nearby Brighton. The trail is never more than a half mile from frequently traveled paved roads.
Land status: State of Michigan Recreation Area. A park fee is required per motor vehicle ($4 daily, $20 annually).
Maps: The Island Lake Recreation Area Trail Map is available at park headquarters.

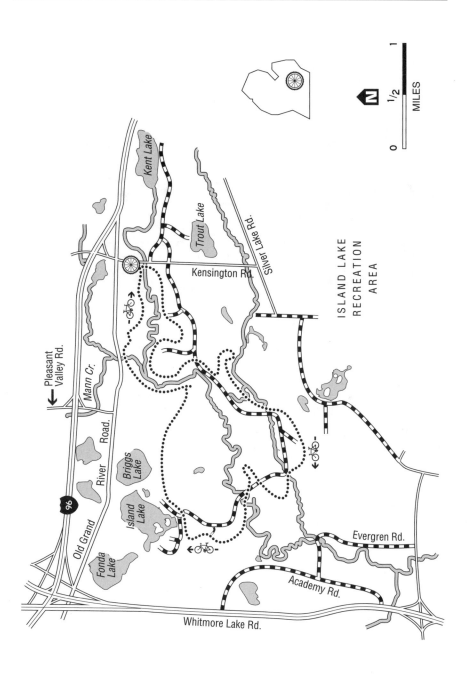

Dusk quiets the waters at Island Lake.

Finding the trail: Island Lake headquarters is located just south of I-96, on the southwest corner of the intersection of Kensington Road and Old Grand River Road. This is also the trailhead. The trail parallels Kensington Road for a few hundred yards, and you must jump back onto the road to cross the Huron River. On the other side of the bridge, the trail heads off west into the Park. If the headquarters is closed, you may pick up a map at the registration center, a bit south of the bridge on the east side of Kensington Road.

Sources of additional information:

Island Lake Recreation Area
12950 East Grand River
Brighton, MI 48116
(810) 229-7067

Greater Brighton Area Chamber of Commerce
131 Hyne Street
Brighton, MI 48116
(810) 227-5086

Notes on the trail: Marking on this one-way, clockwise-only trail is just so-so, but the amount of use makes the path easy to follow. There is no significant amount of sand. About half of the trail can be ridden in the middle chainring, at least by more aggressive riders. The roller coaster sections include whoop-de-doos and banked turns, which are only as challenging as you choose to make them, depending on your speed.

Near the Riverbend picnic area and the Spring Mill Pond, the trail branches into a confusing tangle of footpaths, but the only consequence of a wrong turn is being forced to pop back onto the pavement, where one can use the map to pick up the trail a bit farther along. This easy escape hatch is another feature that makes Island Lake especially attractive to novices or riders with children.

RIDE 53   *PONTIAC LAKE TRAILS*

Look at a topographic relief map of this area, and you will notice that it resembles a crumpled blanket, all ridges and valleys. This makes Pontiac Lake the most challenging course in Detroit's "green belt." This six- to nine-mile loop is the site where experienced competitors tune up for the big races. Those of more modest skills can discover the definition of "somewhat technical," "trials loop," and "grinding hills." All riders will find it challenging.

Not that all nimrods should avoid Pontiac—just plan on pushing your bike a little bit on the uphills, and work those brakes coming down. Most of the tour is quite enjoyable, and the big panoramas viewed from scenic lookouts make the tough parts worthwhile. The one-way, clockwise-only trail is all single-track, firm on the flats, a combination of sand, gravel, and rocks on the hills. In olden days, farmers grew rocks here and scattered their harvest in little piles around the area; these remain to make life interesting for bike riders.

General location: Seven miles west of the Pontiac Silverdome.

Elevation change: Constant. Hills are from 50′ to 90′ tall, and gnarly.

Season: Any time, unless it has snowed or been especially wet. Generally April through November.

Services: All services are available in nearby Pontiac, including a major league football stadium.

Hazards: The hills are washed out, rocky, gravelly, sandy—all the good things that cause falls. Park officials report a steady stream of bumps, bruises, and contusions, but few serious injuries to those who wear helmets.

Rescue index: Help is available at the Recreation Area Headquarters. Because of the terrain, paramedics may have to physically manhandle wracked bodies and bent bikes for the first few hundred yards, but civilization (i.e., paved roads) is always nearby.

Land status: State of Michigan Park / Recreation Area. A park fee is required per motor vehicle ($4 daily, $20 annually).

RIDE 53   *PONTIAC LAKE TRAILS*

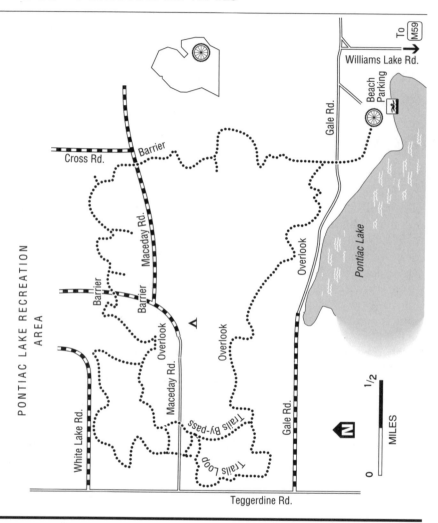

Maps: Pontiac Lake Recreation Area Mountain Bike Trails Map.
Finding the trail: The Park is located west of Pontiac, to the north of Highway
MI 59. The trailhead is located at the beach parking lot at the northeast end of
Pontiac Lake on the south side of Gale Road. The trail immediately crosses
Gale Road and heads north into the Park.

Riders get a workout on the rolling terrain at
Pontiac Lake.

Sources of additional information:

Pontiac Lake Recreation Area
7800 Gale Road
Waterford, MI 48327
(248) 666-1020

Oakland County Chamber of Commerce
1052 West Huron Street
Pontiac, MI 48053
(248) 683-4747

Notes on the trail: This is not the place to initiate novices or juveniles, unless they enjoy overcoming challenges or are eager to test the limits of their equipment. On the other hand, you don't need to be a NORBA champion to have fun here, either. Signs separating horse trails from bike trails appear at most intersections, but there are no "you are here" maps.

The southwesternmost section of trail is a "Trials Loop" that many riders will want to avoid. A bicycle trail sign with arrows points out the alternate trails at this point. To avoid Trials, stay to the right. This is the first such choice that you will come to.

Shortly after this, the trail crosses Maceday Road. Those who have experienced enough gnarlyness can hang a right and head east on Maceday. Take it all the way to the end, past the horse stable and assembly area, to where the bike trail again crosses Maceday road. (Cross Road will be visible through the trees at that point.) Jump back onto the bike trail for the last mile and a half south to the trailhead.

Note: Pontiac Lake officials have completely segregated mountain bike and equestrian trails, a project which should be a model for land managers everywhere.

Northern Lower Peninsula of Michigan

The 45th parallel of latitude cuts across the northern part of Michigan's Lower Peninsula. This invisible line marks the halfway point between the equator and the north pole. There is nothing invisible about the landscape change that results from the diminished sunlight and shorter growing season of the northern latitude. The proportions of land use are just the opposite of the region to the south. Instead of farmland with intermittent wooded areas, you find pine and hardwood forests with intermittent farms.

The continental glacier left its stamp here, carving fjord-like Grand Traverse Bay and leaving the jumbled ridges of the Port Huron Terminal Moraine. The basin of Lake Huron was shaped by the glacier, and rides on two of its islands, Mackinac and Bois Blanc, are included here. The combination of woodlands and glacial terrain that characterizes the northern Lower Peninsula make for very fine off-road riding.

Riding through a dense oak forest is a moderately difficult off-roading experience on the Hungerford Trail. The confines of the Sand Lakes Quiet Area also offer moderate riding. On the trails at Schuss Mountain/Shanty Creek, riders can take on the challenging terrain used for the NORBA (National Off-Road Bicycle Association) National Championships. Shingle Mill Pathway provides a moderate experience in a deep forest where elk may be seen. Riders will have an easy time on the Wildwood Hills Pathway. Wild and scenic Bois Blanc Island can be circled on easy riding roads and trails. Moderate and challenging riding will be found on the motor vehicle–free roads and trails of popular Mackinac Island.

RIDE 54 *HUNGERFORD TRAIL*

Big oaks are common in the rolling hills of this 13-mile cross-country ski trail, making it a prime destination for two-wheeled tree-huggers. Loops as short as four miles combine to form the route. The two-way trail is a bit sandy with short, steep hills, many of which should be walked to prevent further erosion. Horses are in the process of destroying this single-track trail, but the Forest Service says it is aware of the problem and will gradually separate the user groups.

Those parts of the trail that are level to slightly rolling (most of it) are quite rideable, except for sandy ground under the few stands of conifers. Technical

213

RIDE 54 *HUNGERFORD TRAIL*

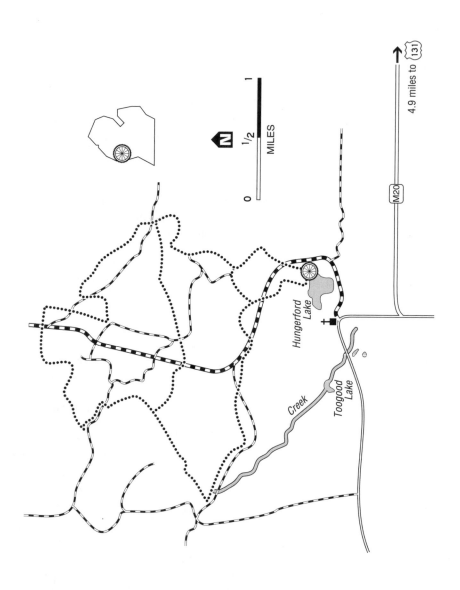

Autumn decorates the forest floor with colorful leaves.

skills are not needed. Riding through such a beautiful forest makes the slight hoof-induced bumpiness and the occasional sandpit worth overcoming. The average rider will find Hungerford to be moderately difficult.

General location: About seven miles west of the town of Big Rapids.

Elevation change: The trail is mostly gently rolling, but scattered about are a number of short, steep hills approximately 50′ high. Many of these hills have become sandy and rutted.

Season: Well-drained soil makes the trail rideable from as soon as the snow melts in March or April until November 15, the opening day of deer season.

Services: All services will be found in Big Rapids.

Hazards: There are a number of road crossings, and horse doo-doo may clog your knobbies. Otherwise, the steepness of a few hills is the only risk.

Rescue index: Help is available in Big Rapids. The access road cuts through the trail loops, so you will never be more than a mile from civilization, although it may feel more remote.

Land status: Huron-Manistee National Forest.

Maps: Hungerford Cross-Country Ski Trail Map, available form the Forest Service office in White Cloud. (Address is below in "Sources of additional information.")

Finding the trail: Take Highway MI 20 and proceed 4.9 miles west of US 131. Where the road bends noticeably to the south, you will see a little town hall building on the right. Turn right, then right again at the cemetery. Follow the road around Hungerford Lake to the trailhead.

Sources of additional information:

> Huron / Manistee National Forest
> White Cloud Ranger District
> White Cloud, MI 49349
> (616) 689-6696

> Mecosta County Area Chamber of Commerce
> 246 State Street
> Big Rapids, MI 49307
> (616) 796-7649

Notes on the trail: There are more trails in the area than can be shown on this map. The trail is very well marked with easy-to-read "you are here" intersection confidence markers. It is intersected at several points by double-track roads that can be used to add distance with a fast out-and-back. It is also intersected by the unpaved access road, which can be used to fashion custom loops. Some dispersed camping sites are located near the trailhead on the north side of the lake.

RIDE 55 *SAND LAKES QUIET AREA TRAILS*

Sand Lakes Quiet Area contains a ten-mile looped, single-tracked cross-country ski trail that winds around a half dozen pretty little lakes. Loops as short as three miles are easily charted, or one can explore the entire area. The trail is very well marked with confidence markers at each intersection, most of which retain their "you are here" maps. Bordering the small lakes are numerous small private coves and beaches that seem to whisper to passing bikers, "Camp here, camp here."

The undulating terrain is gently to moderately steep, and the surface is quite firm. Your derailleurs will get a real workout as you continually shift from the middle to the inside chainring to compensate for elevation changes. The average rider will find the riding to be of moderate difficulty. The second-growth forest here is quite varied and rather young, with large numbers of oaks, red pines, and northern hardwoods, including many maples, which are the highlight of a fall color tour.

General location: Roughly mid-way between the towns of Traverse City and Kalkaska.

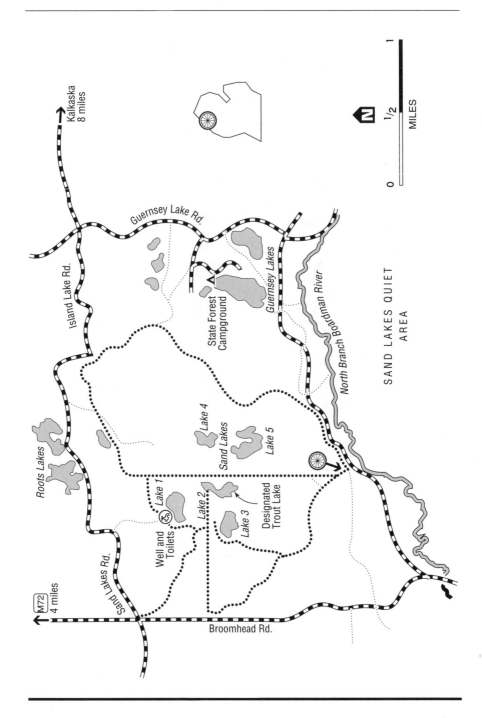

Kalkaska
8 miles

Guernsey Lake Rd.

Island Lake Rd.

Guernsey Lakes

State Forest
Campground

North Branch Boardman River

SAND LAKES QUIET
AREA

Roots Lakes

Lake 4

Sand Lakes

Lake 5

Lake 1

Lake 2

Lake 3

Designated
Trout Lake

Well and
Toilets

M72
4 miles

Sand Lakes Rd.

Broomhead Rd.

MILES
1
1/2
0

N

Riders roll on wide, grassy trails past a scenic lake.

Elevation change: There are no extreme hills here; the biggest is less than 50´ tall. However, total elevation change will be rather high, since this trail has very few flat spots. Many of those uphills will be "freebies" that use the momentum gained on the last downhill.

Season: You can expect the trails to be clear of snow by mid-April and rideable until November 15, the opening day of deer hunting season.

Services: All services will be found in Traverse City, including several full-service bicycle shops.

Hazards: There are no significant hazards on this DNR maintained ski trail.

Rescue index: Help is available in Traverse City, or back on Highway MI 72. The "quiet area" is a bit off the beaten track, but residences are thinly scattered on the roads surrounding the area; you will never be more than a couple of miles from the road.

Land status: Pere Marquette State Forest, managed by the Michigan Department of Natural Resources.

Maps: "Sand Lakes Quiet Area" maps are available from the Michigan Department of Natural Resources. (Address below.)

Finding the trail: The trail is located four miles south of State Highway MI 72. At 1.5 miles east of the village of Willimsburg, head south on Bromhead Road. Bromhead zigs and zags a couple of times, but is easy to follow and leads right to the well-marked parking area.

Sources of additional information:

Michigan Department of Natural Resources
404 West 14th Street
Traverse City, MI 49684
(616) 922-5280

Traverse City Chamber of Commerce
P.O. Box 387
Traverse City, MI 49685
(616) 947-5075

Brick Wheel Bike Shop
736 East Eighth Street
Traverse City, MI 49684
(616) 947-4274

Notes on the trail: There's something inherently appealing to mountain bikers about a place designated "Quiet Area." Sand Lakes lives up to the expectations generated by its name. At "Lake One" there is a pump and vault toilet, and on the eastern border of the area there is a drive-in primitive campground. The trail is all two-way, and signage is the standard Michigan DNR Ski Trail "you are here" style.

The roads surrounding the area are all unpaved, and some will be of interest to cyclists who want to rack up a little mileage without constant gear changes. Groups with riders of varying ability will appreciate the fact that everyone can start and finish at the same location; more aggressive riders may opt for a lengthy, vigorous charge through the woods, while laid-back lolligaggers can leisurely tour as short a loop as they choose.

RIDE 56 *SCHUSS MOUNTAIN / SHANTY CREEK TRAILS*

Ride where the big kids go! Site of the 1993 NORBA Nationals, this resort features a small but rewarding network of well-marked trails that run between the associated resorts of Schuss Mountain and Shanty Creek. The entire loop runs up to nine miles in length. A shuttle service travels between the resorts, making a cycle-out / motor-back ride possible.

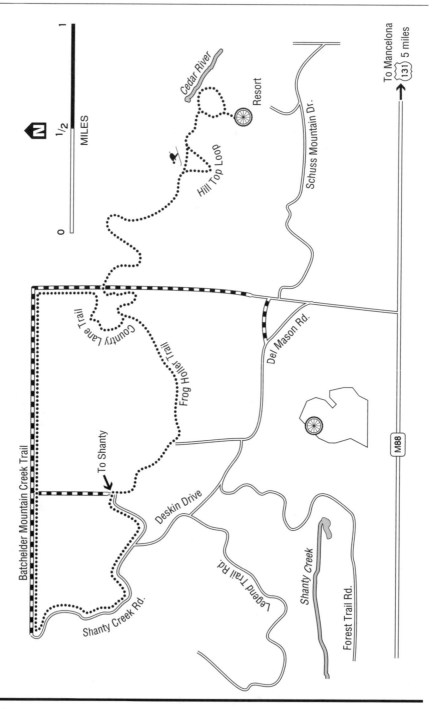

The NORBA Nationals brought top riders to Schuss Mountain. *Photo by John Robert Williams.*

No surprise, the first half mile of this ride climbs straight up, winding around the back side of the ski slopes. It is steep but rideable the entire distance. The single-track trail is a little sandy, but resort personnel have installed perforated rubber mats over the worst sections, something you *won't* see at state parks. Despite the ominous beginning, this ride is only of moderate difficulty for the average cyclist.

General location: near Mancelona, in Antrim County.
Elevation change: Elevation at the top is 1,160′ above sea level. Vertical drop is about 450′. Once off the ski hill itself, the trail remains moderately hilly, nothing that would dissuade novice riders in average shape.
Season: Trails should be rideable from May through October, although the best riding will be from late spring until the trail gets covered with fallen leaves.
Services: All services are available in Mancelona or Bellaire except for a bike shop. The nearest bike shop will be found in Traverse City or Gaylord.
Hazards: Coming down the ski hill, watch for downed limbs and other obstructions hidden by fallen leaves.
Rescue index: Help is available at the resort. There is no ski patrol during bike season, but riders are never more than a half mile from houses or roads.
Land status: Private land controlled by resort management. A $5 trail fee is charged.

Maps: Schuss Mountain / Shanty Creek Mountain Bike Trail Map is available at the trailhead.

Finding the trail: Check in at the lodge of either of the twin resorts to get a trail map, directions, and parking instructions and pay the trail fee.

Sources of additional information:

> Shanty Creek / Schuss Mountain
> Bellaire, MI 49615
> (800) 678-4111, (616) 533-8621

> Bellaire Chamber of Commerce
> P.O. Box 205
> Bellaire, MI 49615
> (616) 533-6023

Notes on the trail: Competitive riders will relish the ski hill climb, but ordinary mortals should not be intimidated. From the top, you can see spectacular rolling hills covered by forests and meadows. The trees are mostly northern hardwoods, and the high meadows traversed by the trail are quite lovely. Those parts of the trail that are not near a road are the most rewarding; some bikers may choose to arrange an out-and-back route that covers only these sections of the trail. Near Shanty Creek a section of paved road is used to complete the loop. The northernmost section of the loop runs alongside an unimproved dirt road.

The two-way trail is very well marked, but the intersections can be confusing; the resort uses coded confidence markers that are different from those used on state land.

RIDE 57   *SHINGLE MILL PATHWAY*

Here be Elk! But the shy creatures will probably hear you coming and disappear without a trace. Located in the heart of the Pigeon River State Forest, the loops that form this ten-mile single-track cross-country ski trail wind through a forest of incredible variety, composed of northern hardwoods, several types of conifer, aspens, and many more. Much of the forest is fairly young; the area was ravaged by fire in the 1930s and shows us again how quickly nature can reassert herself, given a chance.

The terrain is slightly rolling and quite firm, with a handful of short, steep climbs that are part sand. The route is very well marked and non-technical, although it can be a little confusing where it passes through the Pigeon River Campground. The northernmost loop is quite a bit steeper, and trees here are mostly hardwoods. A section of the southernmost loop passes through

RIDE 57   *SHINGLE MILL PATHWAY*

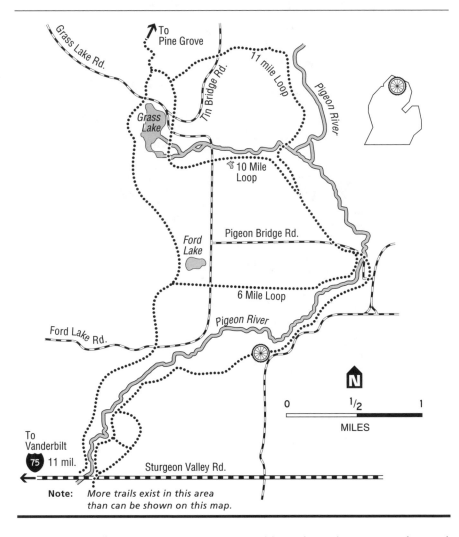

To
Pine Grove

Grass Lake Rd.

Tin Bridge Rd.

11 mile Loop

Pigeon River

Grass
Lake

10 Mile
Loop

Pigeon Bridge Rd.

Ford
Lake

6 Mile Loop

Pigeon River

Ford Lake Rd.

N

0   1/2   1

MILES

To
Vanderbilt
75 11 mil.

Sturgeon Valley Rd.

Note: *More trails exist in this area
than can be shown on this map.*

a wetland, which may or may not be a problem, depending on weather and beaver activity. Overall, Shingle Mill's trails are of moderate difficulty.

General location: About 20 miles northeast of Gaylord.
Elevation change: There are some fairly large hills in the northernmost loop, but overall elevation changes are moderate.
Season: Open year-round, except for the firearms deer season (beginning November 15); skis replace bikes in December.

An easy trail leaves time to enjoy the scenery.

Services: All services are located in Gaylord.

Hazards: Bull elk on the trail? More likely on the access road. The loop crosses several roads open to motor vehicles. There are occasional timber sales, so logging trucks may be present. If so, they will churn the roads into four-wheel-drive affairs.

Rescue index: Because of the remoteness of the area, chances of rescue are slim, although the trail is never more than a mile from open roads. Help is available at the State Forest Headquarters.

Land status: Mackinaw State Forest, Pigeon River Country State Forest.

Maps: Request "Shingle Mill Pathway" from the Michigan Department of Natural Resources.

Finding the trail: Exit I-75 at Vanderbilt, north of Gaylord. Proceed east on what becomes Sturgeon Valley Road. Follow the signs to the Forest Area Headquarters. The trailhead is at the headquarters.

Sources of additional information:

Pigeon River Country State Forest Headquarters
9966 Twin Lakes Road
Vanderbilt, MI 49795
(517) 983-4101

Gaylord Area CTB
125 South Ostego Avenue
Gaylord, MI 49735
(517) 732-4000

Notes on the trail: The best riding is found on the northern half of the trail, the outward legs of the so-called "ten-mile loop" and "eleven-mile loop," starting at the Forest Area Headquarters. (These distances assume a Pigeon River Bridge Campground starting point and are not relevant. Actual distance of this ride is 6 to 7 miles, with possible additions.) The two-way trail twists and turns alongside the Pigeon River for a little less than a mile, then straightens out as it runs into the woods. "You are here" maps remain at most intersections. There are more trails in the area than can be shown on this map.

Several small lakes, impoundments, and streams provide variety. Horses have been banned from the trail, and although earlier equestrian activity left its mark, the damage is fading. There are a few places where the trail crosses unimproved forest roads, but traffic is so light that one is unlikely to encounter motor vehicles. Actually, this trail gives you that Upper Peninsula feeling that you have successfully escaped from civilization.

RIDE 58 *WILDWOOD HILLS PATHWAY*

This lovely cross-country ski area consists of a ten-mile loop with many possible shorter loops. The trail is mostly single-track, part of which is new and part of which is overgrown double-track, that was originally the farm trails of long-departed settlers. There is a little bit of sand, but it's not too bad. The turf growing over the old two-rutters is a little bumpy, but not uncomfortably so. No technical riding skills are required and almost any rider will consider these trails easy.

It may sound "just right," but in one respect this ride is superlative, and that is in the attractiveness of the setting. Nature is rather quickly taking back what man borrowed for a short time. The forests are composed of northern hardwoods with healthy, mature red pines scattered throughout. There are some old CCC (Civilian Conservation Corps) plantations from the 1930s, and the Department of Natural Resources has erected a few signs with interesting silvicultural and historical information.

RIDE 58   *WILDWOOD HILLS PATHWAY*

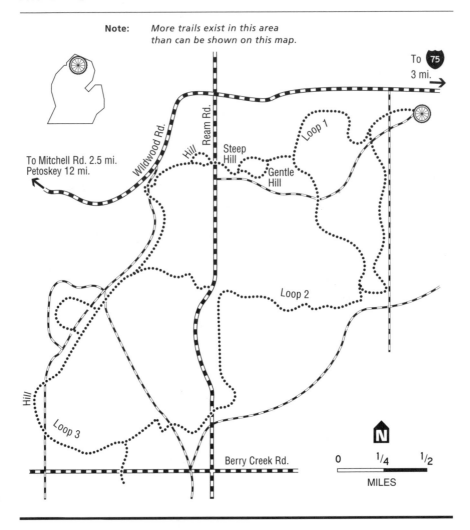

Note: *More trails exist in this area than can be shown on this map.*

To 🛡️75
3 mi. →

Loop 1

Ream Rd.

Wildwood Rd.

Hill

Steep Hill

Gentle Hill

To Mitchell Rd. 2.5 mi.
Petoskey 12 mi.

Loop 2

Hill

Loop 3

Berry Creek Rd.

N

0   1/4   1/2

MILES

Nature doesn't seem to mind the occasional apple orchard planted by far-sighted but long-gone pioneers, and (in season) neither does the passing mountain biker. This trail gets relatively little use during bike season, so there is plenty of fruit left over for the multitude of white-tailed deer that inhabit the area.

General location: Southeast of the town of Indian River.
Elevation change: The terrain is moderately rolling, with a few 50′ to 60′ climbs, enough to raise the pulse rate, but nothing extreme.

Single-track cross-country ski trails plunge into the
woods on the Wildwood Hills Pathway.

Season: Late summer to November 15, opening day of deer season.

Services: Limited services are available in the town of Indian River. All services, including a bike shop, are located about 15 miles west in Petoskey.

Hazards: The area is a hotbed of ATV activity, and some of their designated trails cross the ski trail. Keep your ears open.

Rescue index: Help is available in the town of Eagle River. This is a well maintained cross-country ski trail that never strays more than a few miles from the road.

Land status: State of Michigan, Mackinac State Forest.

Maps: Wildwood Hills Pathway Map, Michigan DNR.

Finding the trail: Exit I-75 and head east at Indian River. Turn south on Straights Highway. About two miles south of town, turn west on Wildwood Road. The trailhead is on the south side of the road, three miles in. There is a second trailhead a mile farther west. Alternatively, wend your way east from Petoskey on Mitchell Road, which will eventually turn into Wildwood Road.

Sources of additional information:

Michigan Department of Natural Resources
Indian River Field Office
Box 10
Indian River, MI 49749
(616) 238-9313

Adventure Sports
Petoskey, MI
(616) 347-3041

Notes on the trail: The two-way trail and intersections are well marked with "you are here" maps, but you must pay attention, because it's easy to get confused among the many twists and turns. The area is also crisscrossed by snowmobile and ORV trails, and many other intriguing double-tracks too numerous to show on this map.

RIDE 59 *BOIS BLANC ISLAND TOUR*

A 27-mile road loop circumnavigates this sparkling Lake Huron jewel, which is just a few miles east of the much more developed and touristy Mackinac Island. Bois Blanc (pronounced "Bob-Lo") has a number of modest cottages and summer homes along the south and east coasts. The north coast is completely undeveloped and features some impressive stands of mature conifers. Most of the island is covered by mixed age hardwood forests that are spectacular in the fall. The road never strays far from the breezy coast, so this is a good ride during the summer bug season. The developed areas are charming, not grandiose or tacky, with some interesting old cottages and other structures.

Six miles of the route consists of smooth gravel road, five miles is loose gravel, six miles is smooth, wide dirt road, and the balance is pure forest floor double-track, with a few sandy or cobble-covered areas near the beach. Although the distance is a bit long, the terrain is flat and no technical skills are required; a tour of Bois Blanc is an easy ride.

General location: Straights of Mackinac, north of Charlevoix.
Elevation change: Practically non-existent.
Season: May through October.
Services: On the island there's one bar, one cafe, one little convenience store, and a few modest rental cabins, but not a fudge shop to be seen. All other services, including two bike shops, are located in Charlevoix
Hazards: Biting insects, motor vehicles.

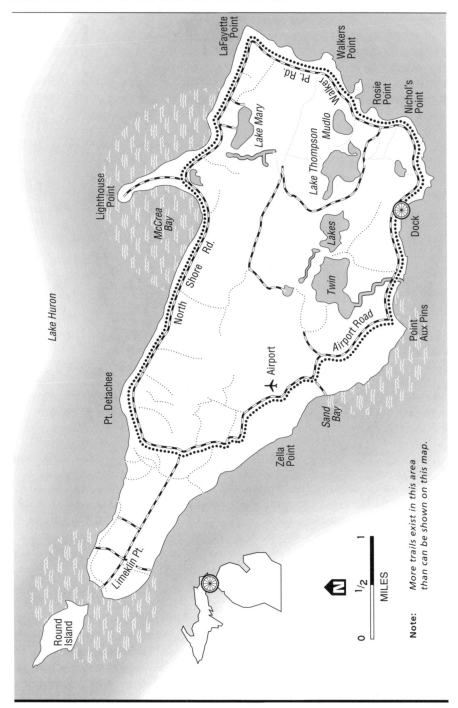

Note: *More trails exist in this area
than can be shown on this map.*

Smooth roads make riding at Bois Blanc Island a
pleasant tour.

Rescue index: Help may be found in the vicinity of the landing. Except along
the north coast, where a catastrophic breakdown may require a long walk back
to more traveled roadways, one is never far from help. Even on the north coast,
one can expect to see the occasional four-wheel-drive or all-terrain vehicle.
This is not wilderness, but "Bob" is a whole lot more woodsy than his resort-
and fudge shop–laden brother "Mac." You'll soon get the hang of these local
nicknames.

Land status: The land is either State Forest or privately owned. The maps
available do not distinguish between the two. For example, one would think
that Sand Bay has a southwest-facing beach that is all state land. However, it
is nothing but cottages and private property. There are campsites at Twin
Lakes, but no State Forest campground as indicated on most maps.

Maps: Michigan DNR maps are the most useful. Some ferry brochures have
a map printed on the back with the location of services indicated. A topo map
would be superfluous, since there is no significant topography.

Finding the trail: Two different ferry companies run the 45-minute crossing from Charlevoix. The boats are car ferries, propelled by noisy diesels. They have an old-time northern Michigan feel about them, as opposed to a polished front for the tourists. Needless to say the boat ride is gorgeous, with Big Mac (the bridge) rising out of the haze, and islands and wooded peninsulas jutting out all over the place. Round-trip fare is $11 per person, and several boats cruise to and fro each day, depending on the season. About 40–50 people winter over on the island and are served by air transport when there is no ice bridge.

Sources of additional information:

The Charlevoix Chamber of Commerce has the boat schedules and the phone numbers of island services, including rental cabins.

> Charlevoix Chamber of Commerce
> 408 Bridge Street
> Charlevoix, MI 49720
> (616) 547-2101

Notes on the trail: This island might be considered a cross between the much wilder Grand Island and the perhaps too civilized Mackinac Island. Along the north coast one can enjoy the feeling of having escaped from civilization, riding narrow double-tracks that are ideal for mountain bikes. The tangle of roads in and around the Lake Mary and Deer Lake area can be a little confusing, but it's hard to get too lost when the big freshwater pond is always near. There are more trails than can be shown on this map.

The north-south road up the eastern shore has unpleasant loose gravel, because it is not shaded like the rest of the roads. Elsewhere the surfaces are excellent, and although you may be passed by the occasional truck or car (usually with a friendly wave), there is no better way to explore this gem of an island than by mountain bike.

RIDE 60   *MACKINAC ISLAND TRAILS*

A tour on the 6.9- or 5.3-mile loops on Mackinac Island is a unique ride in a totally motor vehicle–free environment. Mackinac (pronounced Mac-en-awe) has the only public road system in America that is completely free of cars. People travel by horse-drawn carriage or bicycle. The bicycle is the most popular mode and balloon-tired one-speeds with big, front-mounted paper boy baskets prevail. A paved road circles the entire island at lake level. This is where almost all of the tourists ride. The beauty of Mackinac Island is that, except for the town, most of the rest of the island is a state park. With 300 feet of elevation and steep grades beyond the shore line, the interior is your playground.

RIDE 60 *MACKINAC ISLAND TRAILS*

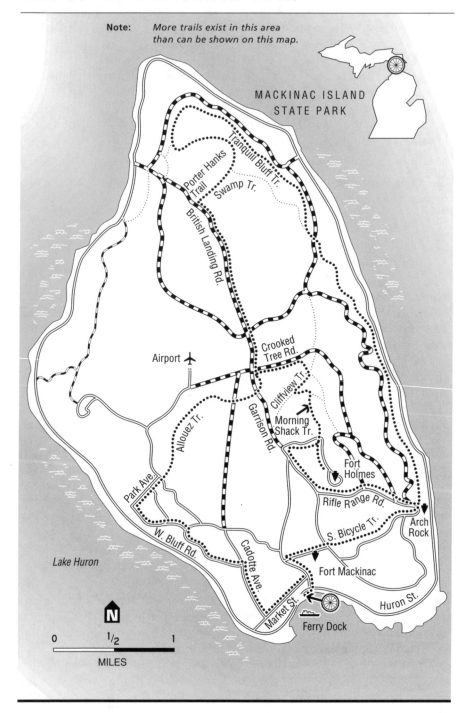

Note: *More trails exist in this area than can be shown on this map.*

MACKINAC ISLAND STATE PARK

Porter Hanks Trail

Tranquill Bluff Tr.

Swamp Tr.

British Landing Rd.

Airport

Crooked Tree Rd.

Cliffview Tr.

Morning Shack Tr.

Allouez Tr.

Garrison Rd.

Fort Holmes

Rifle Range Rd.

Park Ave.

S. Bicycle Tr.

Arch Rock

W. Bluff Rd.

Cadotte Ave.

Fort Mackinac

Lake Huron

N

Market St.

Ferry Dock

Huron St.

0   1/2   1

MILES

Mackinac Island has been a center of tourism for more than one hundred years. Its history as a trading center and military stronghold goes back even farther. As you approach the island by ferry from Mackinaw City or St. Ignace, the whitewashed walls of Fort Mackinac, built by the British in 1780, still appear formidable on the bluff above the town. As the island's military importance waned in the late nineteenth century, vacationers began to flock to it to escape the summer heat. Today over 800,000 people visit the island annually, most of them between June 15 and Labor Day.

Both loops require climbing steep grades. The routes are a mix of paved and gravel roads and single-track trails. No appreciable technical ability is needed on the moderately difficult short loop. The long loop is challenging due to off-camber trails with rocks, roots, and steep slopes. (The trails slope away from the direction of the turns.) Both routes begin with a visit to Arch Rock, a scenic natural bridge.

General location: Mackinac Island lies between the upper and lower peninsulas of Michigan east of the Mackinac Bridge.

Elevation change: Both loops begin with a 145′ climb from the town to the fort. Afterwards you can expect flat to gently rolling terrain on the long loop except for a gradual 70′ climb on British Landing Road. The short loop takes you up another 150′ to the site of Fort Holmes.

Season: Ferry service to the island runs from the second week of May through the third week of October. Expect muddy conditions in the spring and cool temperatures in spring and fall.

Services: All services available in the town of Mackinac Island including bicycle retail, rental, and repair. Bicycle service is also available on the mainland in Mackinaw City.

Hazards: Rocks and roots are common on off-road trails. Windfall trees and branches may be found at any time. Trails are shared with hikers and horseback riders.

Rescue index: Help is available in the town of Mackinac Island.

Land status: Public roads and Mackinac Island State Park land.

Maps: Detailed maps of all roads and trails are available from the Chamber of Commerce and the Mackinac Island State Park Commission.

Finding the trail: Ferry service is available at Mackinaw City on the lower peninsula and at St. Ignace on the upper peninsula. Ferries run 22 times a day from mid-June through Labor Day, ten times daily from mid-May to mid-June and in September, eight times daily in early October, and five times daily in early May and late October. Fare is charged per person and per bicycle.

Arch Rock overlooks Lake Huron.

Sources of additional information:

Mackinaw Area Tourist Bureau
708 South Huron Avenue
P.O. Box 160
Mackinaw City, MI 49701
(616) 436-5664

Mackinac Island State Park Commission
Mackinac Island, MI 49757
(906) 847-3328

Notes on the trail: The tour begins on paved streets and roads. From the ferry
dock, turn right on Huron Street and ride northeast one block. Turn left on
Fort Street and follow it up the steep hill alongside Fort Mackinac. The road
bends around to the right along the north side of the fort. At the junction with

Garrison Road, proceed straight across onto the South Bicycle Trail, which leads to the overlook at Arch Rock, a natural bridge.

To follow the long route, take Tranquil Bluff Trail north from Arch Rock. All trails are well marked with name signs. There are many fine views of the lake from this trail. Use caution—the trail is cambered toward the bluff edge and there are many rocks and roots along it. Farther on you may find soft ground in a cedar swamp area if it has rained recently. After the Tranquil Bluff Trail bends around to the south, turn left onto Porter Hanks Trail. At a **T** intersection turn right onto Swamp Trail, which will lead you to a gravel road named British Landing Road where you will turn left. Just past the airport runway, cross Annex Road and go straight onto Garrison Road. Turn right onto Allouez Trail. When Allouez Trail joins Annex Road go straight across onto Park Avenue, a paved road. Follow Park to Lake View Boulevard and turn left. Turn right on West Bluff Road. Turn right on Cadotte Avenue and descend into the town where you'll turn left at Market Street, right on Fort Street and right on Huron Street to return to the ferry dock.

To follow the short route, head west on Rifle Range Road from Arch Rock. Turn right on Garrison Road and right on Fort Holmes Road. Follow it on a long climb to the high point of the island, the abandoned site of Fort Holmes. Return downhill on the same road and turn right onto Morning Snack Trail when the road swings to the west. At a **T** intersection, turn right on Cliffview Trail. At another **T** intersection, turn left on Crooked Tree Road. Follow it to Garrison Road and pick up the directions for the long route.

Upper Peninsula of Michigan and Ontario

The Upper Peninsula of Michigan is a long way from anything. The people who live there, called 'yoopers' after the abbreviation (U.P.), like it that way. If they didn't want to live there, they would have left. There isn't a lot to hold anyone in the U.P. Most of the turn-of-the-century mines that brought in throngs of Finnish and Italian immigrants have closed down. The new-comers chased the American Dream and found themselves in copper mines one thousand feet below the earth's surface. They were glad to be in there when it was forty below zero above ground. Today you can still find 'pasties' (pronounced pass-tees) at bakeries and restaurants throughout the U.P. This traditional miners' meat and potato pie would stay warm until lunchtime down in the mines. It will stay warm in a fanny pack on a cool day's mountain bike ride, too.

Immigrants weren't the first to mine copper in the U.P. Hundreds of pre-historic Native American surface mines have been identified. They discovered the process of annealing the raw, pure ore to harden it for tools and weapons. In a period of postglacial warming around 4,000 to 3,000 B.C., when the climate in the U.P. was similar to present-day Kansas, the copper culture flourished. Coincidentally, its time frame was nearly identical to the development of copper working in the Mideast and Europe.

Lake Superior is the dominant feature of the U.P. It is the largest body of fresh water by surface area in the world. Superior is much deeper than the other Great Lakes. It averages 489 feet in depth and a maximum sounding of 1,333 feet has been recorded. It is Gitchee Gumi, meaning "big sea water" to the native Ojibwe. More often known as the Chippewa, the tribe made Superior their private lake in the late 1600s when they stopped the New York-based Iroquois at the Sault (pronounce Soo) where Superior flows into Lake Huron. This allowed them to control the western fur trade and become the most populous and powerful nation in the north.

All of the four major continental glaciers of the past million years covered the U.P. They failed to obliterate the ancient ore-bearing mountain cores, and bare rock is often scarred by striae, scratch lines that show the direction of the ice flow. The rugged terrain also gives the U.P. the greatest concentration of waterfalls in the U.S. Over one hundred falls, all with their own unique character, flow north to Lake Superior.

Looking at a map, you would think that the main industry in the U.P. would be state and national forests. Indeed, without forests managed for logging there wouldn't be much work up there. But the impact of logging on an area as vast as the U.P. isn't enough to detract from the tourism experience. There are enough woods to go around.

Riders will find challenging biking and great views of Lake Superior on the Lookout Mountain and Tip of the Keweenaw routes. Spectacular lake views are also part of the moderate riding experience on the Harlow Lake Trails. Off-roaders of all skill levels will enjoy the easy riding of Valley Spur cross-country ski trails. Grand Island is a wild, undeveloped gem just off the Lake Superior shore with miles of moderate riding trails. Riders will have easy going on the Pine Marten Run and Seney Trails. Experiences vary from moderate to challenging on the extensive trails at Searchmont just over the Canadian border in Ontario.

RIDE 61 *LOOKOUT MOUNTAIN TRAIL*

Note on Keweenaw County Snowmobile Trails: Just prior to publication, the author learned from the Baraga office of the Michigan Department of Natural Resources that you must have landowner permission to ride mountain bikes on snowmobile trails that cross private property, including most of the Lookout Mountain and the Tip of the Keweenaw rides. (However, hundreds of bikers are currently enjoying these trails—often at the instigation of individuals in the local tourism industry!)

Vigorous efforts are underway to clarify the legal status of riding on these Conservation Forest Reserve lands, and the rides are included in hope that the situation will be favorably resolved during the shelf life of this volume.

Brockway Mountain Drive is a world-famous paved parkway that provides some spectacular panoramic vistas in the north. Its unpaved cousin, Lookout Mountain, is not so famous, but is of great interest to bikers. A primitive double-track that is a marked snowmobile trail provides a 10-mile out-and-back (total) to the top. The terrain is quite challenging and parts of it are rather technical. The reward is a clifftop outcrop with a spectacular 360-degree view of the entire peninsula and Isle Royale (50 miles away) on a clear day. Steep grades make Lookout Mountain a challenging ride for the average biker.

General location: Just south of the town of Eagle Harbor, Keweenaw County.
Elevation change: Approximately 1,000′ of total climbing. Elevation at the top is 1,336′ above sea level; the trailhead is not far above Lake Superior's 602′ level. There is also a big saddle-like valley that adds to the elevation change.

RIDE 61 *LOOKOUT MOUNTAIN TRAIL*

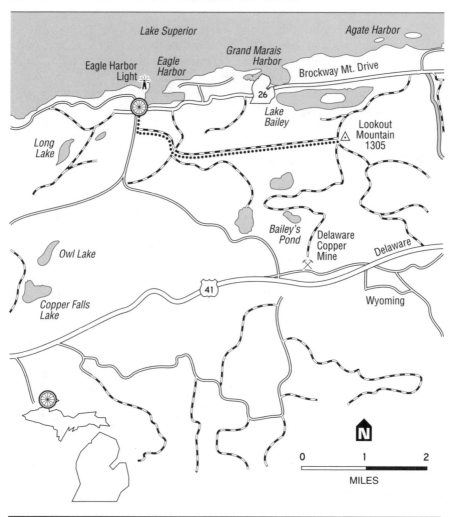

Season: The route should be rideable from mid-May through October. Late summer until snowfall is the best time.

Services: Limited services are available in Eagle Harbor. All other services, including bicycle sales and repairs, are located in Calumet, about 20 miles south on US 41.

Hazards: This is a very technical ride, especially the last stretch down and up the big saddle. Most riders will choose to hike the latter.

Rescue index: Help is available in the town of Eagle Harbor. You're not likely to see another soul on the trail, but it's fairly close to Eagle Harbor.

Lake Superior marks the horizon from the top of Lookout Mountain.

Land status: Private land with DNR easements or similar programs that may allow recreational access.

Maps: DNR County Maps or locally marked-up snowmobile trail maps.

Finding the trail: Park in the town of Eagle Harbor. Head due south one mile from Eagle Harbor on the paved road to Copper Falls. Turn left (east) onto the trail where the snowmobile trail crosses the road, indicated by the characteristic orange and white arrow. An alternate entry point lies a half mile farther south, at the intersection of the Delaware / US 41 cut-across road on the left. At this turnoff, a snowmobile trail begins at a gravel pit located on the northeast corner of the intersection, which makes it easy to find. Just a few hundred yards' ride north of the gravel pit, orange snowmobile trail arrows point out a turn to the east onto the main trail. From here, climb!

Sources of additional information:

Copper Country Vacations
Box 336 HK
Houghton, MI 49931
(800) 338-7982, (906) 482-5240

Michigan Department of Natural Resources
P.O. Box 440, US 41
Baraga, MI 49908

Cross Country Sports
507 Oak
Calumet, MI 49913
(906) 337-4520

Notes on the trail: After the road section, the first three miles is 95% non-technical climbing on a marginal double-track, and leads to an oak-covered hilltop with great views in two directions. The last mile is a purely technical one-rut hiking trail that crosses a big valley.

Don't forget a compass, and be prepared to rough it a bit. However, those who accept the challenge of using mountain bikes to take on the Keweenaw will receive a hundredfold payback for the slight bit of extra effort and preparation required.

RIDE 62   *TIP OF THE KEWEENAW TRAILS*

Note on Keweenaw County Snowmobile Trails: Just prior to publication, the author learned from the Baraga office of the Michigan Department of Natural Resources that you must have landowner permission to ride mountain bikes on snowmobile trails that cross private property, including most of the Lookout Mountain and the Tip of the Keweenaw rides. (However, hundreds of bikers are currently enjoying these trails—often at the instigation of individuals in the local tourism industry!)

Vigorous efforts are underway to clarify the legal status of riding on these Conservation Forest Reserve lands, and the rides are included in hope that the situation will be favorably resolved during the shelf life of this volume.

Copper Harbor is the last town on the tip of the Keweenaw Peninsula. It is the launching point for the Isle Royale Ferry and exists solely to serve the needs of visitors, including huge numbers of snowmobilers. The year-round population of the entire *county* is only 2,000.

Starting at the end of US 41 (yes, the end) two miles east of the town of Copper Harbor, a vast network of double-track, four-wheel-drive, and snowmobile trails crisscross the tip of the Keweenaw Peninsula. Tours of 5 to 50 miles are easily charted, many branching off from the 18-mile loop outlined below. The terrain is steep and rugged, with some fairly technical climbs and descents. Bedrock is never far beneath the surface (and frequently crops out), but there are also long stretches where enough soil has filled in to make riding comfortable.

If you have ever questioned the utility of front suspension, the Copper Country will convince you. This is probably the best Midwest warmup for a Rocky Mountain bike trip. However, those who lack springs in their forks and

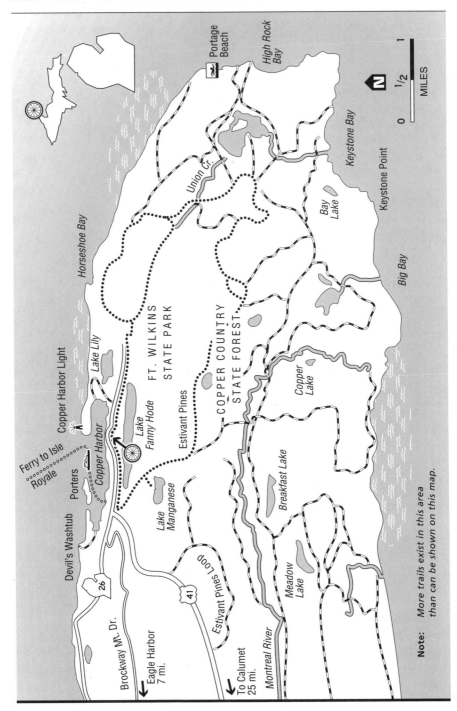

Note: *More trails exist in this area than can be shown on this map.*

steel in their thighs should not turn away from the area—just go a little slower downhill and do a little more walking on the uphills. If you want extreme technical riding it can be easily found, but it can also be easily avoided. No matter how you cut it, the riding on the Keweenaw is challenging.

The area is heavily forested, mostly in thick second-growth hardwoods, but a few stands of virgin white pines remain. Although not technically a wilderness, most visitors won't be able to tell the difference. Nevertheless, it is very accessible to cyclists willing to make a slightly higher commitment to self-sufficiency and prudent precautions. The area is dotted with reminders of its mining and pioneer past, many of which provide historical points of interest.

General location: The town of Copper Harbor.

Elevation change: In the Keweenaw it's hard to find a piece of ground flat enough to pitch a tent, so constant elevation changes are a fact of life for riders. However, since the bigger hills are "ten-minute climbs," from a couple hundred feet to a maximum of about 500′, the heart of a marathoner is not mandatory. Even champion riders sometimes walk up the big ones.

Season: The best time to ride is in the fall, when the "windshield tourists" arrive in great numbers for spectacular color tours. In the summer, black flies and related pests are a problem. Spring only lasts for two weeks between snowmelt and bug season.

Services: All services, except for a bike shop, are located in Copper Harbor. The nearest bike repairs will be available in Calumet, thirty miles back down US 41. (Which way on 41? There is only ONE way!)

Hazards: Nowhere are downhill runs smooth enough to complete without hitting the brakes at some point. You may be flying down an apparently smooth trail, when suddenly a little washout exposes a minefield of skull-sized stones big enough to bend a rim and send you tumbling. Be ready with those brakes!

Rescue index: Help is available in the town of Copper Harbor. If something or somebody breaks, it will not exactly trigger a wilderness survival saga, but one is unlikely to see another soul beyond a mile or two from town. On the other hand, it's tough to get more than about 15 miles away from town, a long but not unreasonably cruel hike. And there are few places that a tenacious emergency-jeep driver could not reach, thanks to the firmness (read rockiness) of the ground. Except for short loops or out-and-backs near town (of which there are scores), big Keweenaw day trips should be considered for adults only.

Land status: Most of the land is privately owned. Department of Natural Resources easements and similar programs imply recreational access, but not necessarily camping access.

Maps: The handiest maps are the locally produced snowmobile trail maps, usually overlaid on the standard DNR county maps that are available at any

Steep, rocky downhills are common on the Keweenaw Peninsula.

DNR office. USGS topo maps are out of date and very sketchy on the subject of double-track roads. The snowmobile trails usually, but not always, follow double-track roads indicated on the DNR maps. Snowmobile trails are marked on the ground by prominent orange and white arrows, which are highly reliable—if they are still standing.

Finding the trail: The trail network begins right in town, where one can park at the Isle Royale ferry boat dock or many other places.

Sources of additional information:

Copper Country Vacations
Box 336 HK
Houghton, MI 49931
(800) 338-7982, (906) 482-5240

Michigan Department of Natural Resources
P.O. Box 440, US 41
Baraga, MI 49908

Cross Country Sports
507 Oak
Calumet, MI 49913
(906) 337-4520

This bike shop has a wall covered with full-size topo maps of the entire Keweenaw.

Notes on the trail: Start with a climb up the last two miles of pavement from Copper Harbor past historic but touristy Fort Wilkins, and enjoy the thrill of blowing by the "windshield tourists" parked at the end of US 41 who have reached the terminus of their adventure just as you are beginning yours. The first few miles of double-track are probably the roughest of the ride, so do not be discouraged.

About 1.5 miles from the end of the pavement, a parallel loop on the left descends down to Horseshoe Harbor, where the Nature Conservancy has purchased land. (Walk in the last few hundred yards to the beach.) Two miles from the turnoff, on the right, a substantial two-rutter steeply ascends the short distance back to the main loop. Those out for a short ride will turn back to Copper Harbor at this point.

About 3 miles farther east and south is the right turn onto the Clark Mine snowmobile trail, indicated by one of the prominent orange snowmobile trail arrows mentioned above. (This is the only type of signage to be found in this area.) Keep in mind that there are many more trails than can be shown on this map. Make the turn, and you will be back in Copper Harbor with an 18-mile ride under your belt.

RIDE 63   *HARLOW LAKE TRAIL*

Five miles north of Marquette lies an area called the "Little Presque Isle Tract." It contains a five-mile loop called the Harlow Lake Cross-Country Ski Trail, as well as a number of hiking trails. The area provides riders with an excellent sample of the rugged terrain of the western Upper Peninsula. It includes some rocky outcroppings high above Lake Superior, with spectacular panoramic views.

The ski trail is divided into two loops, mostly single-track, with a little bit of double-track. The surface is forest floor, quite firm. The southernmost loop, including the out-and-back trail up Hogsback Mountain, is somewhat technical, with a few mucky-mucks that the more fastidious will want to tiptoe

RIDE 63   *HARLOW LAKE TRAIL*

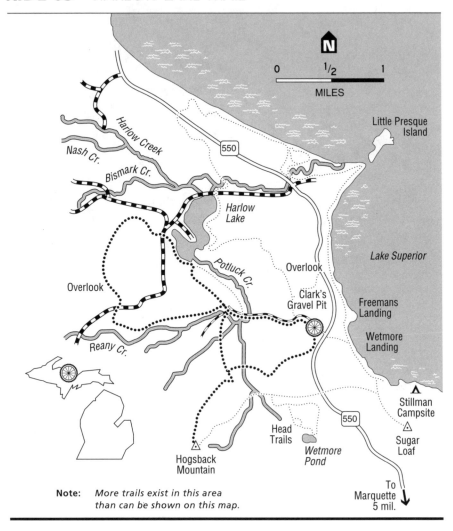

Note: *More trails exist in this area*
than can be shown on this map.

around, but nothing extreme. All of this adds up to a ride of moderate difficulty for the average cyclist.

Vegetation is mostly northern hardwoods plus some impressive stands of oak and hemlock. A babbling brook courses down a steep ravine on the descent from the high overlook. The trail crosses an abandoned railroad grade that goes right on up to Big Bay, as well as a number of four-wheel-drive roads that usually end up on private property.

General location: Five miles northwest of Marquette.

A bridge over quiet waters at Harlow Lake. *Photo by Jack Deo.*

Elevation change: There is one long, gradual ascent/descent, and the balance is sharply rolling, with a series of short, steep hills, but nothing that requires one to dismount. Maximum elevation change is about 150´.

Season: Late summer to when all the leaves fall off the trees in mid-October.

Services: All services, including several bike shops, are available in Marquette, the most "cosmopolitan" city in the Upper Peninsula. You'll know this town is different from the rest of the peninsula when you spot scores of lycra-clad joggers along the lakeshore, and notice that nobody stares at people in funny bike clothes.

Hazards: Parts of the trail are rocky and twist tightly. The greatest hazard is mistakenly getting onto a hiking trail that intersects the ski trail. If you find yourself in a sub-one mile per hour, trials bike zone, you've made a wrong turn.

Rescue index: Help is available in Marquette, 5 miles from the trail, home of the U.P.'s most sophisticated medical facilities. Double-tracks run all around the area, but are infrequently traveled, as is the ski trail itself.

Land status: Escanaba River State Forest, managed by the Department of Natural Resources.

Maps: When the Chamber of Commerce or a local bike shop hands you the Marquette Area Cross-Country Ski Trails map and invites you to use it to ride Harlow Lake, politely (or not so politely) decline. You *need* the DNR's "Little Presque Isle Tract" map.

Finding the trail: Travel 5 miles north from Marquette on County Road 550, a.k.a. Big Bay Road, and look for a hard-to-spot gravel pit and parking lot on the west side of the road. It is 1.2 miles north of the Sugarloaf Mountain parking lot. Alternatively, proceed another 1.2 miles north of the gravel pit and turn left on 550 H.D., an improved gravel road that goes directly to Harlow Lake, and catch the trail as it winds around the back of Harlow Lake.

Sources of additional information:

> Michigan Department of Natural Resources
> 1990 US 41 South
> Marquette, MI 49855

> Marquette Chamber of Commerce
> 501 South Front Street
> Marquette, MI 49855
> (906) 226-6591

Notes on the trail: When starting out at the gravel pit, proceed down the unpaved "Seasonal Road" until you come to the sign pointing right to Harlow Lake. From this point the trail is easy to follow. It is well marked, and confidence markers are in place at intersections, although the "you are here" maps tend to disappear (probably nabbed by poor souls trying to navigate with just the ski trail map). It's a little confusing coming up from the lakeside traverse, but range around a bit and you'll spot the trail with no trouble.

RIDE 64 *VALLEY SPUR TRAILS*

Two unpaved road loops, of five and twelve miles respectively, use one of the Upper Peninsula's finest cross-country ski trails as a launching point. The wide skating track takes riders through the ski area and onto a network of classic U.P. hardwood forest double-tracks. These tend to be smooth, firm tunnels through the trees suitable for riders of any age or skill level.

Once past the ski area, the terrain is level to slightly rolling with just a few long, gradual hills. The short section of ski trail is quite hilly. The ski trail itself traverses a series of folded valleys and is characterized by a combination of short, steep ravines with a few long gradual climbs and descents as well. The roads are slightly rolling, with no drastic changes in elevation. All of this makes Valley Spur an easy ride.

General location: Near Munising.
Elevation change: The longest climb is only about 100 feet.

248

RIDE 64 VALLEY SPUR TRAILS

Note: More trails exist in this area
than can be shown on this map.

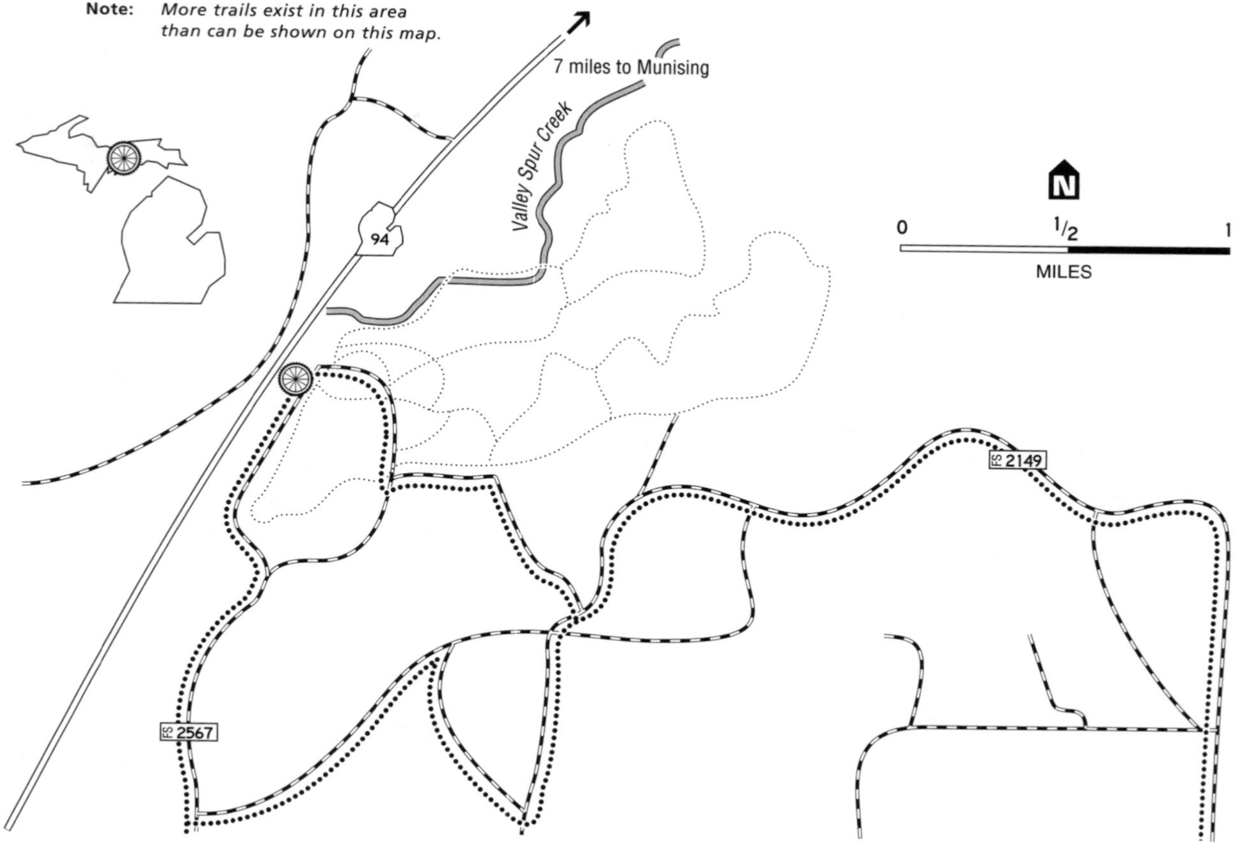

7 miles to Munising

Valley Spur Creek

94

FS 2149

FS 2567

N

0   ¹/₂   1
MILES

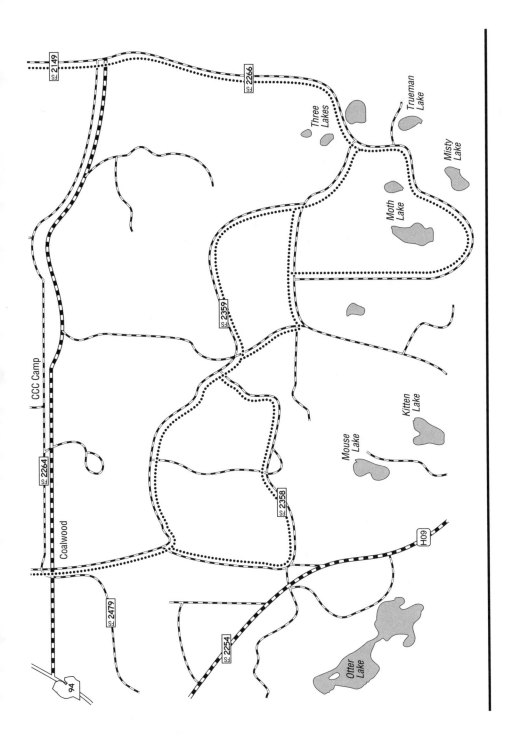

One of the many easy ski trails at Valley Spur. *Photo by Jack Deo.*

Season: The Valley Spur trails should be rideable from mid-May through October. As always in the north country, late summer to fall is best. Biting flies can drive you nuts during the summer, especially in the slower-paced, heavily wooded ski trail sections.

Services: All services are available in Munising, except for a bike shop, of which there are several in Marquette (forty miles to the west).

Hazards: Some of the steep ski trail hills have rather abrupt turns at the bottom. Greatest hazards are bugs in the summer and cold in the fall. The double-tracks are open to motorized vehicles.

Rescue index: Help is available in Munising. The ski trail is never more than a mile from highway I-94. The double-tracks are seldom traveled by motorized vehicles, but are never farther than 3 miles from more substantial, improved roads.

Land status: Hiawatha National Forest, Munising Ranger District.

Maps: The Forest Service in Munising has a Valley Spur Bicycle Route Map available. Be sure also to pick up the big four-color, "Hiawatha National Forest: Western Half" map. It's a bargain at three dollars, and your passport to hundreds of miles of forest double-tracks.

Finding the trail: The parking lot is located on the south side of Highway I-94, 7 miles west of Munising. There are signs on the highway that are easy to spot.

Sources of additional information:

Hiawatha National Forest
Munising Ranger District
400 East Munising
Munising, MI 49862
(906) 387-2512

Alger Chamber of Commerce
Box 405
Munising, MI 49862
(906) 387-2138

Notes on the trail: There are more trails in this area than can possibly be shown on the map. At the time of publication, the Forest Service was well into the process of establishing a particular bike route through the ski area (many are possible), and placing confidence markers on the double-track road sections. The ski trail itself is very well marked.

Riders seeking the adrenaline rush of zooming past big trees on a firm, narrow single-track are welcome to ride the ten-mile ski trail itself, which winds up and down the short but steep hills of Valley Spur Creek. Check out the ladder-like bear claw marks on the larger beech trees.

In the immediate vicinity of Valley Spur there are miles of excellent double-track riding, as well as some challenging single-track, for instance the northern half of the Bay de Noc to Grand Island Trail. Avoid the southern half of the latter, as it is an impassable sandpit, churned to uselessness by heavy equestrian use.

RIDE 65   *GRAND ISLAND TOUR*

This is perhaps the finest mountain bike ride in the Midwest. Most scenic shorelines in the world are either private property or have paved roads alongside. On Grand Island, cyclists cruise a hard gravel double-track through thick second-growth hardwoods, popping out every few minutes to catch breathtaking views of 200-foot cliffs tumbling down to frigid Lake Superior. There is nothing else like it.

RIDE 65 *GRAND ISLAND TRAILS*

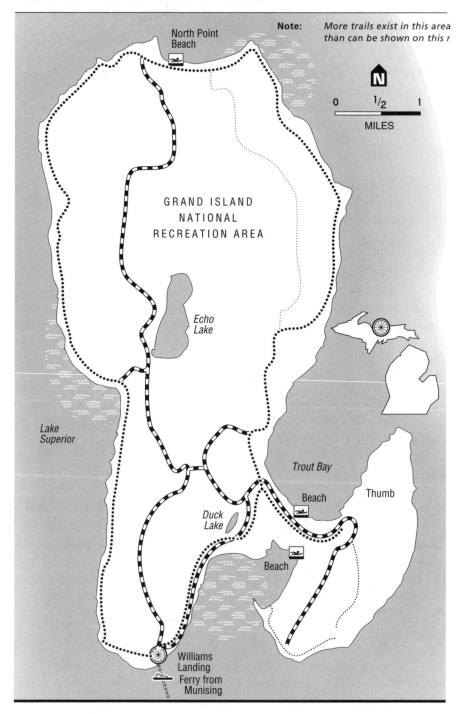

Note: *More trails exist in this area than can be shown on this r*

North Point
Beach

N

0   1/2   1
MILES

GRAND ISLAND
NATIONAL
RECREATION AREA

Echo Lake

Lake
Superior

Trout Bay

Beach   Thumb

Duck Lake

Beach

Williams
Landing
Ferry from
Munising

The wilderness Lake Superior shoreline of Grand Island.

The so-called "carriage trail" that circumnavigates the main part of the island is about 18 miles long. It is firm but a little bumpy—suspension is optional. By skipping the section up to North Point Beach, the ride can be cut back to 10–12 miles. Although the trail does not require athletic or technical ability, occasional riders should work to get their contact points in shape before heading up to Munising. Overall, Grand Island is moderately difficult for the average rider.

General location: On Lake Superior, a half mile offshore from Munising.
Elevation change: Most of the trail is slightly rolling, with a half dozen good climbs and descents (100′ to 250′), and a couple of mile-long, smooth gravel, "Look Ma, no brakes" screaming downhills.
Season: Like all north woods rides, late summer through fall is the best season. The ferry runs from June through early October.
Services: All services are available in Munising except for a bike shop, of which there are several in Marquette, 45 miles to the east. However, when that ferry boat drops you off on the island, you're on your own; a higher degree of self-sufficiency is desirable.

There is no potable water on the island, so bikers are advised to bring a gallon a day per person. A PAIR OF BIKE-MOUNTED WATER BOTTLES IS NOT ENOUGH if the weather is warm. Those planning to camp should pick up a sub-micron water filter and pump.

Hazards: A few big hills are washed out and rutted, so good brakes are important. Make sure you don't fall off the 200′ cliffs. Biting flies can be especially bad when the warm south winds blow, as if they know that if they get blown out to sea, the next stop will be Thunder Bay, Ontario. This is true along the entire southern shore of Hiawatha's Gitchee Gumee (Lake Superior). Weather is EXTREMELY changeable, so even in summer one must be prepared for anything from snow squalls to excessive heat and humidity.

Rescue index: Help is available in Munising. At the southern end of the island there are a number of summer cottages, but north of Echo Lake is "wilderness." Bring some tools, and plan on leaving North Point with enough time before the ferry departure to *walk* the nine miles back to the landing in the event of a catastrophic bike failure. (This rider has established an annual tradition of having a chain come apart near North Point.) There is a phone at the ferry landing.

Land status: National Recreation Area, Hiawatha National Forest.

Maps: Grand Island NRA Map, available at the Ferry Boat office or the Munising Ranger District.

Finding the trail: Pictured Rocks Cruises uses a tour boat to run a fifteen-minute ferry service to and from Munising, two or three times a day depending on the season.

Sources of additional information:

Munising Ranger District
Hiawatha National Forest
400 East Munising Street
Munising, MI 49862
(906) 387-2512

Pictured Rocks Cruises
(906) 387-2379

Alger Chamber of Commerce
Box 405
Munising, MI 49862
(906) 387-2138

Notes on the trail: Although there are a lot more trails on Grand Island than can be shown on this map, the trail (road) is easy to follow and confidence markers are located at some prominent intersections. The island is also criss-crossed by scores of old logging roads, "ghost roads," and two-rutters leading into the forest.

There are probably more black bear than deer on the island, since a previous owner removed the large conifer stands that provided thermal cover in winter. Bears have been seen swimming the half-mile Lake Superior crossing soon after the spring thaw. The Forest Service has placed food-hanging ropes at the campsites located at Trout Bay and Murray Bay—if Trout Bay has not yet been closed to camping when you visit, that is. It is an exquisitely delicate "tombolo" ecosystem, and visitors should be very careful not to damage the "lichen fields" as they approach the gorgeous sand beach here.

RIDE 66   *PINE MARTEN RUN*

Within an area five miles long and three miles wide, there are twelve small lakes, a wild river, an incredible variety of vegetation including monster hemlocks and white pines, and a brand new 26-mile trail network. Although intended for hikers and equestrians, this trail network offers much more to mountain bikers than backpackers, since it is impossible to find a loop that does not cross at least one road open to motor vehicles. Mountain bikers won't mind this, because these roads are seldom traveled and are good biking. The trail itself is partly new single-track, and partly over-grown double-track. No technical skill is required, and the terrain is gently rolling.

This trail is easy to follow with well-marked intersections. Many routes are possible, from four miles in length to forty, with five different access points. A specific five-mile loop is detailed below. The northwest corner contains a very large opening managed for sharptail grouse. The southwest corner contains impressive conifer stands, where the pine martens run. In the center, radiating out from Ironjaw Lake, northern hardwoods prevail. Toward the northeast, the ground becomes marshy and there are wetlands. Some of the lakes are nesting grounds for loons. (I won't say which.) Most riders will find the trails to be moderate in difficulty.

General location: Pine Marten Run is located 17 miles south of Munising, 4 miles east of Forest Highway 13, on the north side of County Road 440.
Elevation change: Moderate. The terrain is gently rolling, with a few modest hills.
Season: Expect the trails to be rideable from mid-May through October. Post-bug to pre-snow is best (mid-August to mid-October).
Services: A couple of convenience stores are located on FH 13, a few miles north of CR 440. All other services, except for a bike shop, are in Munising. All services including a bike shop are in Manistique, 25 miles southeast of the area.
Hazards: The trail gets little use, because the inability to escape motor vehicle roads makes it unattractive to hikers, its intended users. Fortunately there has been very little equestrian activity. As a result, uncleared deadfalls are frequent. Also, the new single-track sections still have some stumps from small trees cut off *almost,* but not quite, at ground level.

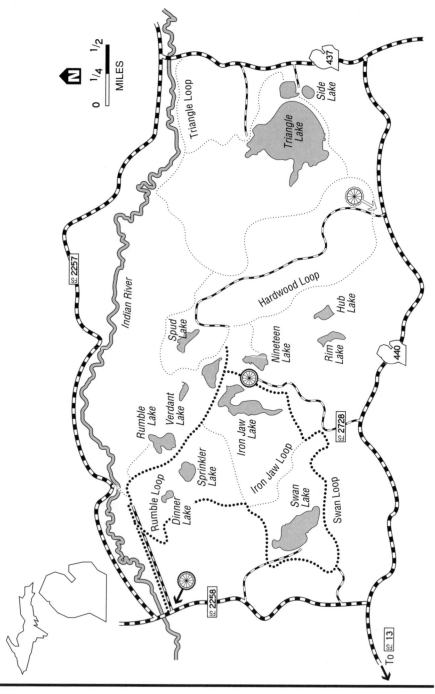

N

0   1/4   1/2

MILES

Triangle Loop

Side Lake

437

Triangle Lake

SR 2257

Indian River

Hardwood Loop

Hub Lake

Spud Lake

Nineteen Lake

Rim Lake

440

Rumble Lake

Verdant Lake

Iron Jaw Lake

SR 2728

Sprinkler Lake

Iron Jaw Loop

Rumble Loop

Dinner Lake

Swan Lake

Swan Loop

SR 2258

To SR 13

Rescue index: Help is available in Munising or Manistique; which are about equidistant from the trail. There are no residences or other inholdings within Pine Marten Run. Except for those lakes open to motor vehicles, the area sees few visitors. Nevertheless, one is never more than 3 miles from a county road.
Land status: Hiawatha National Forest.
Maps: "Pine Marten Run" and "Hiawatha National Forest: Western Half." The former is available in boxes at the trailheads (maybe), or at the Ranger Stations in Munising, Manistique, and Rapid River (definitely).
Finding the trail: Follow the signs pointing north from County Road 440 to either Swan Lake or Ironjaw Lake, or head north from CR 440 on either Forest Road 2258 or County Road 437 to the Indian River. Trailheads are located at each of these locations.

Sources of additional information:

> Hiawatha National Forest
> Manistique Ranger District
> 499 East Lake Shore Drive
> Manistique, MI 49854
> (906) 341-5666

> Alger Chamber of Commerce
> Box 405
> Munising, MI 49862
> (906) 387-2138

Notes on the trail: If I *must* recommend a loop, it will be this one: Park at Ironjaw Lake. Head northeast to the Indian River, past Rumble Lake. Loop back south on the trail east of Dinner Lake. At the next intersection, swoop east around Swan Lake, then back to Ironjaw and the trailhead.

South of CR 440 the double-track roads tend to be sandy and unrideable. North of 440 and east of FH 13 the double-tracks tend to be firm, as the forest here is mostly hardwoods. Use the big "Hiawatha" map to navigate your way around some of the best mountain bike roads in the Midwest.

RIDE 67 *SENEY TRAILS*

Certainly the most accessible ride in the Upper Peninsula for families or less athletic individuals, this is also the *only* area in the state, besides Mackinac Island, where mountain bikes have access to roads and motorized vehicles don't (except for the occasional forest ranger's truck).

The Seney National Wildlife Refuge is traversed by a network of gravel double-track trails that wind in and among pools and ponds used by migrating waterfowl. Practically nowhere is it necessary to shift onto the smallest chainring, making this an easy ride for anyone. Very well-marked trails form

RIDE 67   *SENEY TRAILS*

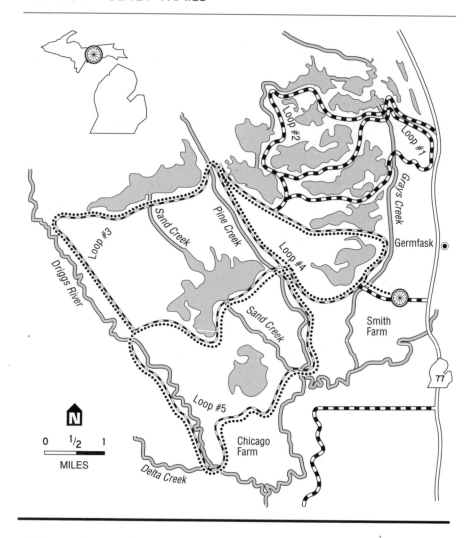

a fifteen-mile loop beginning at the "Smith Farm" parking lot and circling around the southern, nonmotorized portion of the Refuge. Shorter five-mile loops are also possible.

Well, they don't call this a wildlife refuge for nothing; here's a list with some of the many animal species that can be seen: In the late summer / early fall pre-migration period are Canada geese, hooded mergansers, mallards, black ducks, ring-necked ducks, wood ducks, and sandhill cranes. Also present, in addition to the usual north woods cast of white-tailed deer, black

Autumn comes to the Seney cross-country ski trails.

bear, coyotes, beaver and river otters, are ruffed grouse, spruce grouse, sharptail grouse, woodcock, yellow rails, and the majestic bald eagle.

Vegetation is predominantly northern hardwoods; many stands originated after the great forest fires that swept the area in the 1970s. Trail intersections are so well marked that one would have to try to get lost.

General location: Near Germfask.
Elevation change: The terrain is almost flat near the waterholes, and is slightly rolling elsewhere.
Season: Trails should be rideable from mid-May through October, but the best season, as with all north country rides, is late summer to fall. However, during the summer black fly season, the fast riding made possible by solid gravel roads makes Seney a better alternative than destinations where one creeps around single-tracks in granny gear. No, you can't exactly outrun the flies, but you can at least make them work for their meal.

This is a good place to mention that U.P. black flies, stable flies, and deer flies are only amused by bug dope. LONG PANTS and LONG SLEEVES are MANDATORY during the bug season.
Services: Germfask isn't much more than a wide spot in the road, but there are a couple of cafes, a convenience store, a motel, and mountain bike and canoe rentals from Northland Outfitters. The nearest bike shop is in Manistique, about 40 miles away.

Hazards: Almost nonexistent. Busy government workers and your federal tax dollars keep the refuge well manicured.

Rescue index: Help is available in Germfask. It's possible to distance yourself from roads open to vehicles, but at no point would the least capable two-wheel-drive rescue vehicle have any problem gaining access.

Land status: National Wildlife Refuge.

Maps: Seney National Wildlife Refuge, Bicycle Routes.

Finding the trail: A few blocks south of downtown Germfask, there is a sign indicating a cross-country ski area just west of Highway I 77. One may drive partway to the ski trail, to a parking area located where the road is blocked to motor vehicles. This is called "Smith's Farm." Park here and ride west a few hundred yards to the ski area, where the wildlife refuge starts.

One may also start at the Refuge Headquarters, but Loop #1 and Loop #2, which originate there, are open to motor vehicles.

Sources of additional information:

Seney National Wildlife Refuge
HCR 2, Box 1
Seney, MI 49883
(906) 586-9851

Northland Outfitters
Highway I 77
Germfask, MI 49836
(906) 586-9801

Notes on the trail: The Manistique River passes through the refuge on its way to Lake Michigan, presenting a rare opportunity to canoe down a peaceful wilderness river and return on a mountain bike. An unimproved county road parallels the river for about 20 miles. Also, one can easily drop off a canoe and camping gear upstream, then drive downstream, park, and use bikes to execute the upstream shuttle.

City dwellers may shudder, but there is no problem hiding expensive bikes in these remote woods, even for a few days. (Although a resident porcupine once considered my shift lever worth gnawing on—the salt from perspiration must have convinced him that this piece of plastic was food.) Canoe rentals are available at Northland Outfitters.

RIDE 68 *SEARCHMONT TRAILS*

Although it's over the border in the Province of Ontario, Searchmont Resort is no less lovable than the neighboring U.P. Nestled in the rugged terrain bordering Lake Superior's eastern shore, Searchmont offers one of the Midwest's

RIDE 68   *SEARCHMONT TRAILS*

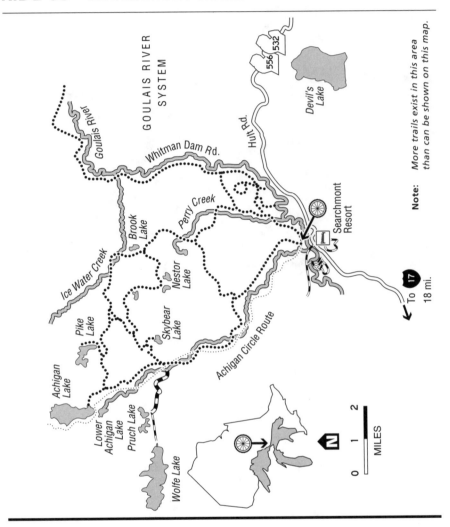

most unique mountain bike "out-and-backs." Riders and bikes can board the Algoma Central Railroad's morning "local," debarking 15 or 30 miles down the line, then bicycle back on an extensive network of double-track and single-track trails. Up to 250 miles of marked mountain bike trails are open, including rides of any distance, suitable for any skill level from novice to gonzo gear-grinder.

The terrain is steep, rugged, and heavily forested with northern hardwoods and many cool, shady conifer groves. Among scenic and historical points of interest is the long climb up an old railroad grade to Christina Lake, site of an

Rolling on bedrock on the Searchmont Trails. *Photo courtesy of Lake Superior Image Productions.*

abandoned copper mine. Or the trail to Nestor Lake, where the resort keeps a canoe hidden for riders who want to take an on-water trail break.

Upon crossing the international border, one leaves behind the flat, alluvial plain that is the eastern Upper Peninsula, and ascends onto the "Canadian Shield," a geologic formation characterized by steep hills, breathtaking gorges, exposed bedrock outcroppings, and tumbling waterfalls. Searchmont is a year-round resort, with alpine and cross-country skiing in the winter months.

General location: Ontario, Canada, northeast of Sault Ste. Marie, Michigan.
Elevation change: The resort is 780′ above sea level. Highest point on the trail system is 1,500′ above sea level. Some rides have very little climbing. On others total vertical rise (and descent) may add up to a couple thousand feet or more.
Season: Mid-May to mid-October.
Services: Limited services, including a lodge, refreshments, and bike rentals are located at the resort. All services, including a bike shop, are located in the two towns named Sault Ste. Marie.
Hazards: Beaver dams may make some trail sections soggy, and the size of the trail system makes it very possible that uncleared deadfalls may be encountered.

Rescue index: Help is available at the village of Searchmont. It is possible to stray far off the beaten trail, and those taking advantage of the longer loops, or the railroad-out, cycle-back tours, should take prudent backwoods precautions in the form of emergency survival kit, bike tools, maps, compass, munchies, extra water or filter, etc.

Land status: Resort or Government Land.

Maps: Various detailed trail maps prepared by the Searchmont Resort are available at the lodge.

Finding the trail: From Sault Ste. Marie, Ontario, head north on Highway 17. Turn right onto Highway 556 and follow it to Searchmont Resort, 25 miles down the road. Register and pick up directions and maps at the lodge.

Sources of additional information:

Searchmont Resort
P.O. Box 787
Sault Ste. Marie, Ontario, P6A 5N3
(705) 781-2340

Notes on the trail: There is an $8 per day (Canadian $) trail fee, and the train ride costs about $5. Over thirty miles of trail are located in and around the resort itself, mostly rated beginner to intermediate. Therefore, to enjoy riding through this geologically fascinating region, it is not absolutely necessary to make the commitment required to step off that train into "wilderness mountain biking." Keep in mind though, there are many more trails in the area than can be shown on this map.

Afterword

LAND-USE CONTROVERSY

A few years ago I wrote a long piece on this issue for *Sierra* magazine that entailed calling literally dozens of government land managers, game wardens, mountain bikers, and local officials to get a feeling for how riders were being welcomed on the trails. All that I've seen personally since, and heard from my authors, indicates there hasn't been much change. We're still considered the new kid on the block. We have less of a right to the trails than horses and hikers, and we're excluded from many areas, including:

a) wilderness areas
b) national parks (except on roads, and those paths specifically marked "bike path")
c) national monuments (except on roads open to the public)
d) most state parks and monuments (except on roads, and those paths specifically marked "bike path")
e) an increasing number of urban and county parks, especially in California (except on roads, and those paths specifically marked "bike path")

Frankly, I have little difficulty with these exclusions and would, in fact, restrict our presence from some trails I've ridden (one time) due to the environmental damage and chance of blind-siding the many walkers and hikers I met up with along the way. But these are my personal views. The author of this volume and mountain bikers as a group may hold different opinions.

You can do your part in keeping us from being excluded from even more trails by riding responsibly. Many local and national off-road bicycle organizations have been formed with exactly this in mind, and one of the largest—the National Off-Road Bicycle Association (NORBA)—offers the following code of behavior for mountain bikers:

1. I will yield the right of way to other non-motorized recreationists. I realize that people judge all cyclists by my actions.

2. I will slow down and use caution when approaching or overtaking another cyclist and will make my presence known well in advance.
3. I will maintain control of my speed at all times and will approach turns in anticipation of someone around the bend.
4. I will stay on designated trails to avoid trampling native vegetation and minimize potential erosion to trails by not using muddy trails or short-cutting switchbacks.
5. I will not disturb wildlife or livestock.
6. I will not litter. I will pack out what I pack in, and pack out more than my share whenever possible.
7. I will respect public and private property, including trail use signs and no trespassing signs, and I will leave gates as I have found them.
8. I will always be self-sufficient, and my destination and travel speed will be determined by my ability, my equipment, the terrain, the present and potential weather conditions.
9. I will not travel solo when bikepacking in remote areas. I will leave word of my destination and when I plan to return.
10. I will observe the practice of minimum impact bicycling by "taking only pictures and memories and leaving only waffle prints."
11. I will always wear a helmet whenever I ride.

Now, I have a problem with some of these—number nine, for instance. The most enjoyable mountain biking I've ever done has been solo. And as for leaving word of destination and time of return, I've enjoyed living in such a way as to say, "I'm off to pedal Colorado. See you in the fall." Of course it's senseless to take needless risks, and I plan a ride and pack my gear with this in mind. But for me number nine smacks too much of the "never-out-of-touch" mentality. And getting away from civilization, deep into the wilds, is, for many people, what mountain biking's all about.

All in all, however, NORBA's is a good list, and surely we mountain bikers would be liked more, and excluded less, if we followed the suggestions. But let me offer a "code of ethics" I much prefer, one given to cyclists by Utah's Wasatch-Cache National Forest office.

Study a Forest Map Before You Ride
Currently, bicycles are permitted on roads and developed trails within the Wasatch-Cache National Forest except in designated Wilderness. If your route crosses private land, it is your responsibility to obtain right of way permission from the landowner.

Keep Groups Small
Riding in large groups degrades the outdoor experience for others, can disturb wildlife, and usually leads to greater resource damage.

Avoid Riding on Wet Trails
Bicycle tires leave ruts in wet trails. These ruts concentrate runoff and accelerate erosion. Postponing a ride when the trails are wet will reserve the trails for future use.

Stay on Roads and Trails
Riding cross-country destroys vegetation and damages the soil.

Always Yield to Others
Trails are shared by hikers, horses, and bicycles. Move off the trail to allow horses to pass and stop to allow hikers adequate room to share the trail. Simply yelling "Bicycle!" is not acceptable.

Control Your Speed
Excessive speed endangers yourself and other forest users.

Avoid Wheel Lock-up and Spin-out
Steep terrain is especially vulnerable to trail wear. Locking brakes on steep descents or when stopping needlessly damages trails. If a slope is steep enough to require locking wheels and skidding, dismount and walk your bicycle. Likewise, if an ascent is so steep your rear wheel slips and spins, dismount and walk your bicycle.

Protect Waterbars and Switchbacks
Waterbars, the rock and log drains built to direct water off trails, protect trails from erosion. When you encounter a waterbar, ride directly over the top or dismount and walk your bicycle. Riding around the ends of waterbars destroys them and speeds erosion. Skidding around switchback corners shortens trail life. Slow down for switchback corners and keep your wheels rolling.

If You Abuse It, You Lose It
Mountain bikers are relative newcomers to the forest and must prove themselves responsible trail users. By following the guidelines above, and by participating in trail maintenance service projects, bicyclists can help avoid closures which would prevent them from using trails.

I've never seen a better trail-etiquette list for mountain bikers. So have fun. Be careful. And don't screw things up for the next rider.

Dennis Coello
Series Editor

Glossary

This short list of terms does not contain all the words used by mountain bike enthusiasts when discussing their sport. But it should serve as an introduction to the lingo you'll hear on the trails.

ATB all-terrain bike; this, like "fat-tire bike," is another name for a mountain bike

ATV all-terrain vehicle; this usually refers to the loud, fume-spewing three- or four-wheeled motorized vehicles you will not enjoy meeting on the trail—except, of course, if you crash and have to hitch a ride out on one

bladed refers to a dirt road that has been smoothed out by the use of a wide blade on earth-moving equipment; "blading" gets rid of the teeth-chattering, much-cursed washboards found on so many dirt roads after heavy vehicle use

blaze a mark on a tree made by chipping away a piece of the bark, usually done to designate a trail; such trails are sometimes described as "blazed"

blind corner a curve in a road or trail that conceals bikers, hikers, equestrians and other traffic

BLM Bureau of Land Management, an agency of the federal government

buffed used to describe a very smooth trail

catching air taking a jump in such a way that both wheels of the bike are off the ground at the same time

clean while this may describe what you and your bike won't be after following many trails, the term is most often used as a verb to denote the action of pedaling a tough section of trail successfully

combination this type of route may combine two or more configurations; for example, a point-to-point route may integrate a scenic loop or out-and-back spur midway through the ride; likewise, an out-and-back may have a loop at its farthest point (this configuration looks like a cherry with stem

	attached; the stem is the out-and-back, the fruit is the terminus loop); or a loop route may have multiple out-and-back spurs and/or loops to the side; mileage for a combination route is for the total distance to complete the ride
dab	touching the ground with a foot or hand
deadfall	a tangled mass of fallen trees or branches
diversion ditch	a usually narrow, shallow ditch dug across or around a trail; funneling the water in this manner keeps it from destroying the trail
double-track	the dual tracks made by a jeep or other vehicle, with grass or weeds or rocks between; mountain bikers can ride in either of the tracks, but you will of course find that whichever one you choose, and no matter how many times you change back and forth, the other track will appear to offer smoother travel
dugway	a steep, unpaved, switchbacked descent
endo	flipping end over end
feathering	using a light touch on the brake lever, hitting it lightly many times rather than very hard or locking the brake
four-wheel-drive	this refers to any vehicle with drive-wheel capability on all four wheels (a jeep, for instance, has four-wheel drive as compared with a two-wheel-drive passenger car), or to a rough road or trail that requires four-wheel-drive capability (or a one-wheel-drive mountain bike!) to negotiate it
game trail	the usually narrow trail made by deer, elk, or other game
gated	everyone knows what a gate is, and how many variations exist upon this theme; well, if a trail is described as "gated" it simply has a gate across it; don't forget that the rule is if you find a gate closed, close it behind you; if you find one open, leave it that way
Giardia	shorthand for Giardia lamblia, and known as the "backpacker's bane" until we mountain bikers expropriated it; this is a waterborne parasite that begins its life cycle when swallowed, and one to four weeks later has its host (you) bloated, vomiting, shivering with chills and living in the bathroom; the disease can be avoided by "treating" (purifying) the water you acquire along the trail (see "Hitting the Trail" in the Introduction)

gnarly	a term thankfully used less and less these days, it refers to tough trails
hammer	to ride very hard
hardpack	a trail in which the dirt surface is packed down hard; such trails make for good and fast riding, and very painful landings; bikers most often use "hard-pack" and "hard-packed" as both noun and adjective, and "hardpacked" as an adjective only (the grammar lesson will help you when diagramming sentences in camp)
hike-a-bike	what you do when the road or trail becomes too steep or rough to remain in the saddle
jeep road, jeep trail	a rough road or trail passable only with four-wheel-drive capability (or a horse or mountain bike)
kamikaze	while this once referred primarily to those Japanese fliers who quaffed a glass of saké, then flew off as human bombs in suicide missions against U.S. naval vessels, it has more recently been applied to the idiot mountain bikers who, far less honorably, scream down hiking trails, endangering the physical and mental safety of the walking, biking, and equestrian traffic they meet; deck guns were necessary to stop the Japanese kamikaze pilots, but a bike pump or walking staff in the spokes is sufficient for the current-day kamikazes who threaten to get us all kicked off the trails
loop	this route configuration is characterized by riding from the designated trailhead to a distant point, then returning to the trailhead via a different route (or simply continuing on the same in a circle route) without doubling back; you always move forward across new terrain, but return to the starting point when finished; mileage is for the entire loop from the trailhead back to trailhead
multi-purpose	a BLM designation of land which is open to many uses; mountain biking is allowed
ORV	a motorized off-road vehicle
out-and-back	a ride where you will return on the same trail on which you pedaled out; while this might sound far more boring than a loop route, many trails look very different when pedaled in the opposite direction; unless otherwise noted, mileage figures are the total distance out and back

pack stock	horses, mules, llamas, et cetera, carrying provisions along the trails . . . and unfortunately leaving a trail of their own behind
point-to-point	a vehicle shuttle (or similar assistance) is required for this type of route, which is ridden from the designated trailhead to a distant location, or endpoint, where the route ends; total mileage is for the one-way trip from trailhead to endpoint
portage	to carry your bike on your person
pummy	volcanic activity in the Pacific Northwest and elsewhere produces soil with a high content of pumice: trails through such soil often become thick with dust, but this is light in consistency and can usually be pedaled; remember, however, to pedal carefully, for this dust obscures whatever might lurk below
quads	bikers use this term to refer both to the extensor muscle in the front of the thigh (which is separated into four parts) and to USGS maps; the expression "Nice quads!" refers always to the former, however, except in those instances when the speaker is an engineer
runoff	rainwater or snowmelt
scree	an accumulation of loose stones or rocky debris lying on a slope or at the base of a hill or cliff
signed	a "signed" trail has signs in place of blazes
single-track	a single, narrow path through grass or brush or over rocky terrain, often created by deer, elk, or backpackers; single-track riding is some of the best fun around
slickrock	the rock-hard, compacted sandstone that is *great* to ride and even prettier to look at; you'll appreciate it even more if you think of it as a petrified sand dune or seabed, and if the rider before you hasn't left tire marks (from unnecessary skidding) or granola bar wrappers behind
snowmelt	runoff produced by the melting of snow
snowpack	unmelted snow accumulated over weeks or months of winter—or over years in high-mountain terrain
spur	a road or trail that intersects the main trail you're following